China's International Relations and Harmonious World

As scholars and publics look for alternatives to what is understood as a violent Western world order, many claim that China can provide such an alternative through the Chinese dream of a harmonious world. This book takes this claim seriously and examines its effects by tracing the notion across several contexts: the policy documents and speeches that launched harmony as an official term under previous president Hu Jintao; the academic literatures that asked what a harmonious world might look like; the propaganda and mega events that aimed to illustrate it; the online spoofing culture that is used to criticize and avoid 'harmonization'; and the incorporation of harmony into current president Xi Jinping's 'Chinese dream'.

This book finds contemporary Chinese society and international relations saturated with harmony. Yet, rather than offering an alternative to problems in 'Western' thought, it counter-intuitively argues that harmony has not taken place, is not taking place, and will not take place. The argument unfolds as a contribution to wider debates on time, space and multiplicity in world politics. Offering analysis of the important but understudied concept of harmony, Nordin provides new and creative insights into wider contemporary issues in Chinese politics, society and scholarship.

The book also suggests a creative and novel methodology for studying foreign policy concepts more broadly, drawing on critical thinkers in innovative ways and in a new empirical context. It will be of interest to students and scholars of IR, Chinese foreign and security policy and IR theory.

Astrid H. M. Nordin is a Lecturer in the Department of Politics, Philosophy and Religion, Lancaster University, UK.

Interventions

Edited by:

Jenny Edkins

Aberystwyth University

and Nick Vaughan-Williams

University of Warwick

The series provides a forum for innovative and interdisciplinary work that engages with alternative critical, post-structural, feminist, postcolonial, psychoanalytic and cultural approaches to international relations and global politics. In our first five years we have published 60 volumes.

We aim to advance understanding of the key areas in which scholars working within broad critical post-structural traditions have chosen to make their interventions, and to present innovative analyses of important topics. Titles in the series engage with critical thinkers in philosophy, sociology, politics and other disciplines and provide situated historical, empirical and textual studies in international politics.

We are very happy to discuss your ideas at any stage of the project: just contact us for advice or proposal guidelines. Proposals should be submitted directly to the Series Editors:

- Jenny Edkins (jennyedkins@hotmail.com) and
- Nick Vaughan-Williams (N.Vaughan-Williams@Warwick.ac.uk).

'As Michel Foucault has famously stated, "knowledge is not made for understanding; it is made for cutting". In this spirit the Edkins–Vaughan-Williams Interventions series solicits cutting edge, critical works that challenge mainstream understandings in international relations. It is the best place to contribute post disciplinary works that think rather than merely recognize and affirm the world recycled in IR's traditional geopolitical imaginary.'

Michael J. Shapiro, *University of Hawai'i at Manoa, USA*

Critical Theorists and International Relations
Edited by Jenny Edkins and Nick Vaughan-Williams

Ethics as Foreign Policy
Britain, the EU and the Other
Dan Bulley

Universality, Ethics and International Relations
A Grammatical Reading
Véronique Pin-Fat

The Time of the City
Politics, Philosophy, and Genre
Michael J. Shapiro

Governing Sustainable Development
Partnership, Protest and Power at the World Summit
Carl Death

Insuring Security
Biopolitics, Security and Risk
Luis Lobo-Guerrero

Foucault and International Relations
New Critical Engagements
Edited by Nicholas J. Kiersey and Doug Stokes

International Relations and Non-Western Thought
Imperialism, Colonialism and Investigations of Global Modernity
Edited by Robbie Shilliam

Autobiographical International Relations
I, IR
Edited by Naeem Inayatullah

War and Rape
Law, Memory and Justice
Nicola Henry

Madness in International Relations
Psychology, Security and the Global Governance of Mental Health
Alison Howell

Spatiality, Sovereignty and Carl Schmitt
Geographies of the Nomos
Edited by Stephen Legg

Politics of Urbanism
Seeing Like a City
Warren Magnusson

Beyond Biopolitics
Theory, Violence and Horror in World Politics
François Debrix and Alexander D. Barder

The Politics of Speed
Capitalism, the State and War in an Accelerating World
Simon Glezos

Politics and the Art of Commemoration
Memorials to Struggle in Latin America and Spain
Katherine Hite

Indian Foreign Policy
The Politics of Postcolonial Identity
Priya Chacko

Politics of the Event
Time, Movement, Becoming
Tom Lundborg

Theorising Post-Conflict Reconciliation
Agonism, Restitution and Repair
Edited by Alexander Keller Hirsch

Europe's Encounter with Islam
The Secular and the Postsecular
Luca Mavelli

Re-Thinking International Relations Theory via Deconstruction
Badredine Arfi

The New Violent Cartography
Geo-analysis after the Aesthetic Turn
Edited by Sam Okoth Opondo and Michael J. Shapiro

Insuring War
Sovereignty, Security and Risk
Luis Lobo-Guerrero

International Relations, Meaning and Mimesis
Necati Polat

The Postcolonial Subject
Claiming Politics/Governing Others in Late Modernity
Vivienne Jabri

Foucault and the Politics of Hearing
Lauri Siisiäinen

Volunteer Tourism in the Global South
Giving Back in Neoliberal Times
Wanda Vrasti

Cosmopolitan Government in Europe
Citizens and Entrepreneurs in Postnational Politics
Owen Parker

Studies in the Trans-Disciplinary Method
After the Aesthetic Turn
Michael J. Shapiro

Alternative Accountabilities in Global Politics
The Scars of Violence
Brent J. Steele

Celebrity Humanitarianism
The Ideology of Global Charity
Ilan Kapoor

Deconstructing International Politics
Michael Dillon

The Politics of Exile
Elizabeth Dauphinee

Democratic Futures
Revisioning Democracy Promotion
Milja Kurki

Postcolonial Theory
A Critical Introduction
Edited by Sanjay Seth

More than Just War
Narratives of the Just War and Military Life
Charles A. Jones

Deleuze & Fascism
Security: War: Aesthetics
Edited by Brad Evans and Julian Reid

Feminist International Relations
'Exquisite Corpse'
Marysia Zalewski

The Persistence of Nationalism
From Imagined Communities to Urban Encounters
Angharad Closs Stephens

Interpretive Approaches to Global Climate Governance
Reconstructing the Greenhouse
Edited by Chris Methmann, Delf Rothe and Benjamin Stephan

Postcolonial Encounters in International Relations
The Politics of Transgression in the Maghreb
Alina Sajed

Post-Tsunami Reconstruction in Indonesia
Negotiating Normativity through Gender Mainstreaming Initiatives in Aceh
Marjaana Jauhola

Leo Strauss and the Invasion of Iraq
Encountering the Abyss
Aggie Hirst

Production of Postcolonial India and Pakistan
Meanings of Partition
Ted Svensson

War, Identity and the Liberal State
Everyday Experiences of the Geopolitical in the Armed Forces
Victoria M. Basham

Writing Global Trade Governance
Discourse and the WTO
Michael Strange

Politics of Violence
Militancy, International Politics, Killing in the Name
Charlotte Heath-Kelly

Ontology and World Politics
Void Universalism I
Sergei Prozorov

Theory of the Political Subject
Void Universalism II
Sergei Prozorov

Visual Politics and North Korea
Seeing Is Believing
David Shim

Globalization, Difference and Human Security
Edited by Mustapha Kamal Pasha

Imagining World Politics
Sihar & Shenya, a Fable for Our Times
L. H. M. Ling

International Politics and Performance
Critical Aesthetics and Creative Practice
Edited by Jenny Edkins and Adrian Kear

Memory and Trauma in International Relations
Theories, Cases, and Debates
Edited by Erica Resende and Dovile Budryte

Critical Environmental Politics
Edited by Carl Death

Democracy Promotion
A Critical Introduction
Jeff Bridoux and Milja Kurki

International Intervention in a Secular Age
Re-enchanting Humanity?
Audra Mitchell

The Politics of Haunting and Memory in International Relations
Jessica Auchter

European–East Asian Borders in Translation
Edited by Joyce C. H. Liu and Nick Vaughan-Williams

Genre and the (Post)Communist Woman
Analyzing Transformations of the Central and Eastern European Female Ideal
Edited by Florentina C. Andreescu and Michael Shapiro

Studying the Agency of Being Governed
Edited by Stina Hansson, Sofie Hellberg and Maria Stern

Politics of Emotion
The Song of Telangana
Himadeep Muppidi

Ruling the Margins
Colonial Power and Administrative Rule in the Past and Present
Prem Kumar Rajaram

Race and Racism in International Relations
Confronting the Global Colour Line
Alexander Anievas, Nivi Manchanda and Robbie Shilliam

The Grammar of Politics and Performance
Edited by Shirin M. Rai and Janelle Reinelt

War, Police and Assemblages of Intervention
Edited by Jan Bachman, Colleen Bell and Caroline Holmqvist

Re-Imagining North Korea in International Politics
Problematizations and Alternatives
Shine Choi

On Schmitt and Space
Claudio Minca and Rory Rowan

Face Politics
Jenny Edkins

Empire Within
International Hierarchy and Its Imperial Laboratories of Governance
Alexander D. Barder

Sexual Politics and International Relations
How LGBTQ Claims Shape International Relations
Edited by Manuela Lavinas Picq and Markus Thiel

Emotions, Politics and War
Edited by Linda Åhäll and Thomas Gregory

Jacques Lacan
Between Psychoanalysis and Politics
Edited by Samo Tomšič and Andreja Zevnik

The Value of Resilience
Securing Life in the 21st Century
Chris Zebrowski

Political Aesthetics
Culture, Critique and the Everyday
Arundhati Virmani

Walzer, Just War and Iraq
Ethics as Response
Ronan O'Callaghan

Politics and Suicide
The Philosophy of Political Self-destruction
Nicholas Michelsen

Late Modern Palestine
The Subject and Representation of the Second Intifada
Laura Junka-Aikio

Negotiating Corruption
NGOs, Governance and Hybridity in West Africa
Laura Routley

The Biopolitics of Lifestyle
Foucault, Ethics and Healthy Choices
Christopher Mayes

Critical Imaginations in International Relations
Aoileann Ní Mhurchú and Reiko Shindo

Time, Temporality and Violence in International Relations
(De)Fatalizing the Present, Forging Radical Alternatives
Edited by Anna M. Agathangelou and Kyle Killian

Lacan, Deleuze and World Politics
Rethinking the Ontology of the Political Subject
Andreja Zevnik

The Politics of Evasion
A Post-Globalization Dialogue
Robert Latham

Researching War
Feminist Methods, Ethics and Politics
Edited by Annick T. R. Wibben

China's International Relations and Harmonious World
Time, Space and Multiplicity in World Politics
Astrid H. M. Nordin

Narrative Global Politics
Theory, History and the Personal in International Relations
Edited by Naeem Inayatullah and Elizabeth Dauphinee

On the Greek Origins of Biopolitics
Contesting Michel Foucault's Genealogy of Biopower
Mika Ojakangas

Insuring Life
Capital Security and Risk
Luis Lobo-Guerrero

The Global Making of Policing
Postcolonial Perspectives
Jana Hönke and Markus-Michael Müller

China's International Relations and Harmonious World

Time, space and multiplicity in world politics

Astrid H. M. Nordin

I look very much forward to more harmonious cooperation and collaboration in the future! You're welcome to Lancaster any time! And I can show you some of those good places to eat in the Lakes.

Astrid

Routledge
Taylor & Francis Group
LONDON AND NEW YORK

First published 2016
by Routledge
2 Park Square, Milton Park, Abingdon, Oxon OX14 4RN

and by Routledge
711 Third Avenue, New York, NY 10017

Routledge is an imprint of the Taylor & Francis Group, an informa business

British Library Cataloguing in Publication Data
A catalogue record for this book is available from the British Library

Library of Congress Cataloging in Publication Data
Names: Nordin, Astrid, author.
Title: China's international relations and harmonious world : time, space and multiplicity in world politics / Astrid H.M. Nordin.
Description: Abingdon, Oxon ; New York, NY : Routledge, 2016. | Series: Interventions | Includes bibliographical references and index.
Identifiers: LCCN 2015047664| ISBN 9781138944879 (hardback) | ISBN 9781315671406 (ebook)
Subjects: LCSH: China–Foreign relations–Philosophy. | China–Foreign relations–21st century. | International cooperation
Classification: LCC JZ1734 .N67 2016 | DDC 327.51–dc23
LC record available at http://lccn.loc.gov/2015047664

ISBN: 978-1-138-94487-9 (hbk)
ISBN: 978-1-31567-140-6 (ebk)

Typeset in Times New Roman
by Wearset Ltd, Boldon, Tyne and Wear

MIX
Paper from responsible sources
FSC www.fsc.org FSC® C013604

Printed and bound by CPI Group (UK) Ltd, Croydon, CR0 4YY

This book is for my parents, Bengt Nordin and Helena Nordin Rudberg

Contents

Figures

Acknowledgements

A large debt of gratitude is owed to my PhD supervisors, Maja Zehfuss and William A. Callahan, for the support in writing the thesis that was the beginning of this book. I also want to thank Roland Bleiker and William Schroeder for helpful and encouraging comments. I am indebted to the editors of the Interventions book series, Jenny Edkins and Nick Vaughan-Williams, as well as three anonymous reviewers, for their helpful feedback.

I have many remarkable peers who have contributed to the book by way of long discussions, probing questions, feedback on drafts and moral support. Part of the research was conducted at the Swedish Institute of International Affairs, where Tom Lundborg, Linus Hagström, Johan Eriksson, Johan Lagerkvist, Mikael Weissman, Björn Jerdén and Johan Englund made me feel welcome and helped me improve my work. Caroline Holmqvist and Dan Öberg also helped make my stay in Stockholm a productive and enjoyable one. Dan deserves special thanks for all the inspiration and feedback he has given me at various stages of this book project – I have Dan to thank for understanding Baudrillard to the extent that I do, and our conversations continue to make my work more challenging and more interesting. Linsay Cunningham also deserves special thanks for patient help with interviews and photographs during fieldwork in the blistering heat of the Shanghai Expo, and for feedback on work at various stages of the writing process. Christopher Courtney, David Tobin, Malgorzata Jakimow, Elena Barabantseva, Shogo Suzuki and Kelvin Cheung have been indispensable in making me better understand different aspects of Chinese life and language. Critical feedback and support was provided by Jamie Johnson, Ronan O'Callaghan, Roisin Read and Julia Welland. The enthusiasm and academic excellence of my colleagues from the British Inter-university China Centre helped spur me on, particularly that of Nicola Leveringhaus, Holly Snape and Isabella Jackson. I am also grateful for stimulating conversations and feedback on various parts of the book to Andrew Slack, Thomas Gregory, Tom Houseman, Kathryn Starnes, Oliver Turner, Chris Hughes, Emmanuel-Pierre Guittet and Kimberley Hutchings. I also owe a debt of gratitude to Ding Chih-Chi and Zhang Xiaoli for helping me properly decipher and translate philosophical texts in Chinese, with which I sometimes struggled. Miriam Nordfors and Marte Svare contributed by way of moral support and inspirational examples out in the real world. Most of all, Graham M. Smith has been a great support, providing critical feedback on the book as a whole, as well as cups of Swedish tea in the final stages of its preparation. Thank you.

Research groups that have helped develop my ideas by way of critical engagement include the Poststructuralist Politics Reading Group and the Poststructuralist and Critical Thought Research Cluster at the University of Manchester, the China Postgraduate Network, the Stockholm International Theory Group, the Research Seminar of the Stockholm University Department of Oriental Languages and the Joint Seminar of the Swedish Institute of Foreign Affairs, the Swedish Defence College and Stockholm University Department of Political Science. Members of these various groups helped improve my work significantly.

For the permission to reproduce their artwork, I thank graphic designer Zhang Facai (Figure 4.2), artist Kenneth Tin-Kin Hung (Figure 4.5) and blogger Keso (Figure 4.6). I thank the *China Digital Times* for granting me permission to reprint cartoons by Crazy Crab (Figures 5.3 and 5.4).

Research for this book was made possible by generous funding from the Economic and Social Research Council UK and the British Inter-university China Centre through a 1+3 studentship award and nine months of Difficult Language Training funds. Additional funding from the Norman Chester research grant fund and the Erasmus Study and Work Placement Grant helped enhance the writing experience.

Parts of this book are revised versions of work I have published elsewhere. Chapter 3 draws on two articles, 'Taking Baudrillard to the Fair: Exhibiting China in the World at the Shanghai Expo', *Alternatives: Global, Local, Political*, 37(2), 2012, 106–20, and 'Space for the Future: Exhibiting China in the World at the Shanghai Expo', *China Information*, 26(2), 2012, 235–49. I thank the publishers for their permission to reuse them here.

Abbreviations

ASEAN	Association of Southeast Asian Nations
BBS	Bulletin Board System
CASS	Chinese Academy of Social Sciences
CCP	Chinese Communist Party
CPPCC	Chinese People's Political Consultative Conference
GFW	Great Firewall
IR	International Relations
NPC	National People's Congress
PSAAC	Public Service Advertising Art Committee
PLA	People's Liberation Army
PRC	People's Republic of China
SARA	State Administration of Religious Affairs
TCM	Traditional Chinese Medicine
UN	United Nations
US	United States of America

Introduction

The Chinese dream of a harmonious world: a story of appearance and disappearance

Harmony is everywhere in China. Anyone who has visited a Chinese city in the last decade will have been surrounded by billboards advertising it, traffic cones suggesting it and popular music extolling it. For the last ten years, China's top political leaders have been urging their foreign counterparts and people around the world to build a harmonious world of lasting peace and common prosperity. Many think this notion will reshape international norms, provide an alternative to predominant political ideas and pave the way for a new world order. Meanwhile, policy makers are using the notion of a harmonious world to promote everything from Chinese fashion to five-year plans. Thousands of academic articles discuss its potential and conceptualization. Massive propaganda events like the 2008 Olympic Games and the 2010 Shanghai Expo use architecture, film, posters and multimedia to illustrate it. Harmony is even the inspiration for a whole range of punning jokes, cartoons, songs and videos created by an online generation that is finding ways to mock, negotiate and avoid digital 'harmonization'. Simply put, anyone who wants to think about China needs to think about harmony.

Yet, it is the counter-intuitive claim of this book that harmony has not taken place, is not taking place and will not take place. This does not simply mean that there is discord and unrest in China and in the world (which, of course, there is). Rather, this book makes a wider philosophical, sociological and political claim that a harmonious world is impossible. This claim is based on the discussions among a large group of contemporary Chinese policy makers, scholars and propagandists who collectively dream of a better and harmonious future world order, in what has been called a 'discourse of harmonism' (Son, 2012: 399). Contributors to this discourse repeatedly make two claims about harmony. First, they suggest that harmony requires difference or multiplicity. This is because harmony is said to be about balance, and if there are not different things that can balance against one another, then balance becomes by definition impossible. Second, they take harmony to also require universality. This is because they do not think it makes sense to speak of harmony at all if some parts of the whole are in disharmony with the rest. Based on these two proposed requirements, this book argues that harmony is impossible in three important senses.[1]

First, 'Western' thought and practice are often criticized because they do not treat 'non-Western' others as *properly different*, but rather as *behind* in a predefined story about modernization and progress. This book will demonstrate that the discourse of harmonism, as expressed in policy documents, Chinese scholarly writing and government propaganda spectacles, repeats the very same logic as the 'Western' discourse to which it is presented as an alternative. If harmony is a balance between different things in the here and now, as is the claim, then this way of imagining difference makes harmony impossible. Those who are different from us in this story are not *really* different, they are just behind. They are an earlier version of ourselves, and will eventually become like us. They are therefore imagined as located in a different time. There is no real difference in the here and now, and therefore no possible harmony.

Second, there is an inherent and irresolvable philosophical contradiction in the two claims about harmony, which makes harmony impossible by definition. In the literature examined in this book, harmony must *by definition* be universal, but its universalization *by definition* makes harmony impossible, because again it disallows the otherness or multiplicity that is its precondition. If everything and everyone has to be harmonized into the one system governed by the Chinese elite, then there is nothing left that can balance against that system, and so harmony cannot be achieved.

Third, this book makes a more sociological claim about the disappearance of the Chinese dream of a harmonious world. It may once have been possible to imagine harmony as a meaningful concept, a dream or an ideal. What this book illustrates is a mass proliferation of harmony, where everything and anything is supposed to be harmonious. In my research for this book, I went to the harmonious world fair on the harmonious high-speed train, where I watched harmonious exhibitions and if I hurt myself I could get a band-aid from the harmonious first-aid kit. This mass proliferation of harmony means that it has been used to mean anything and everything. It has made the term amass so much meaning that it has collapsed into a joke – quite a clever joke that I will analyze in due course – and the possibility of using it as a meaningful concept has disappeared. The threat posed by proliferating harmonization is then not only the disharmonious behaviour that has tended to accompany it: cracking down on dissidents, suppressing ethnic minorities, blocking words online. A more dramatic threat to harmony comes from the excess of communicating harmony itself, which destroys the illusion of the real in the concept. In this sense, mass communication of harmony is dangerous on a larger metaphysical plane. Again, the attempt to universalize harmony and make it encompass everything has actually undermined it and made it disappear.

For these three reasons, a harmonious world has not been, is not and cannot be made fully present, despite attempts to make it so. Sadly, it does not offer a safe space where scholars can find refuge from the difficulties of imagining multiplicity that many have lamented in 'Western thought'. Rather than offer an alternative world order, official visions of a harmonious world replace 'the West' with 'China' at the head of an imagined historical queue. As a consequence, alterity and difference in the here and now are denied. This is an important problem, because without multiplicity, it seems impossible to imagine not only harmony, but choice, different futures and indeed the political itself.

At the same time, this book will suggest, it is the harmonious world's inability to be fully itself that is its most intriguing and redeeming quality. The harmonious world that is imagined in contemporary Chinese discourse is a profoundly self-contradictory concept, which operates on the logic of intermingled self-defeat and self-perpetuation that others have called 'autoimmune' or 'cancerous' (Derrida, 1998: 46; Baudrillard, 1990 [1983]: 12). The things that harmony does are also *un*done by its very own logic. This, the book will conclude, is a good reason to continue dreaming of a harmonious world. By negating itself in this way, harmony reopens itself to alternative futures to come, to choice and therefore to the political. When the irresolvable contradiction at the heart of harmony is recognized, it allows for a repoliticization of the dream of a harmonious world and of China's role in world politics. Therefore, although this book is critical of the discourse of harmonism as it is currently taking shape in China, it nevertheless seeks to hold open the possibility of other harmonious futures to come. Its most important contribution to this discourse is to bring a recognition of the political back into the Chinese dream of harmony.

Before we begin to explore the proliferation and disappearance of harmony, this Introduction explains how and why this book goes about its argument. It first explains the reason for discussing the 'Chinese dream of a harmonious world' as such. It then introduces the imagination of China as the 'other country' to which that discourse responds, and explains the assumptions about time, space and multiplicity that typically go into such an imagination. It thereafter describes the basic approach of this book, before finally outlining its structure.

The Chinese dream of a harmonious world

Although this book argues that harmony has disappeared, this does certainly not mean that it does not have effects or that it is not important. Harmony is a core concept in Buddhist, Daoist and Confucian thought, and as such it carried great weight in Chinese systems of governance for thousands of years. The central term for 'harmony' in this tradition is *he* (和), which was more recently elevated as the Chinese character that 'carries the most meaning for Chinese culture' (Chin, 2010). Scholars call it a 'foundational' or 'key concept' in Chinese thought (Ba Xiang, 2010: 3), and suggest that traditional sayings like 'cherishing harmony' and 'harmony with difference' have penetrated Chinese society to the extent that they now uphold 'a harmonious national disposition and values' (Ni Shixiong and Qian Xuming, 2008: 125).

Although current discussions about harmony draw on a long history of thought, the concept rose to prominence after then Chinese president Hu Jintao established it as an official policy concept in 2003–5 (Hu Jintao, 2005b, 2005c; CCP Central Committee, 2004). Two key policies under Hu have been 'harmonious society' (*hexie shehui* 和谐社会) and 'harmonious world' (*hexie shijie* 和谐世界). They appeared at a time when the Chinese leadership was concerned about growing social unrest, which had emerged as the country's impressive economic growth was accompanied by increased inequality and environmental degradation. Hu was concerned to maintain stability in order to enable continued growth, and to calm the opposition that could otherwise become a serious threat to party rule (Boutonnet, 2009; *Xinhua*, 2007b). 'Harmonious world' generally built on reform and opening up, a renewed focus on 'Chineseness' and an increasing Chinese assertiveness to go beyond being a 'status quo' power. Specifically, harmonious world has been understood as a development and alternative expression of China's 'peaceful rise', the set phrase that had a short period of popularity in the earlier days of Hu's presidency (Di Dongsheng, 2007).

Every generation of leadership of the People's Republic of China (PRC) has used set phrases like 'harmonious society' and 'harmonious world' to make their mark on Chinese politics, and these two slogans were Hu's attempt to encapsulate his vision and leave a legacy for subsequent generations. The language of harmony was already in use in academic debates and in the speeches of previous generations of leadership (Callahan, 2011: 257; see for examples Liu Zhiguang, 1992; Jiang Zemin, 1997), but it was only with Hu's articulation of 'harmonious world' that it came to denote *the* Chinese way of engaging with the world and of articulating the dream of a new world order. Hu's launch of 'harmonious world' sparked lively debate at all levels of Chinese society about what a harmonious world should look like, and the mass proliferation of harmony that is traced in this book ensued. Overall, it has been argued that the policy concept 'harmonious world' became favourably seen in Chinese academic circles because it showed a 'long overdue attempt by China to exercise normative power in international relations' (Guo Sujian and Blanchard, 2008: 9; see also Jian Zhang, 2007).

In 2012, Hu handed over party leadership to current president Xi Jinping, who was quick to launch his own slogan of choice, the 'Chinese dream' (*Zhongguo meng* 中国梦). This new slogan incorporated Hu's concept of harmony as a key component, and further developed propositions of how Chinese actors might bring about a new type of harmonious international relations. Today, both of these state-led slogans are central ingredients of Chinese foreign policy and international relations, and have become part of the generalized 'discourse of harmonism', which is said to express 'the ethos, identities and norms of the East Asian political elite with respect to national, regional, and global governance at the specific historical juncture the world is passing through' (Son, 2012: 399).

This discourse of harmonism is important because it is central to debates taking place in and beyond China about what the world should look like. It is also important because it articulates visions of what China's role should be in shaping the world, and what kind of ideals should guide China's own internal development in the process of engaging that world. Significantly, it is common to suggest that a Chinese discourse of harmonism can offer a new vision of world order. This vision is said to be a better alternative to the current system associated with American world leadership, and with Western thought more generally.

Despite the heavy focus on harmony within China, scholars outside China have paid it relatively sparse attention. This book aims to address that lack of critical consideration of the important harmony concept. It has been common for Chinese policy makers and scholars to state that when China's ideas of a harmonious world are properly understood, belief in the China threat will wane (for example, *People's Daily*, 2006). A significant proportion of academic commentary on the Chinese dream of a 'harmonious world' similarly stresses the absence of *proper* understanding and a 'specific meaning' of the term as an omission that needs to be addressed (Guo Sujian and Blanchard, 2008: 2). However, unlike most analyses of Chinese foreign policy, this book does not try to find out what 'harmony' *really means* – in fact it claims that it does not have one single specific meaning that can be discovered. Rather, it investigates what harmony *does*. In other words, how does the term harmony function in particular texts or contexts, how does the notion structure these contexts in specific ways, and with what political consequences? It seeks to understand how this official language gears us towards imagining the world and China's place and time in that world in particular ways. It pays particular attention to the way in which difference in time and space is ordered in the notion of a harmonious world, but also to the way in which this official language migrates and morphs in other contexts outside policy documents and in wider Chinese society. It therefore investigates not only how things are done with official words in Chinese politics, but also how they are undone – played with, deconstructed and changed – most often by their own logic.

Imagining China as the 'other country'

As suggested above, the discourse of harmonism contains a clear concern with multiplicity. Behind this concern lies a sense of Chinese history where other countries worked to deny China the possibility of being different. Propped up by current government 'thought work' and patriotic education, Chinese politicians, scholars and the general public are acutely aware of what is known as the '100 years of national humiliation'. This term refers to a period before the founding of the PRC, which saw internal division, a semi-colonial relationship to a number of 'Western' countries and an invasion by Japan (Callahan, 2009; Wang Zheng, 2014).

One of the things that arguably made Chinese suffering in this period possible was the way in which 'Western imperialist powers', as they are collectively referred to in this discourse, positioned China as the 'other country' in temporal, spatial and moral terms (Chow, 1991: 81). This construction of otherness relies on a categorization of that which is in the *same* time and space, homogeneity and self, against that which is in an *other* time and space, alterity and difference (Fabian, 1983; Ashley, 1987, 1988; Campbell, 1998; Crang and Thrift, 2000: 7; Hutchings, 2008: 6). Simply put, this type of story imagines spatially separate others as not simply different, but as 'stuck in the past' or positioned in an 'earlier stage of development' than the self. Importantly, this timeline is often taken to imply a moral yardstick, where imagining others as behind comes to connote their moral deficiency and (as a consequence) their lesser value. Moreover, it often implies childlike qualities, which in turn means that 'they' need to be guided, educated and socialized by 'us'. 'They' cannot quite be trusted to make responsible and mature decisions, and so the leadership or 'being ahead' that is stipulated acquires a moral dimension where 'we' *ought to* assimilate, contain or even exterminate 'them' (Inayatullah and Blaney, 2004). As such, this kind of thinking has been complicit with colonial and neo-colonial global relations (Stocking, 1987: 237).

This organization of difference in temporal sequence has been referred to as 'allochrony' in previous literature, at least since Johannes Fabian's *Time and the Other* (1983: 32). If chronology refers to the arrangement of things or events in a linear timeline, allochrony refers to the imagination of de facto contemporary others at a different point on that line. This book is particularly concerned with Fabian's claim that much scholarly writing has been based on the allochronic assumption that

> relationships between parts of the world (in the widest sense of both natural and sociocultural entities) can be understood as temporal relations. Dispersal in space reflects directly, which is not to say simply or in obvious ways, sequence in Time.
>
> (Fabian, 1983: 11–12)

This way of thinking places all living societies on a temporal slope or stream of time, 'some upstream, some downstream' (Fabian, 1983: 18).[2]

Such temporal alignment of spatial difference indicates the absence of what Fabian terms 'coeval multiplicities' (1983: 31, 34), by which he means 'a common, active "occupation", or sharing of time', seeking 'ways to meet the Other on the same ground, in the same Time' (1983: 31, 165).[3] Fabian shows that as it appears possible to refuse coevalness to another person or another people, coevalness is not a transcultural fact or transcendental condition of knowledge. The term was chosen in order to signal the embeddedness of all temporal relations, and thus all contemporaneity, in culturally organized practice (1983: 34). Other scholars who share this concern with finding ways of thinking about multiplicity in the here and now have referred to it in different terms. Naeem Inayatullah and David Blaney write of tendencies to deal with 'simultaneous occupation' through eradication, separation or temporal displacement (2010: 200). Doreen Massey seeks ways of writing in terms of a 'plurality of trajectories', or a 'simultaneity of stories-so-far' (2005: 9, 12, 24, 54, 80, 130). Kimberley Hutchings writes of 'heterotemporality' which refers to 'ultimately neither one present nor many presents, but a mutual contamination of "nows" that participate in a variety of temporal trajectories, and which do not derive their significance from the one meta-narrative about how they all fit together' (2008: 166). All of these terms seem to point to the same kind of coevalness that is Fabian's concern.[4]

The stories that are told about the allochronic timelines of development produce not only the imagination of the timelines themselves, but also the units or identities that are located on those timelines – units or identities like 'China' and 'the West'. One way in which 'China' has been constructed as other to 'the West' has been the refusal to meet on the same ground and in the same time in this manner, instead imagining China as 'behind'. Today, what used to be called 'savage' or 'uncivilized' is referred to as 'developing', 'modernizing' or as 'being socialized'. This shift in language, however, has done little to change the fundamental manoeuvre of convening spatial difference in temporal sequence. For example, one common way of imagining China's relation to the world since the 1990s has adapted the vocabulary of 'integration', 'engagement' and 'socialization' (see for example Shinn, 1996; Johnston and Ross, 1999; Johnston, 2008). In these stories, China is a 'novice' (Johnston, 2008: 32–3), which has only recently 'joined the world' (Oksenberg and Economy, 1999). By drawing on child socialization, Johnston's work (2008: 5) exemplifies how wider International Relations (IR) literature regularly imagines China as a child or awkward teenager that needs to learn to become more like 'us', by way of a 'huge educational effort' (Oksenberg and Economy, 1999: 28). In these stories, China is imagined as an earlier version of our mature selves. On this logic, China's 'joining the world' and 'engagement with world affairs' from the late 1980s onwards (Oksenberg and Economy, 1999) is unsurprising, an inevitable evolutionary step.[5] This imagination is in part what the general discourse of harmonism reacted against.

Another way in which China has been rendered as the 'other country' has been the insistence on Chinese exceptionalism, an attitude that has arisen in recent years and to a significant extent begun to displace the prior focus on integration (Callahan, 2012: 33; see also Ho, 2014). In this story, China offers an alternative to the failures of 'the West'. This imagination is embraced by the general discourse of harmonism. This position also forms the basis for some of the discussion over the last decade of the possibility of a 'Chinese school' of IR (Yu Zhengliang, 2005; Qin Yaqing, 2011). The building of this particular school rests, in some incarnations at least, on the idea that China is radically different from other countries and therefore can only be properly understood through the lens of 'Chinese culture'. Thinkers who are drawn upon (sometimes perhaps reluctantly) as part of this emerging school look to a select mix of concepts and thinkers from China's past as a source of inspiration for developing theories that can better explain China's rise in a globalizing world (see Qin Yaqing, 2007; Yan Xuetong, 2011 for examples; or Cunningham-Cross, 2014 for a discussion).

In this line of thinking there are also ideas about a 'Chinese model' for development, as well as discussion of a 'Beijing consensus' as opposed to the Washington consensus. With regards to these debates, Shaun Breslin argues:

> [t]his idea of China's difference is part of a feedback loop that has seen the idea of the Chinese model both result from, and then reinforce, conceptions of Chinese difference and exceptionalism: the model is both a result of China's unique history and at the same time a manifestation of China's uniqueness and 'difference.'
>
> (Breslin, 2011: 1343)

Those who deploy such a Chinese exceptionalist imaginary may conceive of China as a threat or as an opportunity, but insist on China as a unique case.

From these two strands of imagining China as the 'other country', we can see how difference and multiplicity in time and space can be understood both as posing a threat and offering an opportunity. Multiplicity means the existence of both myself and others. Those or that which is different from myself can of course potentially hurt me, humiliate me, even try to exterminate me completely. But those others may also be precisely what enables my life in the first place, or who can turn it into a better life. Put differently, multiplicity may be a condition of possibility of a violent relation to those who are positioned as 'others'. At the same time, it is the condition of possibility of something new, different and better. Without it, there would be nobody to meet on the same ground and at the same time. Without multiplicity, all that is imaginable is one all-encompassing great unity: the Self, the One (Massey, 2005: 22–3). Indeed, without multiplicity the idea of newness, a different future and by extension time itself seems impossible – for how could something else emerge from something that is all-encompassing and self-same (Nordin, 2016; Massey, 2005)? In Xi Jinping's own words, '[t]he development of things and progress of the world will come to a stop once all things become homogeneous' (Xi in Gardels, 2014). What is more, without multiple viewpoints or positions, the making of choices that constitutes the political becomes unimaginable – for how to choose, if there is nothing to choose between?

In making this suggestion, I draw on a differentiation made elsewhere between politics in the narrow sense (*politics*) and politics in the wider sense (*the political*).[6] The former is used to describe the areas of life that are commonly called politics, like policy making and other government business, what has been called the 'system of Law-and-Sovereign' (Foucault, 1990: 97). The latter concerns instead what gets to count as politics in the first place, shifting the focus from the smooth running of government business to 'an ontological dimension of undecidability and contingency, agonism and difference underlying political reality' (Variasova, 2011). On this view, what shifts the political into politics, or *depoliticizes*, is reducing something to a question of applying rules, since simple application and calculation does not require us to take responsibility for a political choice (Edkins, 1999: 11). To *repoliticize*, following Foucault, is instead 'to interrupt discourse, to challenge what have, through discursive practices, been constituted as normal, natural, and accepted ways of carrying on' (Edkins, 1999: 12; see also Nordin and Richaud, 2014). The imagining of one single developmental path, where others will eventually become like us, depoliticizes in this sense. When difference in space becomes difference in time, the otherness of others (that is, their singularity or alterity, that which makes them unique and ungraspable to my language and imagination) is reduced to graspable difference, to variations on a theme. Choices about the future stop being political, because they become calculable – after all, it is just a question of time before 'they' become like 'us'. This way of imagining difference robs others of their own future. It turns difference into sameness, other into self,

'Their' future is no longer open to choices and to the political, it is already inscribed in the story. And this of course robs 'us' of a different future, too. Because, again, newness must be impossible without otherness: how could something different appear from an all-encompassing sameness (Nordin, 2016; Massey, 2005)?

This is why difference is needed – and the exceptionalist imagination of China as the 'other country' claims to provide it. Most interesting for our enquiry here are claims made in recent years that Chinese thought can offer better ways of thinking about world order, which can help us do away with some of the problems associated with the European traditions that have been criticized for thinking allochronically. Shih Chih-yu, for example, has argued that Eastern thought does not operate on the binary self–other distinctions of Western thought since the European Enlightenment (Shih Chih-yu, 2010), and that the harmonious world idea is incompatible with the teleological view of shared global norms that is embedded in liberalism (Huang Chiung-Chiu and Shih Chih-yu, 2014: 9). Zhao Tingyang has similarly argued that the *Tianxia* system that was China's central worldview prior to being a modern state was a world 'with no outside', no binary 'other' (2005, 2006c). Therefore, China's harmonious thought can allegedly overcome the problems of a 'Western' state system that has dealt with difference by way of containment, assimilation or extermination. Most literature that has criticized the problematic way of imagining difference described above has also been heavily focused on the way it appears in imaginations of the world that are typically understood as Western, in European languages, but suggests that we may find alternatives to such thinking 'beyond the European imperium' (Inayatullah and Blaney, 2004: ix; see also Fabian, 1983; Massey, 2005; Hutchings, 2008). The discourse of harmonism purports to offer such an alternative, which deserves to be taken seriously.

Approach of the book

What, then, are the assumptions behind and political consequences of different ways of articulating the Chinese dream of a harmonious world, particularly in terms of ordering time and space? Are there contradictions in or between different articulations of the harmonious world, and if so, how are these made visible? What is the overall effect of the proliferation of harmony in contemporary Chinese society?

In order to answer these questions this book traces the Chinese dream of a harmonious world across several contexts. First, it outlines how policy documents and speeches established 'harmonious world' as a set phrase under Hu Jintao, and developed it as part of the 'Chinese dream' after Xi Jinping took over party-state leadership. Second, it examines the discourse of harmonism in the academic literature that took it on and asked what a harmonious world might look like. Third, it discusses harmony in propaganda, particularly at the world fair in Shanghai in 2010 that tried to illustrate and popularize it, but also in a more recent poster campaign after Xi became PRC president in 2013. Fourth, it engages artistic expression and a particular form of online expression called *egao* (恶搞), which operates through spoofs, puns and wordplay to unsettle official language, including the language of harmony.

Before I embark on this task, a few notes are in order to clarify what this book is and is not doing. First, this book shows that the contemporary discourse of harmonism fails to escape the patterns it criticizes in what it terms 'Western thought'. However, as the conclusion to this book will argue more fully, this does not mean harmony should be dismissed. It simply means the discourse of harmonism does not provide a ready-made escape from predicaments that are also encountered elsewhere. That does not mean scholars should stop trying to learn something from 'Chinese thought', or from 'Western thought' for that matter.

Relatedly, this book is focused on Chinese dreams of a 'harmonious world' that have been articulated in the wake of Hu Jintao's launch of it as a major policy term. Before this articulation, China already had a rich history of thinking about harmony. So did other traditions, including what many would think of in terms of 'Western thought'. Importantly, this book is not making a hubristic claim about everything that has ever been said, written and thought about harmony. Instead, it limits itself to analysing a specific discourse that is currently dominating much of Chinese politics and international relations. That discourse draws on prior thinking about harmony, but this book does not analyze such prior versions of harmony in their own right. It is from the contexts examined in this book that it draws the two 'requirements' of harmony outlined in its opening pages. The 'all or nothing' logic that is reflected in some of the subsequent analysis is not imposed on harmony by this book, but is a consequence of the requirements of harmony that are articulated in current literature. As this book will demonstrate, the literature that allows for thinking about harmony in terms of degrees rather than absolutes still tends to do so in terms of allochronic hierarchies, which leads back to the same problems. This does not mean that harmony could not be thought about in different ways, perhaps inspired by its articulation in other times or places, but I have not found such an alternative in current debates. Indeed, the conclusion returns to the question of how harmony opens up to such possible (or impossible) future developments, but this book will not give a definitive answer as to what a better way of thinking about harmony would be.

Furthermore, this book will make some more speculative comments as to how the discourse of harmonism, which stresses its own Chineseness, has ended up repeating the problems it criticizes in what it calls 'Western thought'. Perhaps this is because Chinese thinkers have now been too 'Westernized' to think beyond these particular patterns. Perhaps it is because of an enduring legacy of Marxism or of Eurocentric IR scholarship in China. Perhaps it is because Chinese language too operates on a logocentric logic. My inclination is to believe that what people call 'Chinese thought' and 'Western thought' are constructs that have been informing one another so far back in history that the idea of an 'encounter' between the two fails to capture the point. However, the research here does not enable a conclusion beyond such speculation.

While this book leaves these noted questions to be pursued in future research, the scope and amount of material covered by this book are extensive. The choice of contexts in which it explores the concept of harmonious world is designed to reflect its significance to different segments of society, where it has been deployed for different purposes: policy, academic, public educational and popular cultural. Especially, the book examines the deployment of harmony by state actors and promoters more or less closely tied to the state and its purported purposes – what I refer to as the 'party-state'.[7] It also examines the deployment of harmony by those who are thought of as dissident and as challenging the party-state's practice of harmony. Within these contexts, I have examined a vast amount of primary materials. Interested readers can find the details of these materials, the method for collecting them and the rationale for choosing them in the first endnote to each chapter.[8] Throughout, the book quotes extensively from these materials, sometimes at significant length. This is not an accident, but a conscious stylistic strategy of making the language of harmony visible. This enables the book to go along with the demands of harmony, as it is articulated in the contemporary discourse of harmonism, in order to show how they undermine themselves on and through their own terms. It is also a way of performatively contributing to the proliferation of harmony, as part of the writing strategy of this book, which is explained in greater detail in the next chapter.

Methodologically, this book is concerned with two contradictory imperatives in the discourse of harmonism – the urge to acknowledge the promises of multiplicity, and the drive to suppress its dangers. The notion of coeval multiplicities presents itself here as the solution or opposite of the allochrony problem outlined above. However, the conflicting imperatives for how to deal with multiplicity form what has been called an *aporia*, or an irresolvable contradiction that will not let itself be neutralized. Such an aporia

> is not a contradiction which can be brought into the dialectic, smoothed over and resolved into the unity of the concept, but an untotalisable problem at the heart of the concept, disrupting its trajectory, emptying out its fullness, opening out its closure.
>
> (Burke, 2007: 30–1; also cited in Stern and Zalewski, 2009: 620)

Given that the imposition of allochronic thinking seems built into our language for writing world politics, this book is inevitably setting itself up to fail. It will no doubt fail to resolve its dilemma, or to find a satisfactory alternative to offer up to the reader. In this sense, the reading of harmony offered by this book does not surpass or better the accounts that it scrutinizes. The point of critiquing accounts of harmony here is not to dismiss them for falling back on an allochronic imaginary. Rather, this book shows how it is a trope that is pervasive throughout our thinking about China's foreign relations, irrespective of theoretical approach, geographical location or normative predilection. Simply put, allochronism is a deeply ingrained pattern of thought that is difficult to escape, even with our best efforts.

Ultimately, this book fails to escape the performative re-enactment of the problem that it critiques. Yet this failure must be expected, and in it this book also claims some success. After all, the purpose of this book is not only to point this out, but also to suggest that this may be inescapable. It fails to surpass the aporia with which it grapples – it attempts to read how the harmonious world deconstructs, to counter discourses that treat it as though it had only one true meaning, but in doing so it inevitably reinforces certain understandings of the concept, while marginalizing others. It cannot possibly do justice to the multiplicities of what the Chinese dream of a harmonious world can mean and do. In this failing, however, we may 'further disclose the frantic and violent composition of disciplinary demands to produce the impossible: usable sure knowledge' (Stern and Zalewski, 2009: 629). It is not possible to 'know' what harmonious world is, means or does in any complete manner – and writing about it will invariably fail to do justice to the things the term could possibly do. However, through the excessive or subversive proliferation that this book performs, this instability and impossibility of fullness is made visible. Moreover, the aporetic nature of the issues under study here can reveal 'snags, tears, and portals, inviting alternative paths' (Stern and Zalewski, 2009: 629), offering room for 'thinking otherwise' (Stern and Zalewski, 2009: 629; Derrida, 1982, 1993; Burke, 2007: 30–1). In other words, there is always the possibility of another doing and undoing. On this understanding, scholars can achieve a 'successful failure', which may fail to offer the 'comforting reassurances' of totalizing discourse, but succeed in suggesting 'open-ended conclusions and future[s]' (Stern and Zalewski, 2009: 629). Such a repoliticizing 'successful failure' in engaging both the dream of a harmonious world and the possibility of coeval multiplicities is the goal of this book.

Structure of the book

This book then argues that the Chinese dream of a harmonious world has not taken place, is not taking place and will not take place. Rather than offer an inspirational new vision, it is an impossible and profoundly self-contradictory idea that has lost any appeal it ever had. Instead of illustrating a better alternative to a problematic current system led by 'the West', the contemporary discourse of harmonism repeats the imagination of time, space and difference that has led to many of the problems it criticizes in that current order. This allochronic way of thinking denies difference in the here and now, and thereby makes harmony, as the balance between different things, impossible. The repetition of this allochronic imagination of difference undermines the discourse of harmonism's claims to being alternative, to being better and to being harmonious. What is more, the party-state's efforts to promote the Chinese dream of a harmonious world as a meaningful ideal have ironically accelerated the disappearance of the illusion that it could act as such. If it ever had the potential to function as a significant ideal, that ideal or principle of harmony has now disappeared as an effect of its excessive proliferation. All that remains is a transparent, depoliticized and overexposed proliferation of 'the Chinese dream' and of 'harmonious world' that circulates at various levels of Chinese society. The remainder of this book makes this argument by tracing the appearance and disappearance of harmony at those various levels. The argument is organized into five chapters.

Chapter 1 begins to explore the argument by introducing the 'harmonious world' concept as it first appeared in policy discourse under Hu Jintao. It shows how the party-state has dreamed of a harmonious world of multiplicity and difference, which relies both on a separation of cultural-political units like the state, and on an idea of one-world holism. China is imagined as having a privileged position in the construction of a future harmonious world for all, because of its purported harmonious nature based in history. The chapter then explains how we can see the dream of harmony both *doing* and *undoing* things by tracing it beyond this policy context. It suggests a methodological approach to reading and writing concepts like 'harmonious world' and the 'Chinese dream', what I call a 'strategy of excess', which traces and accelerates the simultaneous appearance and disappearance of the Chinese dream of a harmonious world. In this way, Chapter 1 contributes to my argument by laying the conceptual foundations for the subsequent analysis. It also shows how the exclusions, hierarchies and contradictions that produce an allochronic imagination of harmony are there from the outset in Hu Jintao's dream of a harmonious world. The allochronic imaginary denies difference in the here and now, and therefore makes the balance that is harmony impossible.

Chapter 2 traces the organization of time, space and multiplicity in the academic literature that came about in the wake of Hu Jintao's launch of his harmonious policy discourse. It identifies two common imaginations of time and space that underpin the ways in which academics have written about China's relation to the harmonious world. These mirror imaginations under Hu. The first is what I call a 'unit-based cosmology', that of space as calculable bounded space, as containers of societies. The second is what has been referred to as a space 'with no outside', what I call here a 'holistic cosmology'. The chapter demonstrates that both these imaginations repeat the alignment of space in time that many have criticized in 'Western thought'. In this way, Chapter 2 further illustrates how the universalization and difference that are both said to be requirements of harmony come to undermine one another, and make harmony impossible even in the accounts that have focused on elaborating and increasing its possibility.

Chapter 3 continues by tracing harmony through the Chinese world fair that took place in Shanghai in 2010, and which was created as an illustration of the Chinese dream of a harmonious world. It first investigates how the two cosmologies order universal/particular, time/space and self/other through the representation and ideology of a harmonious world. It then reads the world fair on the level of simulation, which provides a different way of relating 'the West' to its 'other country', China. It examines this relation through asking: Where is the world fair? When is the world fair? Who is the world fair? It shows how reading the world/fair as simulation disrupts notions of inside and outside, now and then, subject and object, to the point where these terms are no longer workable. In this way, Chapter 3 continues to show how the discourse of harmonism produces allochronic thinking in propaganda, but also shows how that same propaganda undermines the differentiation of categories on which allochronic thinking there relies. The proliferation of the Chinese dream of a harmonious world through the Shanghai Expo has therefore contributed to the allochronism that makes harmony impossible, but it has simultaneously showed how the attempt to provide such a pure, ordered and distinct harmonious system fails. Through this argument, it begins to show how the omnipresence of the Chinese dream of harmonious world is making it disappear.

Chapter 4 explores some creative Chinese responses to being censored online in Hu's quest for a harmonious online environment, also known as 'being harmonized'. In the context of the satirical online spoofing culture known as *egao*, the chapter traces one homonym for harmony (*héxié* 和谐), the 'rivercrab' (*héxiè* 河蟹). This term encapsulates a playful way of simultaneously criticizing and avoiding 'being harmonized'. The chapter traces reiterations of this rivercrab in order to bring back in elements denied by Hu's dream of harmony, significantly the question of difference and competition implied in the question 'whose dream of harmony?' By way of this reading, it aims to shed light on the doings and undoings of both harmonious world and coeval multiplicities in a system where inside and outside have been thoroughly confused. Through this examination, the chapter shows how the proliferation of harmony in online discourse makes visible the contradictions that make harmony impossible, thereby contributing to the disappearance of harmony as an ideal while simultaneously opening the term up to other possible (multiple and political) readings.

Chapter 5 turns to developments of the discourse of harmonism after Hu Jintao handed over party-state leadership to Xi Jinping, which incorporated the idea of a harmonious world as a part of his Chinese dream of national rejuvenation. The chapter examines how this new slogan has dreamed of world harmony in the kind of contexts that are discussed in the previous chapters: in government documents, in academic writing, in propaganda and in online spoofing culture. The chapter shows that previous ways of imagining time, space and multiplicity persist under this new formulation, and that harmony has continued to disappear through excessive communication of the Chinese dream. Now, it suggests, all that remains of the ideal or aspiration of the Chinese dream of a harmonious world is a set of empty slogans, whose primary function is to cover up the fact that there is nothing there behind them.

The Conclusion returns to the research questions outlined above, and excavates the implications of my claim that China's harmonious world organizes multiplicity allochronically in the contexts studied in this book. Rather than offer an alternative political dream of world order, official visions of 'harmonious world' simply replace 'the West' with 'China' at the head of an imagined historical queue. As an effect, alterity and difference in the here and now, and the openness of the future, are denied. This in turn makes the political appear unthinkable. The conclusion also outlines the potential and limits for thinking about both harmony and coeval multiplicities – its successful failures. What the Chinese dream of a harmonious world does is also *un*done by its own logic. Most importantly, as an effect of the mass proliferation of this 'harmonious world', the term has amassed so much meaning that the possibility of using it as a meaningful concept has disappeared. The fantasy and reality of a harmonious world have collapsed into one another, and harmony finds it increasingly difficult to appear as an attractive dream for China and the world. In this way, the truly spectacular effect of the proliferating Chinese dream of a harmonious world is the destruction of the dream itself, the disappearance of the illusion of the real within it. Ultimately, however, it is my hope that this self-destruction may open up for new Chinese dreams, of different futures and of a harmonious world that is open to the political.

Notes

1 The first requirement of harmony, which is said to be multiplicity, is clearly articulated in, for example, Ruan Zongze (2005: 14), Liu Xinyu (2005: 41), Yu Xiaofeng and Wang Jiangli (2006), Fang Xiaojiao (2008: 69), Ni Shixiong and Qian Xuming (2008: 125), Yu (2010: 25–6), Li (2010: 49) and Barr (2010: 75). The second requirement of harmony, which is said to be universality, is clearly articulated in, for example, Qin Zhiyong (2008: 68), Zhou Jianming and Jiao Shixin (2008: 28), Li Chenyang (2010: 49), Neville (2010: 69) and Yan Xuetong (2011: 62). These and other examples are discussed in more detail in the chapters of this book.

2 Fabian traces this thinking through evolutionist anthropologists (who '*spatialised* Time' as a taxonomic tree; 1983: 15), on to functionalism, culturalism and structuralism (that did not solve the problem of universal human Time, but 'ignored it at best, and denied its significance at worst'; 1983: 21), further to models of communicatory or Durkheimean sacred Time (that 'project, between sender and receiver, a temporal distance'; 1983: 31). To Fabian, relativists like Ernst Bloch avoid coevalness through 'walling-in the Time of others so that it cannot spill over into ours', which contrasts with the strategy of cultural taxonomy, exemplified by the structuralism of Levi-Strauss, which 'preempts the question of coevalness. Its strategy is to eliminate Time as a significant dimension of either cultural integration or ethnography' (1983: 52). For some recent critiques and appraisals of Fabian's coevalness and research that has tried to develop it since his book, see Birth (2008).

3 When I look 'coeval' up in a Chinese dictionary (Yellow Bridge, 2010), I get the translation 同时代的人, which literally translates as 'people of the same era'. 'Synchronous' gives 同步, or 'same step'. 'Simultaneous' gives 同日, or 'same day/date'; 'simultaneously' gives 同时, or 'same time'. 'Contemporary' gives 同代者, or 'same era person'; 同时代, or 'same era'; 同时期, or 'same phase'; or interestingly also translates as 近人, which literally translates as 'near person' or 'close person' and can also mean 'modern person', 'close friend', 'associate' or 'intimate'. It is worth noting that these terms refer to time in different ways, but that all except the last one contain the character *tong* 同, which indicates sameness, and appears in traditional Chinese cosmologies such as the ideal state of 'Great Harmony' or 'Great Unity' (*Datong* 大同) (for a discussion of the idea of unity in *Datong*, see Callahan, 2004, 2011: 172, 2015a). The role of *tong* in discourses on harmonious world is further discussed in Chapter 2 of this book.

4 Blaney and Inayatullah (2010) trace this temporal displacement from the ethnologies of Lafitau, through Scottish Enlightenment thinkers Smith, Steuart and Ferguson to Hegel and Marx. Massey (2005) examines a range of social thinkers, including Lévi-Strauss,

Sartre, Braudel and Ricoeur, de Certeau, Laclau and Mouffe, and Althusser's critique of Hegel, and finds them unable to furnish us with theoretical resources for such a project. Hutchings shows how in turn Kant, Hegel, Marx; Arendt and Benjamin; Popper, Fukuyama and Huntington; Habermas, Hardt and Negri; Virilio and Agamben 'all render world politics a unitary object for analysis and judgement by privileging a Eurocentric interpretation of the western trajectory of world-political time' (Hutchings, 2008: 23).

5 Elsewhere I have suggested, with Nicola Horsburgh and Shaun Breslin, that 'innovation' may provide an alternative to these allochronic narratives (Horsburgh *et al.*, 2014).

6 The distinction between politics and the political has been discussed by a number of writers, including Ernesto Laclau (Laclau and Zac, 1994), Philippe Lacoue-Labarthe (1990), Claude Lefort (1988) and Fred Dallmayr (1993), to name but a few.

7 I follow Johan Lagerkvist here in referring to governmental, bureaucratic and Chinese Comminist Party (CCP) agencies at all levels of the political system as 'the party-state', unless directly referred to by their level-specific titles. Like Lagerkvist, I take the party-state to indicate 'the power complex consisting of different entities that in different ways design and make policy and laws, plan and monitor' China's harmonious world and society (Lagerkvist, 2010: 11, fn. 3).

8 For these and other sources in this book, I use official English language versions as well as Chinese language ones where possible. I insert simplified characters and pinyin romanization where appropriate. In a few cases I indicate tonal markers to clarify my argument, as in the explanation of 'harmony' (*héxié* 和谐) and 'rivercrab' (*héxiè* 河蟹). Where I make claims about set formulations in China's diplomatic relations, I have checked the English and Chinese language use against some other languages (French, Spanish, Italian, Portuguese and German). Unless referenced to a non-Chinese language source, translations are my own.

1 Policy discourse under Hu Jintao

Doing and undoing things with words in Chinese politics

'The Prince is never casual in his choice of words', Confucius tells us (Analects: 12, iii, 5–6). The Chinese sage famously argued that when names are not correct, state affairs will not be successful and ordinary people will not know how to do what is right. If language is important anywhere, then, Chinese leaders and thinkers may have recognized this more than most. Since the communist revolution, a particular form of linguistic power has gained strength in formalized language known as *tifa* (提法), which may be variously translated as set phrases, formulations, mantras or slogans. Formalized political language exists, of course, in most if not all countries or cultures, but in China these formulations are extraordinarily prevalent and important. As one commentator notes, 'in a political system that is closed and opaque, these are more than just catch phrases – they define the goals of the nation' (Beck, 2007). 'Harmonious world' is one such formulation, which has been central to Chinese foreign policy in the last decade.

This chapter provides the conceptual foundation for the exploration in this book of the 'harmonious world' slogan and subsequent 'discourse of harmonism'. It begins by introducing the 'harmonious world' set phrase in the policy discourse under Hu Jintao. It then explains my basic understanding of what it means to do and undo things with words in Chinese politics, where an utterance is a performance (Austin, 1979) that is ultimately unstable and escapes our intentions (Derrida, 1988). It finally introduces the approach in this book through what I call a 'strategy of excess', which traces and accelerates the simultaneous appearance and disappearance of its object of study.

'Harmonious world' in Hu's policy discourse

Where the prior policy phrase 'peaceful rise' has been understood as an early and somewhat fumbling attempt by Hu to make a permanent mark on Chinese politics, it is said that 'harmonious society' and 'harmonious world' came to define party-state discourse during his time in power (Sow Keat Tok and Zheng Yongnian, 2007: summary).[1] Hu emphatically launched the 'harmonious world' idea to the United Nations (UN) at its sixtieth anniversary summit in September 2005. He emphasized respect for diversity and multiplicity:

> [w]e should do away with misgivings and estrangement existing between civilizations and make humanity more harmonious and our world more colorful. We should endeavor to preserve the diversity of civilizations in the spirit of equality and openness, make international relations more democratic and jointly build towards a harmonious world where all civilizations coexist and accommodate each other.
>
> (Hu Jintao, 2005a)

It continued themes from the 'five principles of peaceful coexistence' advocated by Mao Zedong, including mutual respect for sovereignty and territorial integrity, mutual non-aggression, non-interference in each other's internal affairs, equality and mutual benefit, and peaceful coexistence (Hu Jintao, 2005a). This launch of the harmonious world concept was quickly developed in a white paper, published in December the same year. It is worth citing that white paper here at some length, because it is Hu's speech to the UN and the ensuing white paper that laid the foundations for the vast propagation of harmonism that has since been seen in policy discoure.[2]

The 2005 white paper was titled *China's Peaceful Development Road*, and expanded the rationale for international harmony:

> [p]eace, opening-up, cooperation, harmony and win–win are our policy, our idea, our principle and our pursuit ... China's road of peaceful development is a brand-new one for mankind in pursuit of civilization and progress, the inevitable way for China to achieve modernization, and a serious choice and solemn promise made by the Chinese government and the Chinese people.
>
> (State Council, 2005b)

The future is imagined in terms of an 'inevitable choice', grounded in the particularism of Chinese history and culture:

> [i]t is an inevitable choice based on China's historical and cultural tradition that China persists unswervingly in taking the road of peaceful development. The Chinese nation has always been a peace-loving one. Chinese culture is a pacific culture. The spirit of the Chinese people has always featured their longing for peace and pursuit of harmony.
>
> (State Council, 2005b)

It is said that although an explicit aim is to 'make the country powerful ... China did not seek hegemony in the past, nor does it now, and will not do so in the future when it gets stronger. China's development will never pose a threat to anyone' (State Council, 2005b).[3]

Furthermore, the trait described above as particular to the Chinese people, nation and culture is broadened to make a harmonious world the *wish* of people throughout the world, but the *goal* of China:

> [m]ankind has only one home – the Earth. Building a harmonious world of sustained peace and common prosperity is a common wish of the people throughout the world as well as the lofty goal of China in taking the road of peaceful development.
>
> (State Council, 2005b)

In this way, common interest is imagined as preconstituted, yet needs to be expanded. China is portrayed as a sometimes misunderstood leader of this process: 'China is working hard to bring about a *just* and *rational* new international political and economic order', and is 'working harder to get the rest of the world to understand China' (State Council, 2005b, my emphasis).[4]

In the years after 2005, the term 'harmonious world' was endlessly repeated in speeches by government officials including President Hu Jintao,[5] Premier Wen Jiabao[6] and Foreign Minister Yang Jiechi,[7] along with lower ranking officials[8] and ambassadors.[9] Wen used it in each of his annual reports on the work of government,[10] and more white papers used it to describe People's Republic of China (PRC) relations to the world.[11] Then Vice-President Xi Jinping also used the concept in the run-up to taking over as supreme leader in 2012–13 (Ministry of Foreign Affairs of the PRC, 2011b). In this period, the notion of a harmonious world has been used to encourage and promote a range of views and things, including the official PRC view on the Nanjing massacre (Embassy of the PRC in the UK, 2011a), border politics (State Council, 2009b: VIII) and cybercontrol (Liu Xiaoming, 2011b), and things like the twelfth five-year plan (Liu Xiaoming, 2011a), Confucius Institutes (Embassy of the PRC in Chile, 2011) and even Chinese fashion (Embassy of the PRC in the UK, 2011b). In October 2007 the Seventeenth National Congress of the Chinese Communist Party (CCP) wrote the concept into its constitution, stating its aim to build 'a harmonious world characterized by sustained peace and common prosperity' (*Xinhua*, 2007a, 2007b).[12]

Many of these documents redeploy precise phrases from Hu's speech and from the 2005 white paper (State Council, 2006). It is said that in order to build a harmonious world, there must be political equality and democracy,[13] 'win–win' development and mutually beneficial economic cooperation,[14] as well as cultural exchanges that promote common progress.[15] It is often repeated that countries of the world must work together in friendly cooperation to address traditional and non-traditional global security threats,[16] and bring about 'lasting peace and common prosperity'[17] for the whole world. A stated commitment to multilateral diplomacy,[18] the UN and its millennium development goals[19] are constant. It is claimed that building harmony is a 'guarantee' for social and economic development (Wen Jiabao, 2006).

It is also said that being locked in an integrated holistic system requires a harmonious world to be built (State Council, 2009c: III, 2011c) – a reformulation, perhaps, of the earlier statement that mankind has 'only one home'. Building harmony is 'in line with the trend of the times in the world'[20] and it 'reflects the common interests and aspirations of people across the globe'.[21] At the same time that it stressed this holistic outlook on the Earth, where harmony is said to be everybody's dream, Hu's governmental discourse of harmonism also continued to emphasize that it is a value specific to the Chinese people, state and civilization, because the Chinese people have a history of thinking about harmony and demonstrating their harmonious behaviour.[22] This evaluation is aligned with the more explicit implication of a civilizing mission of sorts, because in order to build harmony there is a need to 'develop a culture of harmony, carry out the program for improving civic morality and foster civilized social conduct' (Wen Jiabao, 2008).

In 2011 a second white paper was issued on *China's Peaceful Development*, which has since been extensively cited and stressed in the PRC's foreign policy work.[23] It reiterated themes of previous reports, and elaborated on the theme of multiplicity and difference in the party-state leadership's vision of a harmonious world through the notion of 'harmony with difference' or 'harmony without uniformity' (*he'er butong* 和而不同):

> [t]he Chinese people have always cherished a world view of 'unity without uniformity,' 'harmony between man and nature,' and 'harmony is invaluable'.... Under the influence of the culture of harmony, peace-loving has been deeply ingrained in the Chinese character.... Imbued with the belief that one should be as inclusive as the vast ocean which admits hundreds of rivers, the Chinese nation has embraced all that is fine in foreign cultures.... The Chinese ... respect different cultures and views, treat others in the same way as we expect to be treated, and do not impose our will upon others. We treat all foreign countries with courtesy, foster harmonious ties with neighbors and make friends with distant states. The Chinese people have inherited the fine tradition of Chinese culture of over 5,000 years and added to it new dimensions of the times.[24]
>
> (State Council, 2011c: IV)

In combination with China's 'basic conditions' and its fundamental national and long-term interests, this predisposition to harmony is said to have created an 'innate force' that drives China's peaceful development (2011c: IV).

There is clearly an emphasis here on wanting to preserve diversity of some sort, but the proud declaration that the Chinese 'nation has embraced all that is fine in foreign cultures' raises the question of the aspects of (foreign) cultures that were not deemed 'fine' by Chinese power holders (Nordin, 2016). A glance at the 'mutual learning' and 'integration' that the party-state calls 'harmony' in the domestic context makes it appear significantly less 'equal' or 'democratic' than what may at first have been supposed. When discussing the harmony of 'ethnic unity', for example, a 2009 white paper demands:

> all China's ethnic groups, in the big family of the unified motherland and on the basis of equality, are required to ... promote peaceful coexistence and harmonious development, continuously strengthen and develop socialist

> ethnic relations based on equality, solidarity, mutual assistance and harmony, devote all to the construction of socialist modernization, and make our country strong, our nation thrive and our people happy.
>
> (State Council, 2009a: III)

The gist of this white paper is that the party-state treats everybody equally, but only to the extent that they conform to party-state standards, as articulated in terms like 'peaceful coexistence', 'harmonious development', 'mutual assistance and harmony' and 'the construction of socialist modernization'. The heavy promotion of harmonious society and world has coincided with waves of violent protest, such as riots and self-immolations among members of China's ethnic minorities (Wong, 2009; Cui Jia *et al.*, 2012). If nothing else, this should make it clear that not everyone wants to be equal on the party-state's terms (Nordin, 2016).

Along similar lines, a white paper on *China's Political Party System* uses 'the multi-party cooperation system' as an illustrative example of harmony with difference, since, it is claimed, '[i]t reflects the fine cultural tradition of the Chinese nation, which features all-embracing and harmony while reserving differences' (State Council, 2007: I). Whatever one thinks of the one-party system, any argument that China's 60 years of CCP rule exhibits equality between parties is clearly unsustainable. What the example does demonstrate is the extent to which the party-state version of 'harmony with difference' is hierarchically ordered. In this unequal organization of difference, decisions in the Chinese People's Political Consultative Conference (CPPCC) are rubber-stamped by other parties. Simultaneously, actual opposition is resolutely and often violently opposed, as is evident in the treatment in this period of imprisoned Nobel Peace Prize winner and pro-democracy activist Liu Xiaobo, or the exiled Dalai Lama who advocates increased autonomy for Tibet. The party-state has tried to delegitimize their respective causes by labelling both these critics as not 'harmonious'.[25] At a few points, it is admitted that harmonious relations build on 'active communication, enhanced cooperation and elimination of differences' (State Council, 2010: V).

As we have seen, then, the party-state version of harmonious world has been used to do a variety of tangible things in Chinese politics and international relations. At the level of imagining difference, it appears to be concerned with diversity and multiplicity. Entities to which this diversity refers include states, but also civilizations and cultures. These are imagined through a hierarchical order that David Kerr describes as 'blending diversity under universalism' (Kerr, 2011: 171). This particular organization of multiplicity is moreover aligned with some spatial and temporal terms, most notably spatial 'opening up', and temporal 'progress' and 'modernization'. This imagination of time and space coincides with the idea of one-world holism, and the idea of a *Geist* of sorts: the 'wish of mankind' or 'the trend of the times in the world', at the end of which we find the Chinese dream of a harmonious world. In this story, China is imagined as having a privileged position in the construction of the future harmonious world that it has inevitably chosen. The reason for this is said to be its purported harmonious nature based in its historical experience.

Against this background, some scholars say that the policy concept 'harmonious world' indicates 'an increasingly confident China relinquishing its aloofness to participate and undertake greater responsibilities in international affairs' (Sow Keat Tok and Zheng Yongnian, 2007: 4.4). Nevertheless, the term is to a significant extent a nice-sounding 'catch-all' phrase. One, albeit not the only, reason for the decline of previously popular term 'peaceful rise' was the association of 'rise' with 'threat' in Chinese as well as non-Chinese discourses (Suettinger, 2005: 6; Glaser and Medeiros, 2007: 304). 'Harmonious world', on the other hand, may be workable not despite but because of its unspecified implications, which nonetheless sound pretty good to people both inside and outside China. Indeed, 'who could argue against global peace and prosperity?' (Callahan, 2011: 262).

Doing and undoing things with words in Chinese politics

As can be seen from party-state discourse, 'harmonious world' often acts as an aspirational and normative concept, the Chinese party-state's articulation of the kind of world order that it wants to build. A key mechanism for facilitating its growth is the communication of this concept and its ideals to the Chinese people and to the world. If anyone thinks of China as a threat, it is said to be because they have not properly understood its dream of a harmonious world (*People's Daily*, 2006). The solution that the party-state has envisaged to this lack of understanding is more and better communication.[26] Therefore, the call to build a harmonious society and a harmonious world has been spread en masse throughout Chinese media, public discourse and public space.

In the same way, a majority of academic writing on the harmonious world concept has also focused on providing better understanding, through what can broadly be divided into two approaches. The first approach takes the relative vagueness of the harmonious world concept as a problem to be solved and tries to find out what the term *really means* (Blanchard, 2008: 165; Tao *et al.*, 2010b: 4). It stresses the absence of a *proper* understanding of the term as a lack to be filled, calling for academics to find out its 'specific meaning' (Guo Sujian and Blanchard, 2008: 2). In such analyses the task of scholars is to 'investigate why and when China favors particular policy tools', 'conduct comparative analyses' to determine the 'varying effectiveness' of the term and to what extent it can 'empower or constrain foreign policy decision makers' (Guo Sujian and Blanchard, 2008: 16; Ding Sheng, 2008).

The second approach focuses on how a harmonious world can be built or realized. This approach presupposes that harmonious world has a specific meaning, often to the point where this meaning is left undefined. It moreover assumes harmonious world to be benign and good. The question in this line of enquiry, then, is not whether or not China should build a harmonious world, but how this can best or most quickly be done. This approach to studying harmonious world is largely part of the Chinese exceptionalist line of thought that was outlined in the Introduction to this book (see for example Liu Guoli, 2008: 151). The aim is to show how a focus on harmony in Chinese history will (naturally) lead to a different (and better) international order as China becomes more powerful (see Kang, 2007; Jacques, 2009 for examples, and Callahan, 2012 for a critique). China, on this view, is naturally harmonious and peaceful, and the task ahead is to make others understand this 'truth' (Liu Jianfei, 2006; Yu Xiaofeng and Wang Jiangli, 2006; Ni Shixiong and Qian Xuming, 2008: 125). It is following this line of thought that policy makers and scholars have claimed that when China's ideas of a harmonious world are *properly understood*, belief in the China threat will vanish (see comments in *People's Daily*, 2006). Like the previous line of thought, then, this approach stresses the absence of proper understanding of the term as a problem that needs to be remedied. The only difference between the two approaches is that the first sees the absence of a clear meaning as a problem for everybody, whereas the second assumes that a clear meaning that Chinese people know already exists, and the only reason for seeking clearer articulation and examples is because foreigners need to be taught.

Both of the previous approaches thus rest on the assumption that 'harmonious world' can have, or indeed has, one single meaning. Furthermore, they assume that this meaning can be discovered by careful study of the behaviour and speech acts of the PRC leadership, or of Chinese historical-philosophical texts. In what follows, an alternative approach is pursued. This approach shifts emphasis from what 'harmonious world' *really means*, to what it *does* (Austin, 1979). In doing so, it draws on a significant tradition of thinking in social sciences and humanities about what it means to do or perform things with words.[27] Asking about harmonious world in these different terms can allow us to think differently about its politics and its futures.

We have seen Hu Jintao articulate 'harmonious world' as a set phrase. Before moving on to tracing that particular set phrase outside Hu's policy discourse, the rest of this chapter lays the foundation for that tracing by looking at how we might understand the 'doings' of set phrases more generally. One of the earliest writings that discussed the particular power of Chinese set formulations at some length is Michael Schoenhals' *Doing Things with Words in Chinese politics* (1992). Schoenhals argues: '[b]y proscribing some formulations and prescribing others, they [the CCP propaganda apparatus] set out to regulate what is being said and what is being written – and by extension what is being done' (1992: 3). He argues that formulations have been deployed in China in an attempt to make the party-state's language the only legitimate medium of political expression (Schoenhals, 1992: 3; see also Apter and Saich, 1994: 5, 68, 108, 114). As such, he takes it to represent one of the most aggressive aspects of CCP propaganda (Schoenhals, 1992: 3). Schoenhals also shows how the nature and intensity of CCP control over appropriate and inappropriate language has fluctuated throughout its rule. Immediately after it seized power in 1949 there was an attempt to stamp out all 'unhealthy language', followed by a reaction against 'excessive formalization' by the mid-1950s, which reached its extreme during the Cultural Revolution (1966–76).[28] At this point Lin Biao, then Vice-Chairman and Mao's unofficial successor, declared: 'one sentence of Chairman Mao's is worth ten thousand of ours'.[29] As Schoenhals explains, between 1966 and 1970 the use of set phrases reduced the 10,000 alternative sentences that individuals may choose to express themselves to 'the one' – and not just any 'one', but the one that Mao was recorded as having said (1992: 19).

In this way, the set phrase restricts what is said through limiting form, the precise words in which things can be said. Schoenhals draws on Maurice Bloch to argue 'this type of restriction is … much more powerful than a direct one on content, since it goes right through the whole range of possible responses' (Bloch, 1975: 5, cited in Schoenhals, 1992: 21). On this view, the type of set phrase that is under scrutiny here not only inhibits the emergence of something new, but also reinforces that which is already established and conventional. To Schoenhals, this is how 'the CCP achieves far more with far less by manipulating the form rather than the content of discourse' (1992: 21).

Importantly, the establishment of the PRC that brought this language practice into the shape seen today was explicitly and from the outset engaged in the kind of 'world making' that is explored here. In the spring of 1949, at the Second Plenum of the Seventh CCP Central Committee, Mao expressed that the communists of China had shown themselves eminently capable of destroying an 'old world', and had now come to the point where they needed to create a 'new world' (*Tianjin shi geming weiyuanhui zhengzhibu*, 1969 [5 March 1949], cited in Schoenhals, 1992: 103). Moreover, Schoenhals refers to the web of intelligibility and possible expression that is formed around these set phrases in terms of a 'semantic map of the real world represented by these formulations' (1992: 27). This chimes with the focus in this book on doing *time and space* with words in Chinese politics, as well as the question of distinction between reality and representation that will be discussed at greater length in Chapter 3.

The present analysis and examination of 'harmonious world' and the 'Chinese dream' draws from Schoenhals' informative research. Importantly, Schoenhals establishes two things. First, the proscription of words may have an inhibiting effect on the emergence of alternatives (*other* alternatives, multiplicity). Second, the CCP prescribes its set phrases, including 'harmonious world' and the 'Chinese dream', in order to reinforce a discourse and logic that is favourable to the existing system. However, I also want to develop Schoenhals' analysis further by supplementing it with an additional line of argument: the party-state is not only doing things with words in Chinese politics, but it is simultaneously *un*doing things and having its own text undone.

We can begin to unpack this claim by way of Jacques Derrida's discussion of signifier and signified. Drawing on Ferdinand de Saussure (1960), Derrida has critiqued the correspondence theory of language where any sign consists of both a signifier (a word) and a signified (the thing itself). In this theory every word means something specific. Put differently, a signifier points to a signified. Derrida has disturbed this logic by showing that every signifier, or word, signifies *not* the thing itself, but another signifier. That signifier in turn signifies another signifier, which in turn signifies another signifier and so on. The chain of words or signifiers reveals the absence of the signified, the absence of the thing itself (Derrida, 1976 [1967]: 61, 73).

Looking at 'harmonious world' through this logic changes the way it makes sense to approach and study the concept. When a scholar (or foreign policy maker, or some other commentator) says or writes the words 'harmonious world', it is to signify a specific thing ('harmonious world' *itself*), even if this thing is as yet only partly constructed or even utopian. However, when the scholar tries to explain what 'harmonious world' is, in itself, he or she can only refer to more signifiers, such as 'cooperation', 'assertiveness', 'pragmatism' and so on. Therefore, although many scholars try to make 'harmonious world' *in itself* present, what their writing actually reveals is the impossibility of making the thing itself present in language. What we see, then, is not the practice or ideal of 'harmonious world' *itself* at the origin of the chain of signifiers (cooperation, assertiveness, pragmatism), but the absence of harmonious world and the impossibility of presenting harmonious world *as such* (cf. Bulley, 2009). In this way, meaning is always deferred. It is promised endlessly from one word to the next, but it is never delivered. As a result, approaches that seek to establish the 'true' meaning of 'harmonious world' are misguided. There is no stable meaning to which the signifier 'harmonious world' refers. Harmonious world does not exist as a thing in itself. Rather, 'harmonious world' is what emerges in the interweaving of chains of signifiers with no signified: a text (Derrida, 1987 [1972]: 26).

Therefore, 'harmonious world' should be read as text. This implies, in a very particular way, that 'harmonious world' loses, or rather *defers*, its meaning. This, however, does not imply that it does not have concrete effects, because a term or text can operate and do things even if it does not have one specific meaning. Moreover, it does not mean that there are not continuing attempts to fix and stabilize the 'true' meaning of harmony. Finally, to treat the dream of harmonious world as a text is to consider much more than spoken or written words. As will be demonstrated, images, artefacts, architecture, videos, music, as well as other visual and digital materials, are part of the text of 'harmonious world' (and these form a focus of discussion in Chapters 3, 4 and 5). The point of studying 'harmonious world' as text is rather to recognize how profoundly our making sense of the world is bound up in language, and how this in turn has effects on our being in the world and on how we relate to others.

Moreover, this language through which we make sense of the world can only make sense to us insofar as it can do so also in a different context, even if the communicator or receiver is not there then. In other words, it must be repeatable in other contexts (Derrida, 1988: 9). This means it is possible to remove its repeatable meaning from the specific context in which it was first deployed and 'recognize other possibilities in it by inscribing it or grafting it onto other chains' (Derrida, 1988: 9; cf. Massey, 2005: 19). The purported or intended meaning of a term like 'harmonious world' is structurally capable of being lost or changed, so that it means something other than the author's intention. Indeed, this is not only possible, but inevitable. Therefore, not only does 'harmony' not have one fixed meaning, but we can also play with it, graft it into other chains of signification that can reveal meanings that were always already potentially there in harmony in the first place.

Harmonious world, then, has no fixed meaning, and is capable of being relocated in multiple contexts. As a result, we can observe a proliferation of the Chinese dream of a harmonious world. Some scholars who do not agree with the official dream of a harmonious world have shown their disagreement with its proliferation through simply refusing to use the term. In this way, they have used silence, the refusal to further proliferate the concept, as a way to resist it. In contrast, an alternative argument is developed here: that harmonious world has also countered itself by way of its excessive mass proliferation. Jean Baudrillard, whose work will be instrumental to this analysis, has written of the effects of excess and proliferation in many forms. One form that will be of significance to the development of this book is his writing on excess in the form of cancer: 'hypervitality in only one direction' (Baudrillard, 1990 [1983]: 12). Just as cancer cells multiply and spread through a biological system through growth and multiplication, so too will we see how 'harmonious world' proliferates as an endlessly repeated promise, communicated again and again through the system, en masse. However, as with cancer, the excessive spread and growth of this promise may backfire against the system in ways that those who dream of a harmonious world have not intended or foreseen. Chapter 4 of this book will demonstrate how harmony, like cancer, has gone from building or production to excessive hyperproduction, uncontrolled proliferation, excrescence and outgrowths. These outgrowths come to threaten, or *undo*, the promise of a future harmonious world order (while simultaneously and paradoxically keeping it alive).

In Schoenhals' study, the formalized language of the set phrase becomes 'a form of power for the already powerful', because '[o]nly a few CCP leaders are able to manipulate rather than be manipulated by formulations, that is, to have the formulations they favor be designated "appropriate" and the formulations they disapprove of be labelled "inappropriate"' (1992: 22). Although Schoenhals' point is well taken, scholars need not stop at acknowledging and studying the attempt by those in powerful party-state positions to fix language and what it does. Following Baudrillard, the *doing* of things with words in Chinese politics may also carry with it an *undoing* of things, with the very same words.

Baudrillard's interest in the potential of texts to be undone by their very own logic is shared by Derrida. The general approach of Derrida's work springs from his 'general strategy of deconstruction' (1987 [1972]: 41), which observes a 'double movement' of simultaneous reversal and displacement of terms that are formed in apparent binary opposition in a given text.[30] It involves a first movement of *overturning* because:

> in a classical philosophical opposition we are not dealing with a peaceful coexistence of a vis-à-vis, but rather with a violent hierarchy. One of the terms governs the other (axiologically, logically, etc.), or has the upper hand. To deconstruct the opposition, first of all, is to overturn the hierarchy at a given moment.
>
> (Derrida, 1987 [1972]: 41)

Importantly, however, this is not a 'once and for all' resolution, but a move one needs to continuously go through since the hierarchical binary re-establishes itself (Derrida, 1987 [1972]: 113). Moreover, the second move of *displacement* is equally important, and moves towards a new term that is not part of the previous hierarchy (Derrida, 1987 [1972]: 42; see also Nordin, 2012b: 3). Both these moves are thus crucial to the 'double gesture' of deconstruction, one of the two on its own is not enough (Derrida, 1988: 21).

Although this can be thought about as a kind of strategy, deconstruction is something that takes place in texts, rather than something that is applied to them – it is the assumptions already there in the text that undermine it. For this reason, we can think of reading a text as 'another act of writing' (Zehfuss, 2007: 23). This does not mean a text can be read to give *any* meaning, or to *do any thing*. However, no text has one single predetermined meaning that one can uncover. In other words, a plurality of possible doings are always already there in a text, and responsibility for what the text means, or rather *does*, falls on both 'writer' and 'reader' (or, following Zehfuss, 'the other writer'). My reading/writing of the Chinese dream of a harmonious world, of Derrida and Baudrillard, and of the other texts under scrutiny here, is similarly not intended to uncover their one 'true' meaning or doing, but rather to pose a challenge.

Strategy of excess

Both Derrida and Baudrillard write of a 'double reading' or 'reversal' of sorts from which this book draws inspiration in formulating its own challenge. In Derrida's deconstruction, this double reading consists of reading a given text as closely as possible to its own explicit logic, but then also with attention to the way deconstruction takes place in it, how the text's logic works against itself. Baudrillard does something similar in his 'reversibility', an 'absolute weapon' against determination and teleology (Baudrillard, 1990 [1983]: 82). Reversibility is a kind of 'evil spirit' in Baudrillard's thought that ensures that every system (like the texts Derrida was concerned with) can and will be overturned, precisely by its own functioning (Baudrillard, 2005 [2004]; see also Coulter in Smith, 2010: 181–3). Indeed, some have commented on Baudrillard's approach to theory as 'a form of deconstruction'.[31]

This book thus reads both Derrida and Baudrillard as emphasizing the possibility of a double reading of tensions at play in language – and in turn the play with this tension as a strategy of sorts.[32] This book will point throughout towards what Baudrillard would term the 'objective irony' that 'arises from within things themselves', from a system 'functioning against itself' (Baudrillard, 1987). This focus on systems is shared by Derrida, who insists that deconstruction always has to do with systems and their destruction so as to disclose other 'possibilities of arrangement' (1995 [1989]-b: 212).

Together, these approaches amount to what may be thought of as the analytical strategy of this book. In a proliferating system, which I suggest is what we are dealing with, traditional approaches that resist falsity with truth (what

Baudrillard calls 'banal theory') are no longer workable (Baudrillard, 1990 [1983]). Such truth-seeking approaches include the two approaches to studying 'harmonious world' that were outlined earlier in this chapter. In 'fatal strategy', in contrast, 'the system's own logic turns into the best weapon against ... its own logic to total perfection' (Baudrillard, 2001: 126). Baudrillard tries to access this through a form of 'provocation' that 'plays (along) with the system by accelerating its logic so as to "precipitate" it towards its end' (Rajan, 2002: 271):

> [o]ne goes therefore in the same direction as the text – but one accelerates, one goes much faster towards the end of the text. And one plays on the logic itself to be able ... to reach a point beyond it, so as to make the system reveal itself more clearly.... One produces ... meaning *as if* it arises from the system (even if in fact the system lacks meaning) in order precisely to play that meaning against the system itself.
>
> (Baudrillard, 1987: 52, 40–1, cited in Rajan, 2002: 271)

Like Tilottama Rajan, I read this passage as resonating with Derrida's account of deconstruction as using 'the instruments or stones available in the house' against 'the edifice' itself (Derrida, 1982 [1972]: 135).

This book draws on this way of reading on several levels. First of all, it makes a double reading of the concept of 'harmony' within each chapter. It reads each 'text' closely to remain true to that text's own logic and purported message. In Chapter 2 these are academic texts on China's harmonious world. In Chapter 3, they are the symbols, layout, architecture and texts produced at the Shanghai Expo. In Chapter 4 they are the Chinese characters for 'harmony'. In Chapter 5 it is all of these in the context of the 'Chinese dream' slogan. In each case this book reads an intended message within the text's own logic, but then performs a second reading, which presents the text 'otherwise' than that purported message. In the chapter on the Expo, for example, I read it first in terms of representation and then as simulation. This multiple reading strategy is also at play between the different chapters of the book, where each supplements and defers the meaning of the other.

Together, the chapters form what Michael Shapiro has called 'disruptive writing', which involves approaching an issue by a set of alternative texts and narratives to the well-rehearsed debates that they usually engage (Shapiro, 1997: ix, 38). These readings perform a take on Baudrillard's 'fatal theory', which involves an acquiescence to the power of the 'object' of this study in the hope of pushing its meanings to their limits so that they collapse or are reversed. On this understanding, this book follows what Marc LaFountain has called Baudrillard's 'ethics of excess' (LaFountain, 2008). I give in to harmony. Rather than bin it, I recycle it, again and again. I comply with the demand that everything should be harmonious and so I read harmony anywhere and everywhere that it appears. However impossible, I try to seek out all its meanings and doings. I follow it in a way that hopes to take its demands to their limits, where excessive following becomes transgressive to the demands themselves. Thus pursuing the object according to its provocation has the potential of making it 'obese' or 'overripe' with meaning to the point where it collapses or reverses 'under the weight of its own desire and machinations' (LaFountain, 2008). As pointed out with reference to Derrida's deconstruction, this reversal cannot be a 'once and for all' – as soon as my object may be seduced and reversed, it will mutate, metastasize and return once again in recycled form. Through deconstruction and reversibility, both Derrida and Baudrillard thus emphasize the point that the system itself (here 'harmony') contains the seed of its own destruction. It itself produces that which threatens it. This thinking runs through the entirety of the book, but is further developed in Chapter 4, which draws on the two writers' thought on cancer and the autoimmune, to show how 'harmonious world' produces the elements that destabilize it.

In this way, through reading the notion of a 'harmonious world' in terms of both its doing and its undoing, its appearance and its disappearance, this book suggests a novel way in which scholars of Chinese international relations may study foreign policy concepts in general and Chinese set phrases in particular. It thus contributes to the literatures on 'doing things with words' in Chinese politics through emphasizing ways of examining the undoings that doings necessarily imply, and the disappearance that begins as soon as a concept appears. It moreover contributes to literatures on time, space and multiplicity in International Relations (IR) through showing how the thought of Derrida and Baudrillard may help us shake up the manner in which questions of multiplicity and politics can be formulated, and foreign policy concepts can be studied in terms of excess and disappearance (cf. Nordin and Öberg, 2015; Nordin, 2014a, 2014b; Öberg, 2013, 2014).

Finally, it should be acknowledged that the writing here is not structured purely chronologically, nor simply thematically. I have in my writing tried to maintain awareness of how my structuring of the text plays with and draws on the notions of time that the text itself also discusses. This book critiques the spatio-temporal taxonomy and chronology that structures the discourse of harmonism, and at the same time it (re)taxonomizes and (re)chronologizes it through its own analysis. The irony of this move is not lost on the author, but is part of the struggling with these concepts and the attempt to write the world more critically in a way that explores the possibility of multiplicity in the here and now – to perform a successful failure.

Conclusion

This chapter has introduced the policy discourse of 'harmonious world' under Hu Jintao. It has suggested that this term does not have one single meaning that researchers can pin down, but that we can nonetheless study what it does in and to Chinese politics. The chapter has proposed that this policy discourse has done a number of different things. Of particular interest has been the emphasis on preserving multiplicity and difference, an emphasis that sits in tension with the simultaneous tendency to hierarchical ordering or even elimination of that difference. The chapter has also pointed towards some violence and exclusion that has taken place at the hands of the party-state in the name of harmony. Most notably, we have seen that harmony is positioned at the endpoint of a purported 'trend of the times', but also that China or (some) Chinese people are understood to have privileged access to harmony because of history.

This chapter has also suggested that the things that are done by Hu's discourse of harmonism may ultimately be undone by their own logic. We can read both the doings and undoings of the policy-driven discourse of harmonism by tracing how harmony has continued to proliferate outside policy discourse under Hu. This will be the task of the rest of this book. Pursuing this continued and excessive proliferation in other contexts – in academic discourse, propaganda and online spoofs – will enable an analysis of the simultaneous appearance and disappearance of the Chinese dream of a harmonious world. Pursuing such a strategy will also performatively enact this double move of appearance and disappearance. This chapter has suggested that deconstruction and reversibility, as discussed by Derrida and Baudrillard, speak to the same potentials for such a performative reading. These two thinkers can be read in different ways, in ways that point to closures and ways that point to openings. As they would insist, drawing inspiration from their work cannot be a question of application, but of working in dialogue with and emerging with something appropriately different. I draw on them here to put forward a performative 'strategy of excess', through which this book engages with harmony and contributes to the acceleration of its symbolic disappearance.

Notes

1 The policy discourse examined here is important because it set off the wave of proliferating harmony that is under study in this book. Because this book is interested in how the party-state itself wants to portray its view of 'harmonious world' to wider global and domestic audiences, the data here consists in official publications, speeches and policy documents. I have processed all Chinese government white papers published from 1991 to mid-2015 (90 in total) in the Chinese and English languages, as well as the annually published Reports on the Work of Government for 2000–15. I have moreover sought out additional speeches made by key figures such as Presidents Hu Jintao and Xi Jinping, Premiers Wen Jiabao and Li Keqiang, and Foreign Ministers Yang Jiechi and Wang Yi, especially at key state visits or significant gatherings in national bodies such as the National People's Congress (NPC) or the CPPCC, as well as international bodies like the UN. I have processed written and video materials from Chinese and international news media. Finally, I sourced a significant portion of materials through speeches and documents that were made available by the Chinese Ministry of Foreign Affairs and that include permutations of the term 'harmonious world' in English and Chinese. I also processed all documents referring to the term that were made available on the websites of individual Chinese embassies, in English, Chinese, French, Spanish, Portuguese or German (166 embassies in total). The analysis of government discourse in this chapter, and the section on policy discourse under Xi Jinping in Chapter 5, relies primarily on English language documents, and has used the sources in other languages to 'check' for significant deviations that may contradict these. These sources are limited to ones where my own language skills are enough to provide an understanding of the text. Having said this, these languages cover all of the Americas, Africa and Oceania, as well as a majority of Europe, and

those not covered have documents available in the Chinese language. In addition, many embassies do not provide documents in the official language(s) of the state to which they are deployed (for example, embassies to Scandinavian, Arabic and many Asian countries provide documents in English or French, as well as Chinese). Some of the arguments and evidence in this section are discussed with a different focus in Nordin (2016).

2 It has been deployed for similar purposes and retaining the same formulations in numerous languages. A number of PRC embassies make such examples available, for example in French (Zhang Guoqing and Kadieh, 2010; Wang Yingwu, 2011), Italian (Ding Wei and Cubeddu, 2010), German (Embassy of the PRC in Germany, 2010), Spanish (Yin Hengmin, 2007) and Portuguese (Chen Duqing, 2007; Qiu Xiaoqi, 2011a, 2011b).

3 Nordin (forthcoming a) examines the Chinese discourse of hegemonism, and urges caution with regards to accepting this common claim.

4 In subsequent publications these claims to China's vision being uniquely just and rational is common. Unlike other, less harmonious countries, China 'will never seek hegemony' (State Council, 2005a, 2009b), but simply needs to focus on 'safeguarding China's sovereignty' (Wen Jiabao, 2007, 2008, 2009; State Council, 2011c). 'Safeguarding China's sovereignty' in a harmonious world typically implies recognition of the 'one China' principle, according to which there is only one China, and Taiwan is part of China (Central People's Government of the PRC, 2008). This will bring about a future world order where China will always stand for 'fairness and justice', an order that is also rational due to the application of China's 'scientific outlook on development' (Hu Jintao, 2007). The 'scientific outlook on development' (科学发展观) is one of the guiding principles of the CCP, incorporating sustainable development, social welfare, a humanistic society, increased democracy and, ultimately, the creation of a harmonious society. Together with 'harmonious society', it marked the shift of emphasis under Hu Jintao from 'socialism' to 'Chinese characteristics' (Cheung, 2012). Chinese scholars have argued that the 'scientific outlook on development' provides the theoretical basis and guidance for the building of a harmonious society, while the latter represents the concrete implementation of such a perspective (Guo Jianning, 2006). The two phrases were together ratified into the CCP constitution at the Seventeenth Party Congress in October 2007 (Communist Party of China, 2007). The term was also associated with the building of a harmonious society in earlier documents, such as Wen's 2006 and 2007 work reports (Wen Jiabao, 2006, 2007).

5 Hu Jintao (2009, 2010, 2011a, 2011b). See also *Xinhua* (2009b, 2009c, 2011), Foreign Ministry of the PRC (2011).

6 Wen Jiabao (2010a). See also *Xinhua* (2010d).

7 Yang Jiechi (2011). See also Embassy of the PRC in the USA (2011).

8 Some examples include Wu Bangguo, Chairman of the Standing Committee of the National People's Congress (2010), State Councilor Dai Bingguo (2011, 2012) and Ye Xiaowen, head of the State Administration for Religious Affairs of China (SARA) (*Xinhua*, 2008).

9 For a small selection, see examples from Antigua and Barbuda (Liu Hanming, 2011), Bahamas (Hu Dingxian, 2010; Hu Shan, 2011), Bangladesh (Embassy of the PRC in PR Bangladesh, 2011), Barbados (Embassy of the PRC in Barbados, 2010; Wei Qiang, 2012), Botswana (Liu Huanxing, 2011), Brazil (Chen Duqing, 2007; Qiu Xiaoqi, 2011a, 2011b), Chile (Embassy of the PRC in Chile, 2011), Commonwealth of Dominica (Embassy of the PRC in Commonwealth of Dominica, 2011; Wang Zonglai, 2011), Democratic Republic of Congo (Wang Yingwu, 2011), Djibouti (Zhang Guoqing and Kadieh, 2010), Ethiopia (Liu Guijin, 2010), Germany (Embassy of the PRC in Germany, 2010), Italy (Ding Wei and Cubeddu, 2010), Lesotho (Hu Dingxian, 2012), Liberia (Zhou Yuxiao, 2011), Mexico (Yin Hengmin, 2007;

Embassy of the PRC in Mexico, 2011), Micronesia (Zhang Weidong, 2010, 2011), Nepal (Yang Houlan, 2012) and Tanzania (Liu Xinsheng, 2010).

10 Since 2000, the only mention of harmony in a government work report prior to Hu's 2005 speech to the UN was by then Premier Zhu Rongji in 2003, where it was briefly mentioned with reference to creating a standardized administrative system and to justify the postponement of raising government salaries and pensions, pending the need to 'harmonize relationships among the interests of all quarters' (Zhu Rongji, 2003). Harmony gained significantly more prominence in Wen Jiabao's 2005 work report, where one of the 'basic ideas' for the work of government in that year was to 'build a harmonious socialist society' (Wen Jiabao, 2005). The work report in the subsequent year, the first one after Hu's speech to the UN, mentioned 'harmonious world' for the first time (Wen Jiabao, 2006). Work reports in 2007, 2008, 2009, 2010, 2011 and 2012 continued to use 'harmonious world' as a marker and descriptor of the government's foreign policy ambitions (Wen Jiabao, 2007, 2008, 2009, 2010b, 2011, 2012). The work reports after Xi Jinping's leadership takeover in 2013 have used the term 'harmony' repeatedly, but not 'harmonious world' (Wen Jiabao, 2013; Li Keqiang, 2014, 2015).

11 The term 'harmonious world' has been key to two particular white papers: *China's Peaceful Development Road* (State Council, 2005b), and *China's Peaceful Development* (State Council, 2011c). Harmonious world is given a foundational position at the outset of other white papers, such as China's first foreign policy white paper on Latin America and the Caribbean Region in 2008 (Central People's Government of the PRC, 2008), and a white paper elaborating on the Chinese government's policies and positions on arms control, disarmament and non-proliferation (State Council, 2005a). In general terms, 'harmony' has featured in white papers at least since the early 1990s, but saw a sharp rise in popularity after 2005. In the 14 years before 2005, 22 white papers used the term 'harmony' (*hexie* 和谐, or, in English, some other grammatical permutation of the word), and 19 did not, as follows: in 1991 1 of 1 paper used the term; 1992 1 of 2; 1993 0 of 1; 1994 1 of 2; 1995 2 of 3; 1996 1 of 3; 1997 2 of 3; 1998 1 of 3; 1999 1 of 1; 2000 4 of 7; 2001 1 of 3; 2002 2 of 2; 2003 2 of 4; and 2004 3 of 5. In the seven years after 2005, 30 white papers used the term, only seven did not, as follows: 2005 7 of 7; 2006 3 of 4; 2007 1 of 2; 2008 2 of 4; 2009 5 of 6; 2010 5 of 5; 2011 7 of 9. From Hu's retirement to the time of writing, seven white papers have used the term, five have not (2012 2 of 5; 2013 3 of 4; 2014 2 of 4; 2015 2 of 2).

12 Note that this refers to the constitution of the CCP (Communist Party of China, 2007: General Program), not that of the PRC (National People's Congress of the PRC, 2004). The latter contains no reference to harmony.

13 Wen Jiabao (2007), Central People's Government of the PRC (2008), State Council (2011c).

14 Wen Jiabao (2007). For this prominent 'win–win' theme, see also Wen Jiabao (2008, 2009), Hu Jintao (2010), Central People's Government of the PRC (2008), State Council (2009b, 2011c).

15 Wen Jiabao (2007), State Council (2011c).

16 Wen Jiabao (2007, 2011), State Council (2009b, 2011c: IV).

17 This set definition of the goal of Chinese foreign policy being to 'build a harmonious world of lasting/durable/enduring peace and common prosperity' is reiterated more or less verbatim in each of Wen's government reports after Hu's 2005 speech to the UN (Wen Jiabao, 2006, 2007, 2008, 2009, 2010b, 2011, 2012). It is frequently reiterated in government white papers (Central People's Government of the PRC, 2008; State Council, 2006, 2009b, 2011b, 2011c), Joint Communiqués (Ministry of Foreign Affairs of the PRC and the Ministries of Foreign Affairs of the Caribbean countries having diplomatic relations with China, 2010), and in speeches by Hu Jintao (2011b; Foreign Ministry of the PRC, 2011), government officials (Dai Bingguo, 2011; Yang

Jiechi, 2011) and ambassadors (Embassy of the PRC in Barbados, 2010; Hu Dingxian, 2010; Hu Shan, 2011; Liu Hanming, 2011; Qiu Xiaoqi, 2011a, 2011b; Yang Houlan, 2012).

18 Wen Jiabao (2006, 2008, 2009), Hu Jintao in *Xinhua* (2011), Central People's Government of the PRC (2008), State Council (2011c).

19 State Council (2011a, 2011c), Hu Jintao in *Xinhua* (2011).

20 Wen Jiabao (2007), Central People's Government of the PRC (2008), State Council (2006, 2009b, 2011c: IV).

21 Wen Jiabao (2007), Hu Jintao (2011b), Central People's Government of the PRC (2008), State Council (2006, 2009b, 2011c: IV).

22 State Council (2005a, 2007: I, 2011b, 2011c) and Zhang Weidong (2011).

23 The white paper itself frequently appears on embassies' websites, more than any other document relating to harmonious world. It has been explicitly referred to in many speeches, for example by ambassadors to Nepal (Embassy of the PRC in FDR of Nepal, 2011) and the UK (Liu Xiaoming, 2011c). Embassies also frequently link to speeches and symposia held in China to draw attention to the white paper (Dai Bingguo, 2011; Embassy of the PRC in the USA, 2011; Yang Jiechi, 2011).

24 Advocates of this view include Ambassador Wang Xuexian, to whom

> 'Seeking harmony while acknowledging differences' means that a country or an ethnic group, while preserving its own cultural heritage, should be open and tolerant to other civilizations.... In Chinese culture, harmony is underpinned by diversity and there will be no harmony without diversity.
>
> (Wang Xuexian, 2008)

The theme is developed closely with the concept of peaceful coexistence and mutual respect between civilizations (Ye Xiaowen in *Xinhua*, 2008; Hu Jintao, 2005a; *Xinhua*, 2009b). Historical examples that are used to back up the claim that the Chinese are a naturally peaceful people include the elsewhere recurring examples of Admiral Zheng He and the Silk Road (State Council, 2011c: IV). For similar comments in policy discourse about Chinese people's harmonious nature due to the purported 5,000 years of harmonious civilization, see Wu Yi (2006).

25 For the case of the Dalai Lama, see *Xinhua* (2009a) for an example, and Callahan (2011: 173) for a discussion related to 'harmonious world'. For a press release that equates supporting Liu with not being harmonious, see Embassy of PRC to the USA (Embassy of the PRC in the US, 2010).

26 See for example Wen Jiabao (2007), Central People's Government of the PRC (2008), State Council (2011c: IV).

27 The study of 'doing things with words' draws on a rich tradition within the humanities, with this formulation being used particularly in the footsteps of John L. Austin (1979 [1961]). This is not to say that this tradition focuses time, space and multiplicity in the way that I do in this book, which is why I leave a more detailed discussion thereof to others.

28 David E. Apter and Tony Saich have shown this focus on 'health' and 'cleansing' of the body politic to be a marked trait from the initial consolidation of the Chinese communist movement as a Maoist party at Yan'an (1936–47). It was no accident, they claim, that Mao's first published writing was concerned with the need to purify and restore collective health (Apter and Saich, 1994: 92, 102, 104).

29 This quotation from Lin Biao can be found in a collection of his quotations by the People's Liberation Army (PLA) General Political Department (1970: 17, cited in Schoenhals, 1992: 19). The formalized language of this period has been discussed in a number of books that take delight in the humorous effects the awkward use of set phrases often had (for example, Jin Chunming *et al.*, 1989).

30 'Text' here 'implies all the structures called "real", "economic", "historical", "socio-institutional", in short: all possible referents' (Derrida, 1988: 148).

31 For such a reference, see Hegarty (2004: 7). This book highlights a significant commonality and complementary difference between Baudrillard and Derrida, especially as they touch on terrorism, 9/11 and the autoimmune discussed in Chapter 4 of this book (see for example McMillan and Worth, 2003, or a summary of their meeting to discuss these questions in Daubigny, 2003). Some readers of Baudrillard have found Derrida too attached to the real, and as too driven by a productivist impulse (Coulter, 2005; see also Baudrillard, 1981 [1972]: 160). On this view, Baudrillard is more interested in subtraction, Derrida (ironically) in deconstructive addition and accumulation (Coulter, 2005). I think of any such difference as usefully complementary. Reading Derrida alongside Baudrillard can help guard against an interpretation of the former as too enchanted with the 'real' and with prioritizing 'positivity' over 'negativity' (as Massey does in her own argument for space, see Nordin, 2012b). If Baudrillard can add something to a reading of Derrida, so too can Derrida be drawn on to read Baudrillard in a way that avoids the totalizing logic and closure that some have read into his work. Most notably, some have read Baudrillard's 'phases' of the image as implying a linear notion of time, a taxonomy of stages. For example, Jeppe Strandsbjerg argues that if we take him literally, 'Baudrillard's statement logically presupposes a time where the territory preceded the map', which Strandsbjerg goes on to show is inaccurate, because maps cannot be understood as ever simply representing space – their relation is one of 'construction' (2010: 87–8). Strandsbjerg's reading of Baudrillard is plausible, if indeed 'taken literally', and I agree with his point about the map never having been a representation. Nonetheless, I think (with Derrida's help) that we can read Baudrillard differently. Despite attempts to marry Baudrillardian temporality with notions of teleological time (Hughes, 2011), Baudrillard thinks of time in terms of recycling, rather than linearity or teleology (I expand this argument in Chapter 3). As a consequence, we need not read Baudrillard's successive phases of the image, or orders of simulacra, as aligned in linear time (this point has also been argued by Hegarty, 2004: 49–51). Likewise, when Baudrillard writes of the territory 'no longer' preceding the map (1994 [1981]: 1), or of metaphysics being 'lost' (1994 [1981]: 2), we do not need to take this to imply that 'once' the real was fully present and true, or that metaphysics was once unproblematically possible. The 'era of simulation' (Baudrillard, 1994 [1981]: 2), then, need not be understood as temporally fixed or discreet. Baudrillard's description of the simulacrum as 'pure' (1994 [1981]: 6) should be similarly qualified, as it is not 'pure' in the sense in which the term is commonly used, but is always contaminated by recycling. Derrida seems more insistent on the incompleteness of any such 'stage' and explicit that these moments 'cannot be distinguished; they feed into and overdetermine one another. They are, at bottom, the same' (2003: 100). In this way, Derrida is more explicit about the 'mutual contamination' that Hutchings emphasizes, which is why he can help reinforce a reading of such traces or impurities as always already there in Baudrillard's work. Derrida helps me follow Baudrillard's 'recycling' through and read the simulacrum as always contaminated. I am not claiming that Derrida does *not*, too, slip into the occasional all-too-easy mobilization of 'pure' and 'always', as when he writes to the effect that '[t]he word "history" doubtless has always been associated with the linear consecution of presence'. He too deploys 'stages', for example when he describes three moments of the autoimmune (Derrida, 2003: 94ff.). Nonetheless, reading Derrida and Baudrillard together helps me maintain necessary tensions in thinking through coeval multiplicities.

32 By using the word 'strategy' I do not mean to imply the separation of agent and target (subject and object), or the causal relation between them, that some have taken the term to imply. It could equally well be called a 'tactic' (Bleiker, 2000: 212).

2 Chinese academic discourse

Reinventing a hierarchical world order

When Hu Jintao's twin policy concepts of 'harmonious society' and 'harmonious world' were first used in minor contexts in 2003–4 and more forcefully launched in 2004–5, they reinforced an interest among scholars in traditional readings of 'harmony' as a basis for rethinking China's relation to the world. A (perhaps unintended) consequence of Hu's vague concept has been the emergence of a vibrant scholarly debate over what a harmonious world might look like. This debate has been particularly strong within, but not confined to, the discipline of International Relations (IR), where discussion was already under way over the possibility, necessity or even inevitability of building a 'Chinese school' of IR based on Chinese thought and experience (see for example Ni Shixiong and Xu Jia, 1997; Wang Yizhou, 2005; Yu Zhengliang, 2005; Qin Yaqing, 2007). It is these academic debates that deploy the 'harmonious world' concept that are under scrutiny in this chapter.

Specifically, this chapter explores the assumptions about time, space and difference that underpin the deployment of 'harmonious world' in these debates. A significant portion of academic publications emphasize the need for multiplicity and heterogeneity in order to have *proper* harmony (for example contributions in Tao *et al.*, 2010a, especially Li, 2010: 49; Barr, 2010: 75; and Yu, 2010: 25–6). One proponent of harmonious world, Professor Wang Yiwei of Renmin University, puts the term forward as a better alternative to a Western view that imagines others as behind in a historical queue, where

> patriotism and nationalism became separated into a symbol of advanced and backward, sameness and difference. This is a typical case of 'logic of taking initiative' (*xianfa luoji* 先发逻辑), the implication is 'your life is in our history'.
>
> (Wang Yiwei, 2006: 16)

The Introduction to this book has indicated how a number of academic commentators have criticized the tendency to think of time and space in an allochronizing way, in the types of literature that Wang is attacking here. As it also noted, it is commonly claimed in the wider literature that Chinese thought does not operate through radical dichotomization and binaries, which seems to indicate that Chinese imaginations of a harmonious world may be able to move outside the allochronic way of thinking (Huang Xiaoming, 2001). That is to say, there are indications that Chinese thought does not imagine others as 'behind', and that it can therefore avoid all the baggage such thinking entails (depoliticization, foreclosing futures, moral hierarchies and a tendency towards the containment, assimilation or annihilation of others). This chapter explores this proposition. In doing so, it draws on Chinese academic texts, chosen as examples of wider tendencies in the debates.[1] In these texts this chapter identifies two common ways of thinking about time and space, or 'cosmologies', that underpin the ways in which academics in the Hu era have written about China's relation to the world. The first is what I call 'unit space', or a 'unit-based cosmology', that of space as calculable bounded space, as containers of societies. The second is what has been referred to as a space 'with no outside' (*wuwai* 无外), what I call here 'holistic space' or a 'holistic cosmology'.

The first kind of space comprises common conceptualizations of nation states, modernization and development. 'Cultures', 'societies', 'civilizations' and 'nations' are imagined as having an integral relation to bounded spaces, internally coherent and differentiated from each other by separation. 'Places' are seen as bounded, with their own internally generated authenticities, defined by their difference from other places that lie outside, beyond their borders (Ashley, 1987; Campbell, 1998).

The second kind of space, 'holistic space', has parallels with some extreme ideas of globalization as free unbounded space, where everything is always already networked and connected to everything else (Massey, 2005: 81). It is, moreover, prominent in versions of the Chinese concept of *Tianxia*, or 'All-under-heaven', which has become increasingly popular with both a domestic and an international audience, and which was developed at least partly in response to perceived problems in the state system.

The two spatial imaginaries are commonly described as opposites in the wider literature on China in the world, with one replacing the other. First, it is said, pre-modern China had a holistic view of space. This cosmology was replaced by a modernist territorial imaginary when China had to transform into a modern (nation-)state. Now, it is claimed again, the territorial notion of space is no longer plausible under globalization (Agnew, 1998). Following Callahan's work on maps of national humiliation (2009: 141–73, 2010: ch. 4), this chapter challenges such notions through arguing that both these spatial imaginaries are working simultaneously in contemporary China with particular effects for thinking multiplicity and the political.[2] Although the two cosmologies are neither opposed nor mutually exclusive, this chapter discusses them in turn for the sake of clarity.

A view from China: unit-based political cosmology and harmonious world

A cosmology that has been predominant in writing on China and its relations to the world is what I call here a unit-based cosmology. What I mean by this is the bounded space of separate and mutually exclusive units that are recognized in particular from much of traditional state-centric IR literature, but which is widespread throughout today's social sciences. This book is by no means the first to identify or criticize this mode of spatialization. Many have done so before and surely many will do so again in the future. Yet, the hold of the unit-based spatial imaginary is strangely strong on our thought, and it is therefore indispensable to an examination of the way in which China and harmonious world are thought about in terms of time and space.

What, then, is this unit-based cosmology? The term 'unit-based' is used here to refer to a particular way of imagining the world akin to a jigsaw puzzle, made up of separate and mutually exclusive units. These units take the form of what some people would call territories, or geobodies.[3] The imaginary of discrete state units, with their associated nations, has been of particular concern to the discipline of IR. As Ruggie already explained two decades ago, traditional IR takes as given 'the modern form of territoriality ... based on linear, fixed boundaries separating continuous and mutually exclusive spaces' (1993: 168). Thus, '[i]t has been the geographical division of the world into mutually exclusive territorial states that has served to define the field of study' (Agnew and Corbridge, 1995: 78). Of course, particular units are often contested. Yet, for territorial units to 'function', the basic assumptions of the unit-based cosmology cannot be seriously questioned. The boundaries and meanings of particular units may be under frequent discussion within IR, but the spatial imaginary that makes this discussion possible is less often scrutinized or paid due attention, particularly in publications specifically concerned with China. For the sake of clarity, the assumptions on which the unit-based cosmology operate are discussed here in turn. We will first examine the assumption of spatial units (positing a clear distinction between the inside and outside of these units). We will then see an assumption of temporal sequence (where harmony is established first on the inside, then on the outside). Then we will interrogate the positing of an endpoint (and that endpoint is harmony, often conceived of as a form of compliance). Finally, we will see how the method of achieving harmony is said to be its active promotion (through hard- and/or soft-power tools).

Spatial units: inside/outside division

A vast majority of academic commentary treats 'harmonious world' as a straightforward state policy or inherently Chinese idea promoted by the People's Republic of China (PRC) under Hu Jintao, against the backdrop of the state-centric assumptions that are embedded in our most common approaches to IR.[4] The imagination of separate state units rests on the possibility of imagining a separating border between them. Inayatullah and Blaney (2004) argue that the European experience of religious wars of the seventeenth century imbued the idea of difference with connotations of enmity and radical othering. The state system, which is perhaps the clearest example of the unit-based political cosmology and the consolidation of this kind of imaginary, is said to have emerged from this particular European experience (Krasner, 2001; Teschke, 2003).

Furthermore, the division of space into units is typically thought of in terms of dichotomies mapping onto the inside/outside of these bounded entities (Massey, 2005: 64). Within the discipline of IR the boundary of the state is closely tied to the idea of sovereignty (Walker, 1993) and also traditionally marks the border distinguishing community from anarchy (Ashley, 1987, 1988). Traditional IR theory, then:

> not only assumes a particular conception of territory (as clear, closed, fixed) but also tends to render territory in strongly dichotomous terms by way of mapping order/chaos, identity/difference, presence/absence, politics/power, and so on onto the lines and spaces through which global social life becomes intelligible.
>
> (Delaney, 2005: 37)

Even where there is talk of connection and mutual construction, geographical variation is preconstituted. First the differences between places exist, then those different places come in contact. Social relations may change the preferences and identity of an actor, but the spatial units of interaction are not allowed this same construction (see Xiao Feng, 2005 for an example).

This imagination of space and society remains common in the study of China and its relations to the (harmonious) world. It is this conceptualization of space that provides the basis for the supposed coherence, stability and authenticity to which there is such frequent appeal in discourses of nationalism. This tendency is particularly clear in the Chinese calls for (Yu Zhengliang, 2005) and predictions of (Qin Yaqing, 2007) a 'Chinese school' of IR (see also Hilal, 2001; Cheung, 2014; Schneider, 2014; Noesselt, 2015b). As Gloria Davies (2007) has demonstrated, Chinese scholarship is characterized by a 'patriotic worrying' (*youhuan* 忧患) that makes this nationalism a marked trait of Chinese IR literature and certainly of those that follow Hu Jintao in arguing for the construction of a harmonious world. In this tradition, an argument's strength is judged on how well it helps promote China's national interest (Cunningham-Cross, 2014).

In fact, the very analytical division between 'harmonious society' for domestic use and 'harmonious world' for international deployment, which is almost universally accepted also by more 'critical' scholars, reflects a classical inside/outside understanding, where a state border separates off national space. Such domestic/international divisions are common in writing about Hu's harmonious policy in both English language literature on harmonious world (for example Sow Keat Tok and Zheng Yongnian, 2007: 4; Zou Keyuan, 2011: 8) and in the corresponding Chinese language texts (for example Hang Lihua, 2010: 20–1; Yan Xuetong, 2006: 14–15), as well as in party-state descriptions (for example State Council, 2006, 2011b: II).

As previously indicated, what is particular about the 'inside' Chinese space in this division is the privileged access to and understanding of harmony. As seen in the policy discourse, this privileged access is taken to stem from the 'culture', 'tradition' or 'history' of harmony in China. That harmony is something that 'Chinese people', or 'China', has always understood and cherished is an implication, and often explicitly stated 'fact', of most literature on harmonious world. For example, to Zhang Yunling, 'from ancient times until today, China has possessed traditional thought and a culture of seeking harmony' (Zhang Yunling, 2008: 4). This claim is taken to be mutually supportive with the idea that 'the Chinese nation' (*Zhonghua minzu* 中华民族) has always been a peaceful nation (see Ni Shixiong and Qian Xuming, 2008: 125; Liu Jianfei, 2006; Yu Xiaofeng and Wang Jiangli, 2006 for examples).[5]

As explained in the previous chapter, many debates about harmonious world hinge on the idea of achieving a proper understanding of harmony, and the notion that the Chinese nation, or at least a part of it, has privileged access to such understanding. This claim that there is a Chinese essential culture that is by nature peaceful, harmonious, benevolent and non-violent is problematic in many ways on both conceptual and empirical levels. Such claims have been criticized from a range of theoretical and historical-empirical viewpoints, by prominent critics such as Alastair I. Johnston (1995), Yu Bin (2008), Wang Yuan-Kang (2011), William A. Callahan (2012) and Peter Purdue (2015). Recalling the violent riots, crackdowns and attempts at isolation of border regions like Tibet (Human Rights Watch, 2010) and Xinjiang (AFP, 2011) during the phase of promoting 'inter-ethnic harmony' should temper such belief, as should the fact that most of those who argue that China is by nature peaceful draw their evidence from the aptly named 'Warring-states period'. Nonetheless, this trope of the naturally peaceful China remains popular and is repeated in different versions in a majority of texts on harmonious world, both in Chinese and English – which indicates that it is intended both for China's domestic discussions and for an international audience. It is from this assumption that the arguments outlined in what follows draw much of their rhetorical force, as well as many of their problems.

Temporal sequence: first inside, then outside

In this unit-based cosmology, not only is space conceived as divided into bounded units, but that system of differentiation is also organized in a particular way. Different 'places' are interpreted as different stages in a single temporal development. As argued by Massey, '[a]ll the stories of unilinear progress, modernisation, development, the sequence of modes of production … perform this operation' (2005: 68). This manoeuvre is often recognized throughout the social sciences and humanities, yet remains strong in the academic discipline as well as popular discourse of China's IR. For example, it has long been seen in debates on China's rise as a form of 'catching up' with the West, as outlined in the Introduction to this book. It also appears in studies of Chinese relations with those conceived of as temporally 'behind' inside and outside China. Descriptions of China 'exporting development' to parts of Africa is a notable example of this

(Nyíri, 2006). So are representations of relations between more and less prosperous parts of China, where 'receiving' areas are characterized as spaces of 'lower quality' (populated by 'low quality people') that similarly need to catch up (Bakken, 2000). Precisely who or what is ahead or behind may differ in these debates, but the underlying imaginary of spatial difference aligned in a historical queue remains the same.

This logic of forerunners and those that lag behind is a similarly common feature of the debates concerned with harmonious world. Much literature writes in terms of a 'first inside, then outside' movement of harmony. For example, one early English-language analysis writes of how '"building a harmonious society" became "building a harmonious world"' (Sow Keat Tok and Zheng Yongnian, 2007: 9). Yan Xuetong puts it in more normative terms, and suggests that '[i]f the Chinese government cannot establish a society facing harmony under the circumstances of controlled state power, then nobody can believe that it can construct harmonious world policies in the international' (Yan Xuetong, 2006: 15). Yan attributes this thinking to Ancient Chinese thought, and approvingly takes Mencius' point that '[i]f a state is harmonious domestically then its army, even though it be weak, will nonetheless be victorious over strong armies' (Yan Xuetong, 2011: 54). In other words, in order to make the world harmonious, the PRC needs first to establish a harmonious society at home.

Another English-language analysis narrates the same linear-causal movement from 'internal harmony (harmonious society)' to 'external harmony (harmonious world)', where 'the doctrine of "harmonious world" is just an extension of that of "harmonious society"' (Zou Keyuan, 2011: 8). This paper simultaneously identifies Hu's first expression of 'harmonious world' with a speech to the Moscow Institute of International Relations on 28 May 2003 (Zou Keyuan, 2011: 2, fn. 2), and his first mention of 'harmonious society' with the Fourth Session of the Sixteenth Party Congress in September 2004 (2011: 8, fn. 30). The linear inside/outside imaginary that projects 'external' harmony as 'just an extension' of 'internal' harmony is thus so strong that it contradicts the linearity of posited 'launch dates' that the author himself identifies, where 'harmonious world' was clearly announced before 'harmonious society'.

The point here is not to claim that the idea of harmonious world *really* appeared before that of harmonious society and that the movement was in fact the reverse. Various 'launch dates' are identifiable for both concepts, and harmonious society certainly appears as the more developed concept in party-state deployments. Nonetheless, the consistency with which the external is portrayed as a mere extension of the internal is striking; indeed, there does not appear to be an analysis that discusses both policy terms and treats them otherwise. Surely, there could be other ways of imagining the spatio-temporal relation between harmonious society and harmonious world. Chapter 4 of this book examines some such possibilities. The point is that the near-complete absence of such alternative accounts in the academic literature on harmonious world goes to show that this particular way of imagining time and space is deeply ingrained.

The force of this imaginary can also be seen in the tendency in literature on harmonious world to emphasize how China 'itself' needs to be harmonious 'first', before it can work for a harmonious world. This is associated with a linear movement, China's literal 'going out' (*zouchuqu* 走出去) (for example in Sow Keat Tok and Zheng Yongnian, 2007: 10). In this way, many Chinese-language articles argue that harmonious world is a 'natural extension and development' of harmonious society (Hang Lihua, 2010: 20; cf. Liu Xinyu, 2005: 41). Wang Yiwei, in a slightly different formulation, emphasizes that the real achievement of harmonious world originates from China, but belongs to the world, where other countries are 'backwards' or 'lagging behind' (*luohou guojia* 落后国家) (Wang Yiwei, 2006: 16).[6] Others follow the attitude towards 'fine' culture found in the *China's Peaceful Development* white paper, and take harmony to imply the acceptance only of *advanced* culture into China, in the process of making China and the world harmonious (Ni Shixiong and Qian Xuming, 2008: 125). This spatio-temporal move seems natural if one accepts the common assumption that (some) Chinese have a natural predisposition to and understanding of harmony. In such a narrative, China is the creator of 'harmonious world' theory, and is 'inevitably the principal practitioner of harmonious world' (or that which brings it about) (Ruan Zongze, 2005: 15).

Elena Barabantseva has convincingly argued that in state-led narratives that draw on a predominantly Marxist legacy, 'Chinese dominant discourses on development are trapped in the teleological thinking about a modernization process, constructing the Chinese nation as somewhat inferior to the "developed West"' (2012: 65). The unit-based imaginary of harmonious world repeats the spatio-temporal logic of such stories, but draws on broadly Confucian thought to replace 'the West' with 'China' at the head of its linear imagination of constructing a harmonious world.

Endpoint: harmony as compliance

This linear 'going out' of China moreover has an endpoint, or telos, towards which its movement is directed. As Barabantseva's comment shows, teleological thinking is not unique to discussions of 'harmonious world'. Some reflections on China emanating from other parts of the world still regularly reflect, in Fukuyama's footsteps, a linear thinking that asks 'how' and 'when' China will become a democracy, will become like 'us' (for one clear example, see Gilley, 2004). Nonetheless, this way of thinking does remain strong in academic debates surrounding 'harmonious world', where the term itself is positioned simultaneously as the end and the means to that end, a 'blueprint' for future world development (*fazhan lantu* 发展蓝图) (Liu Dongjian, 2006: 46). What more precisely it is that is being promoted by this Chinese 'going out' varies with different authors, as the meaning of 'harmony' is often left undefined and changing in each deployment, or generalized into meaning the production (rather than presumption) of consent (Pierre, 2010), or simply 'a good social order' (Zhang Qianfan, 2010: 284).

As already noted, a significant portion of the literature that discusses the prospects of a harmonious world stresses multiplicity as a prerequisite of harmony. Some see the common conflation of 'harmony' with 'conformity' or 'subservience' as a problem (especially highlighted by contributions in Tao *et al.*, 2010a, particularly Barr, 2010: 74–5, 77). This multiplicity is typically that of 'nations', 'civilizations' or 'cultures', the key units on which the unit-based cosmology operates in the academic literature and in the policy discourse described at the outset of this book. A significant number of texts deploy the term 'harmony with difference' (*he'er butong* 和而不同) to express the need for difference in order to have the balance of separate elements that is harmony (Liu Xinyu, 2005: 41; Ruan Zongze, 2005: 14; Yu Xiaofeng and Wang Jiangli, 2006; Fang Xiaojiao, 2008: 69; Ni Shixiong and Qian Xuming, 2008: 125). Some also use the term 'Great Harmony' (*Datong* 大同) to denote the idea of harmonious world based in Chinese history, which may have less association with underscoring the need for difference (Liu Xinyu, 2005: 40; Yu Xiaofeng and Wang Jiangli, 2006; Ni Shixiong and Qian Xuming, 2008: 125; see Callahan, 2008, 2015a for a discussion). Inequality is often seen as the biggest challenge to building a harmonious world (Shi Yinhong, 2008a: 81), and respecting cultural multiplicity is emphasized as the only way to a harmonious world and the development of 'human civilization' (Ni Shixiong and Qian Xuming, 2008: 125).

Having said this, the harmonious world is clearly a universal ideal in this rhetoric. As Yan Xuetong explains, 'a theory of harmonious world diplomacy will have difficulty attaining any great influence on international relations or in acquiring historical vitality unless it presents a universal vision' (2011: 62). On this logic, several scholars state that harmony theory, or sometimes Confucianism more broadly, aims towards the 'ultimate goal of harmonizing the world' (Li Chenyang, 2010: 49), or entertain the notion that various or all aspects of society need to be 'harmonized' within the larger whole (Neville, 2010: 69). In a world of de facto difference and contradiction, this means that contradiction needs to be resolved. A common theme in literature concerned with the notion of a harmonious world has therefore been a focus on the resolution or melting away (*xietiao* 协调, *jiejue* 解决, *huajie* 化解) of contradiction and divergence (*maodun* 矛盾, *fenqi* 分歧) (Liu Dongjian, 2006: 43; Qin Yaqing, 2006: 31; Wang Yizhou, 2008: 14; see Nordin, 2016 for a more detailed demonstration).

As a consequence, much of the literature that begins by suggesting that harmonious world envisages a tolerant, open and equal form of 'harmony with difference' then tries to perfect its realization by listing things that need to be harmonized (excluded, rejected or transformed) to achieve harmony. To Qin Zhiyong, that list consists of a whole range of attitudes that are 'resolutely to be guarded against and rejected', including 'extreme individualism, money worship, hedonism, Anarchist mentality and concept in the Western culture' (Qin Zhiyong, 2008: 67). Ni Shixiong and Qian Xuming similarly want to respect civilizational differences while, again, accepting only *advanced* culture in China (2008: 125). Significantly, this also involves opposing terrorists. It will be clear to the article's Chinese-language audience that these 'terrorists' should be read to denote the ethno-civilizational others who are experiencing the more brutal edge of harmonious policy in border regions like Tibet and Xinjiang, while seeking increased or complete autonomy from the PRC. In wider Chinese culture, they are also imagined as 'backward' in relation to the 'advanced' cultures that should be accepted (Lafitte, 1999: §§ 4, 5, 6; Nyíri, 2006: 92; Kaltman, 2007: 2; Barabantseva, 2009: 231, 2012; Nordin, 2016).

It is clear, then, that harmony is not unprincipled compromise. Certainly, striving to spread harmony to the world requires discipline and morality from its leaders. Yan Xuetong makes this clear when he remarks that 'only when a society upholds morality can it be a harmonious society, only then become a model (*yangban* 样板) for the world' (2006: 14). Achieving such morality furthermore requires that those who want to establish harmony refer to predefined principles or rules. As Kam Por Yu puts it, 'the *right* kind of harmony is achieved by referring to some principles of proper conduct … [n]ot all claims can be treated as equal' (Yu, 2010: 22). To Ding Sheng, the virtue of noble families is that they 'do not worry about poverty, but worry about discontent' (2008: 196). The noble and excellent leader, in turn, will 'subjugate the enemy's army without doing battle', in order to have 'no rivals in the world' (2008: 196, 197; see also Nordin, 2016). As a consequence of this type of narrative, it is not unusual to equate 'harmonious' with 'consensual' (Rockman, 2010: 199), and to portray this as an 'inevitable choice' (Liu Jianfei, 2006: 38) and 'the only correct goal and the only reachable goal' (Qin Zhiyong, 2008: 73). Once this endpoint has been assumed, the patriotic worry about discord or competition leads many to begin listing disharmonious groups, ideas or behaviours, and creating a distance from those who have not kept up with the times, but lack 'advanced' culture or even turn to 'terrorism'. This, then, often comes to undermine any commitment to an open and tolerant 'harmony with difference'. Indeed, as Yu tells us, the interaction between the entities imagined should be governed by principles of proper conduct, presumably decided by the true gentleman leader who 'stands his ground, and is not moved by popular opinions' (2010: 22). Indeed, we get the impression throughout that it is the Chinese elites who *properly and correctly understand* harmony. It is these elites who should decide on those principles that determine whose claims should be treated as equal and whose claims should not (Nordin, 2016). Certainly, such decisions cannot be left to the foreigners who lack 'harmonious disposition', or even the popular opinion of China's own people (whose poor and non-Han communities are often considered 'backward' or of 'low quality'). These groups need instead to act harmoniously, in a way that is not discordant with the harmonious aims of the Chinese political and intellectual elites. As Ding has explained, there are no enemies in such a state, because they have been subjugated, and have therefore vanished as such. If this happens, as I have put it elsewhere, 'an end-state can be imagined where everyone complies with, or is co-opted by, the Chinese elite's notion of what is an advanced culture and a "win-win" solution: a harmonious world' (Nordin, 2016).

Method: promoting harmony through hard- and/or soft-power tools

How, then, can such a harmonious world be realized? There appears to be near consensus in the literature on harmony and harmonious world that the term should be opposed to conflict. This leads Shi Zhongwen to stress that the doctrine opposes going to extremes, and therefore contradicts what Shi calls 'the philosophy of struggle' (Shi Zhongwen, 2008: 40, where 'struggle' implies Marxist ideology). Qin Zhiyong similarly stresses the need to turn away from collisions and put the emphasis on 'merging different cultures' (2008: 73). However, as we have seen, the end result towards which we should strive, on these views, is a telos to which Chinese people, culture or leaders have privileged access, which leaves little room to ponder whose culture should 'merge' into whose (or better, perhaps, be subsumed by whose).

In respect to many parts of the world (such as Ding's 'global south'), the spatio-temporal designation as being 'backwards countries' or 'countries lagging behind' is often enough for the ideas emanating from that unit not to merit further attention in the merging of cultures (remember, China should accept only advanced culture). The vast majority of literature on harmonious world instead focuses on how this ideal can be merged with, or win out over, 'Western culture' or 'Western civilization'. For several writers, there is therefore little doubt against whom any effort to build a harmonious world is directed, and they claim that increasing Chinese soft power can 'smash' (*dapo* 打破) Western influence (Fang Xiaojiao, 2008: 68). At the same time, with a few exceptions (such as Tao *et al.*, 2010a), 'China' and 'the West' are commonly taken as representative of 'the world'. The civilizational essentialism with which posited units are approached means that key thinkers of each of these two 'civilizations' are taken to represent 'the values' of large swathes of people. To simplify slightly (but not much): if Plato and Confucius both talked about harmony, that means that it is a universalizable value, and that all people can agree on it (for a clear example, see Ba Xiang, 2010).

Scholars typically hold that where the realization of 'peaceful coexistence' could be achieved rather passively, building a 'harmonious world' requires the *promotion* of harmony. There is often a recognition that although the endpoint of harmony is a state free of discord and competition, this ideal has to compete against other ideas of world order before it can be realized. Most literature rejects the idea of subjugating the opponents of 'harmonious world' through military force, but do, like Ding, retain the idea that they need to be 'subjugated' – it is just that such subjugation is better achieved through 'soft' rather than 'hard' power. Thus, efforts to promote harmonious world identified in the literature typically include the setting up of Confucius Institutes (Cai Liang and Song Lilei, 2010: 38; Zou Keyuan, 2011: 11), the 2008 Beijing Olympics (Zou Keyuan, 2011: 11), Shanghai Co-operation Organization activity (Ruan Zongze, 2005: 14; Qin Yaqing, 2006: 32; Yu Xiaofeng and Wang Jiangli, 2006) and Expo 2010 Shanghai China, which is discussed in Chapter 3 of this book (Zou Keyuan, 2011: 11). Others imply that a panoptical form of power will suffice to make deviant others conform to the norms of harmony: '[p]owerful societal control will be exerted on individuals by public opinion and by public disapproval of things contrary to good moral standards' (Shi Zhongwen, 2008: 40). What is clear throughout is the need for 'reformation' and 'education' of elements deemed disharmonious. For example, Zhang Qianfan takes the purported need for reformation to mean that 'we need a government that honours virtuous gentlemen and actively inculcates the virtues among people' (2010: 302). In the call for education, the hierarchical-temporal relationship between ruler-father and people-infants is often highlighted (for example by Roetz's commentary on Xunzi, which also challenges such a reading; Roetz, 2010: 316).

Having said this, the call to build a harmonious world has also been used to argue in favour of Chinese military capacity, including its naval power (Deng Li, 2009). Although Chinese policy documents stress that violence or threat of violence should be avoided (State Council, 2011c; Wen Jiabao, 2010b, 2011), they similarly appear to leave room for means that would traditionally be understood as both 'hard' and 'soft'.[7] It has also been argued that the dichotomization of 'hard' and 'soft' power, or 'coercion' and 'attraction', is unstable (Bially Mattern, 2005; Nordin, 2012a). One reason for this is that language games can be rhetorically set up in a manner that leaves only one 'inevitable choice' as a conceivable option (Bially Mattern, 2005). Another reason is that the imagery of 'hard' military power is empirically intermingled with 'soft' messages to simultaneously coerce and attract at events that are described as 'soft power tools', such as Expo 2010 (Nordin, 2012a). Whatever the means, there is apparent consensus within the literature that to establish its ideal of harmonious world, China needs to become strong and influential (see for example Zhang Yunling, 2008: 5).

We have thus seen how the literature on harmonious world that is underpinned by a unit-based cosmology tells a story that organizes time and space in a particular way. An assumption is made about the division of space into bounded units, where inside and outside come to respectively connote the presence and absence of community, harmony and so on. This division lies at the very core of the analytical separation between 'harmonious society' for the inside and 'harmonious world' for the outside. Moreover, a timeline is imagined that runs from inside to outside. China is ahead, a forerunner in the establishment of harmony that will first be built on the inside, then on the outside. 'Harmonious world' becomes both the means and the end to China's relation to that outside world. What 'harmony' means is often left unsaid or implicit and varies from one account to the other, but there is a tendency to conflate harmony with compliance and the absence of discord. However, on the way to establishing the harmonious world that will be agreed on by all, China will have to 'subjugate' its opponents through hard and/or soft power. This is a most common way of imagining China's relation to the harmonious world.

A view from the world: holistic political cosmology and harmonious world

The previous section discussed a discursive rendering of space, common in approaches to Chinese IR with close ties to a Western experience of *modernity*, that some would understand as conquered by time. Today, however, in times that some would call *post*modern, we are simultaneously presented with a political cosmology that in many ways contrasts radically with the modernist one. It is said that we have now moved on instead to spatial times. This involves an imagination of a world of holistic space, where everything is already connected to everything else.

This imaginary resonates in particular with some discussions of harmonious world that go further in drawing on Chinese *pre*-modern notions of world order. Dissatisfied with the problematic rendering of difference in the state-centric thinking of what I have called a unit-based cosmology, these thinkers try to imagine a new world order without bounded units. Instead, they imagine a world without radical self–other distinction, a space without bordered difference, what I call a holistic cosmology.

Zhang Yunling elaborates on the notion of 'harmonism' (*hehe zhuyi* 和合主义), which is of course instrumental to the 'discourse of harmonism' under scrutiny in this book. Zhang clearly articulates it as a holistic concept:

> in Chinese culture, 'harmony' (*he* 和) has many layers of meaning of 'kindness' (*heqi* 和气), 'reconciliation' (*hehao* 和好), 'amity' (*hemu* 和睦), 'peace' (*heping* 和平), and so on, and 'unity' (*he* 合) also has the many layers of meaning of 'merging into one' (*heyi* 合一), 'being agreeable' (*heyi* 合意), 'co-operating' (*hezuo* 合作).
>
> (Zhang Yunling, 2008: 5)

The harmony that emerges through this chain of signification emphasizes the 'merging into one' or 'unification' that leads to a holistic understanding (Nordin, 2016).

To others, the basis of their holistic treatment of the harmonious world is found in their understanding of an extreme globalization where everything is always already connected to everything else in a borderless world. To Yu Xiaofeng and Wang Jiangli, for example, the need to build a harmonious world derives from their particular understanding of globalization (*quanqiu yitihua* 全球一体化). This particular way of expressing the term 'globalization' emphasizes the global as 'one unit' (*yi ti* 一体), which gives it a different stress than the more common *quanqiuhua* (全球化). To these authors:

> [t]he development of globalization (*quanqiu yitihua* 全球一体化) will certainly cause people's field of vision to change from nation, state or region to the globe, taking the shape of a kind of 'global identity' [or 'whole world identification', *quanqiu rentong* 全球认同].... It demands making people

> cast off the fetters of nation-centric theory, representing a theory of humanity holism and world-centric harmony theory, and then gives prominence to a 'group ethics' (*leilunli* 类伦理) value system.... Only the entirety of humankind (*quan renlei* 全人类) is the focus and kernel to which we should pay close attention, only the joint construction of a 'harmonious world' is the value objective that we should pursue.
>
> (Yu Xiaofeng and Wang Jiangli, 2006: 59)

Clearly, here, there is an attempt to break with the state-centrism of the unit-based cosmology, although the explicitly Chinese goal of building a 'harmonious world' remains the goal towards which everyone should jointly strive. In Chinese, 'holism' is usually translated as *zhengti zhuyi* (整体注意), literally 'whole-unit-ism'. This terminology resonates in these concepts for globalization and 'humanity holism'.

This globalized, harmonious whole unit is moreover associated with the new territorial understanding of networked space, '"network space" (*wangluo kongjian* 网络空间) became the new territory' (Ni Shixionḡ and Qian Xuming, 2008: 124). In this type of holistic rendition of harmonious world, space is imagined without a radical other, but rather as one all-inclusive unit where everything is connected to everything else in a networked space.

Within the literature that draws on Chinese historical concepts, this type of all-inclusive space has come to be associated in particular with the concept of *Tianxia*. *Tianxia*, usually translated as 'All-under-heaven', is a concept that is occasionally deployed by authors discussed above, and which was frequently used by the pre-Qin thinkers that focused on discussions of harmony. It is also taken to express a pre-modern Chinese idea of world order. With the renewed focus on Ancient Chinese thought as a source of inspiration for rethinking the world order it has become increasingly popular as the search for a Chinese school of IR theory has gained momentum. It is regularly deployed in the literature concerned with harmonious world, and a number of scholars stress that harmony calls for such a holistic approach (for example Li Chenyang, 2010: 38).

Some authors who imagine a harmonious world reliant on a unit-based cosmology refer to *Tianxia* as an unbounded space, but then use it to perform a traditional analysis based on the state unit. In such accounts, *Tianxia* is deployed merely as a harmonious inter-state space of bounded units. Others, however, go further in developing a seemingly more boundless idea of *Tianxia*, which is said to be 'completely different from Western civilization, since Chinese civilization insists on its own subjectivity, and possesses inclusivity' (Zhou Jianming and Jiao Shixin, 2008: 28). To Zhou Jianming and Jiao Shixin, in the *Tianxia* outlook that they associate with harmonious world:

> China's '*Tianxia*' concept includes everything in the entire world, including matter and consciousness. Starting off from the position of *Tianxia*, China and other countries are all a part of *Tianxia*, so [the attitude of] 'nothing outside the mind' (*xinzhong wuwai* 心中无外) can consider questions from

> the holistic interest (*zhengti liyi* 整体利益) of the world, at the same time as considering its own interest it can also consider the interests of other countries. From the point of view of world outlook this kind of civilization recognizes the multiplicity of civilizations and the pluralism of interests, that is 'nothing outside *Tianxia*' (*Tianxia wuwai* 天下无外), it also stresses the peaceful coexistence of many kinds of civilizations, shared development, namely 'working together with one heart' (*hezhonggongji* 和衷共济).
>
> (Zhou Jianming and Jiao Shixin, 2008: 28)

Based on such a view, Fang Xiaojiao takes a feeling of *Tianxia*-ism (*Tianxia zhuyi* 天下主义) to form the basis of harmonism. Fang describes *Tianxia*-ism as:

> admitting differences, stressing that different civilisations, states of different development levels, different social systems and ideologies can get along in harmony and peace. This kind of peaceful thought respects multiplicity and difference, it is not the unification of *Tianxia* (*bushi yitong Tianxia* 不是一统天下), conceited, but is mutual forgiveness, mutual respect.
>
> (Fang Xiaojiao, 2008: 70)

Even though this passage appears to sidestep the holistic idea of *Tianxia*, readers are subsequently told that harmonious world incorporates the interests of the other as well as the self:

> in this sense, the thought embodied in harmonious world expressed a new concept of Chinese diplomacy, it is Chinese traditional culture and universal world value notion, China's own interest and the other's interest, the outcome of combining the goal of harmony and the method of peace.
>
> (Fang Xiaojiao, 2008: 71)

In a similar manner, Li Baojun and Li Zhiyong take *Tianxia*-ism to signify an identification with all of humankind, without ethno-national classification, and without distinction (*qubie* 区别) or differentiation (*tongdeng* 同等) between people. Therefore, although there can be a conflict of individuals' interests, there can be no conflict of group interests (Li Baojun and Li Zhiyong, 2008: 82). Spatially, this means seeing the world or *Tianxia* as a common political space (Li Baojun and Li Zhiyong, 2008: 82). Therefore, they claim, 'only by understanding the world as an inseparable a priori unit can it be possible to see and define a permanent interest belonging to the world' (Li Baojun and Li Zhiyong, 2008: 82). In arguing for such an a priori holistic understanding of harmonious world, this cosmology differs distinctly from the unit-based cosmology.

A thinker whose deployment of the *Tianxia* concept has been particularly influential is Zhao Tingyang, Professor of Philosophy at the Chinese Academy of Social Sciences (CASS). Zhao is a prominent scholar and a public intellectual whose work has received significant critical attention in China and internationally (Barabantseva, 2009; Callahan, 2004, 2008; Nordin, 2014b). Zhao is one of the few thinkers who have taken the purported 'unbounded' imagination of *Tianxia* seriously. He criticizes the state-system for being Western-centric and would reject a notion of *Tianxia* that was advocated 'from China's point of view' (2005, 2006c). Instead, he argues that *Tianxia* can offer 'a view from nowhere' or a view 'from the world' (Zhao Tingyang, 2003). Zhao's 2005 book *The Tianxia System* (*Tianxia tixi* 天下体系) put his worldview on the global academic agenda (Callahan, 2008).

There are some initial indications that Zhao's proposed worldview may accord well with the notion of coeval multiplicities. Importantly, Zhao argues that his 'political conception could find a strong argument in Chinese ontology, the ontology of relations, instead of the western ontology of things' (2006c: 33). Throughout his discussions of *Tianxia*, Zhao plays with the definition of this ancient and often vague term, sometimes reading it as 'the World', and at other times understanding it as 'Empire', but always as a political cosmology that explicitly tries to break with the problematic self–other relations of discourses of modernity in general and that of the nation-state system in particular (2006c: 31).

Writing about the harmonious world concept and policy, Zhao stresses that the concept derives from *he* (和), which he, like other scholars discussed above, claims has always been treasured by China (2006a: 1). In his interpretation of harmonious world, Zhao emphasizes *he* (和, harmony) over *tong* (同, sameness or unity):

> in the Spring and Autumn period there was a dispute of rich academic significance concerning harmony, which in contemporary academic language can be expressed as: given that the world is in a state of existing difference, and difference can take the form of conflict, there are at least two kinds of schemes of resolution (*jiejue fang'an* 解决方案), one is 'unity' (*tong* 同), that is the unification (*tongyi* 统一) of value systems and ideologies. This scheme is unworkable, because 'unity cannot endure' (*tongzebuji* 同则不继). The other kind is 'harmony' (*he* 和), that is establishing maximized mutual benefit of mutual coordination in the midst of difference.
>
> (Zhao Tingyang, 2006a: 1)

From this passage, it is clear that Zhao shares the concern here with acknowledging and accommodating difference, and that he wants to prioritize it over unity.

Key to Zhao's criticism of the state system is that '[s]uch projects have essential difficulties in reaching the real integrality of the world … due to the lack of a vision of world-ness' (Zhao Tingyang, 2006c: 33). In contrast to the unit-based cosmology, '[w]orld-ness cannot be reduced to internationality, for it is of the wholeness or totality rather than the between-ness' (2006c: 39). This worldview is an image of wholeness, integrality and connection: 'All-under-Heaven presupposes the Oneness of the world … Oneness of the world is also reflected in the political principle of "inclusion of all" in All-under-Heaven' (2006c: 37). In this way, the imagined space is all-inclusive.

Could this, then, be a relational space of coeval multiplicities? Any such possibility seems doomed as an effect of Zhao's insistence that 'any inconsistency or contradiction in the system will be a disaster':

> [i]n a very Chinese way, politics aims at a good society of peaceful 'order' (*zhi* 治), which is the first condition for any possible happiness of each and all, and at keeping a society from the 'disorder' (*luan* 乱) that destroys all possibilities of individual happiness.
>
> (Zhao Tingyang, 2006c: 33)

As a result of prioritizing order, Zhao comes to insist on the *homogeneity* of his all-inclusive space, where 'all political levels ... should be essentially homogenous or homological so as to create a harmonious system' (2006c: 33). Similarly, '[t]he world's effective political order must progress from All-under-Heaven, to state, to families, so as to ensure universal *consistency and transitivity* in political life, or the *uniformity of society*' (2006c: 33, emphasis in original). The end-goal of the *Tianxia* system is therefore to achieve a single uniform and homogeneous space. In order for the existing world with all its heterogeneity to pass into such homogeneity, someone must change (Nordin, 2014b). Zhao explains that:

> one of the principles of Chinese political philosophy is said 'to turn the enemy into a friend', and it would lose its meaning if it were not to remove conflicts and pacify social problems – in a word, to 'transform' (*hua* 化) the bad into the good.
>
> (Zhao Tingyang, 2006c: 34)

The bad will transform into the good through 'voluntariness' – they will simply see how good the *Tianxia* elites are and will want to become like them without anybody needing to become a missionary (2006c: 36). This idea of transforming the bad into the good in order to achieve *Tianxia* and a harmonious world is particularly important because it has been influential with other scholars using the *Tianxia* concept to imagine a harmonious world (for example Li Baojun and Li Zhiyong, 2008: 84).

How, then, should 'the good' to which all others must conform be determined? Zhao states quite frankly that 'most people do not really know what is best for them, but ... the elite do, so the elite ought genuinely to decide for the people' (Zhao Tingyang, 2006c: 32). As a result of these elites turning 'the bad' into 'the good', there will eventually be no other, the 'many' will have been transformed into 'the one'. According to Zhao, only then will there be a 'world' at all (2005: 13; see also 2006c). Zhao's utopia, then, envisages a world of 'complete and perfect' understanding, that has literally 'no outside' (Callahan, 2007: 7).

However, as pointed out by Callahan, when Zhao says that the benefit of such a 'civilization/barbarism' interaction in Chinese history (that between the converted and the converters) was an 'objective discussion of the long term advantages and disadvantages of different cultures' (Zhao Tingyang, 2005, cited in Callahan,

2008: 755), it 'certainly sounds like a hierarchy of cultures analogous to modern racism and the PRC's current concern with the "population quality" of its ethnic minorities and of the peoples of the world' (Callahan, 2008: 755).

Finally, Zhao argues for a prioritization of time over space:

> [t]he comprehensive view of the world as All-under-Heaven surely takes the whole world as a single political system that is much greater and higher than a single country or nation/state. Consequently, the empire of All-under-Heaven highlights the problem of time rather than of space, that is, the problem of its duration rather than of its territory; and it has been apparent in the Chinese concern for the legitimacy of its dynasties rather than actual territorial conquest.
>
> (Zhao Tingyang, 2006c: 34)

Not only does Zhao's vision of *Tianxia* conceive of space as one single, interconnected system. It cannot think time and space properly together, but needs to prioritize one over the other in its imagination of a harmonious world. Spatial difference becomes unimportant, subsumed under the singular temporality of his harmonious world.

The idea that harmony can only be achieved by way of extreme unity, the inclusion of all in its system, is not unique to Zhao's analysis, but is recurring in the wider literature on harmony. Qin Zhiyong, for example, stresses that 'an incomplete harmonious society obviously does not hold up to high standards' (2008: 68). We have thus seen how a number of texts, including Zhao's elaboration of *Tianxia*, imagine one holistic system, a single space where everything is already connected to everything else. This conceptualization thus seems (at first glance at least) to imagine a relational space, constituted through interactions. However, if 'the many' are indeed turned into 'the one', how can interaction or any form of relation be possible? Furthermore, and just as in the unit-based cosmology, (spatial) differences are convened under the sign of temporal sequence. Among the 'barbarians', where the values and rule of *Tianxia* are not 'yet' accepted, people will soon see the error of their ways and choose to follow the magnanimous brilliance of the all-knowing *Tianxia* elite.

This view of the coherence of space is problematic because it 'enables the existence of only one history, one voice, one speaking position' (Massey, 2005: 41–2). In Zhao's account this voice claims to speak not 'from China', but rather 'from the world' or 'from nowhere'. It leads to an imagination of causal closure, since there are no others, no outside. Everything is already connected to everything else.

Conclusion

This chapter has discussed scholars' two most common ways of thinking about China in the harmonious world, what I have called a unit-based cosmology and a holistic cosmology. The unit-based cosmology conceives of a jigsaw-puzzled world of bounded and mutually exclusive units. We have seen how these units are built in the discourse of harmonism by first separating off an inside from an outside, and then imagining a movement of harmony from its inside to its outside, so that spatial difference is aligned in temporal sequence. China is a forerunner and blueprint to others that lag behind. Although this movement is often described as an inevitable choice, we have also seen the need to promote it through hard- or soft-power tools, and a tendency towards the elimination of deviant elements in this process.

The holistic cosmology conceives instead of a world where everything is already connected to everything else and there is no outside. It refers to a political cosmology that is thus aspatial. The potential differences of trajectories are occluded, the multiplicities of the spatial are denied and it cannot allow for a distinct and separate other within its system. This chapter has shown how both these cosmologies, as they are deployed in the literature that surrounds the notion of a harmonious world, operate through turning other into self. All spaces are assumed to be following the same, 'our', path. Hence, because space has been marshalled under the sign of time, other places have no space – precisely – to tell different stories, to follow other paths.

Moreover, the aspatial character of these political cosmologies makes impossible the temporal, since the multiplicity of the spatial is its precondition. The homogeneous, uniform and other-less system of *Tianxia* conceives of space as a seamless coherence. It conveys an image of the essential section of what has been referred to as 'a slice through time' (Massey, 2005: 23). In this formulation temporality becomes impossible – 'how to pass between a series of self-contained presents?' (Massey, 2005: 76). If this is the imagination that is to replace 'Western modernism's' temporal alignment of places, then it is a move straight through from a billiard-ball world of essentialized places to a claustrophobic holism in which everything everywhere is already connected to everywhere else, where there can be no coeval multiplicities.

In these conceptions of singular progress, temporality itself is not really open. The future is already foretold, inscribed into the story. The temporal convening of space thus reworks the nature of difference. Coexisting heterogeneity is rendered as (reduced to) place in a historical queue. Drawing on Fabian's critique, a crucial aspect of the manoeuvre is that many students of IR and harmonious world, by placing an other that is observed in a time which is different from 'the Time of the observer' (Fabian, 1983: 25), 'sanctioned an ideological process by which relations between the West and its Other [between China and its other, IR and its object] were conceived of not only as difference, but as distance in space *and* Time' (Fabian, 1983: 147, emphasis in original).

It adds to this sense of hierarchical separation when scholars describe other people, places or civilizations that are physically separate from the projected 'us' as *behind* (whether through bordered separation or relative distance in a holistic network). The temporal convening of space is hence being used to increase distance and in the process creates a hierarchy where the difference and otherness of others does not need to be taken seriously. These discordant elements are positioned as the excluded other of harmony, its constitutive outside. This greater distancing moreover has the effect of decreasing the actuality (the challenge) of difference. The temporal convening of space refuses to recognize the challenge that space and time could present us with: coeval multiplicities.

Notes

1 The texts that I examine in the academic discourse on harmonious world are important as an example of how actors more or less closely tied to the state have used and developed the concept and theorized it in more explicitly spatio-temporal terms. The texts that I focus on are particularly significant because they come from scholars and publications that have been influential both with the Chinese leadership and their academic colleagues in China, and in the international field. I examine a significant volume of academic texts, most of which are in the Chinese language and were available via the Chinese-language academic database, China National Knowledge Infrastructure (CNKI). I have read all the documents that mention 'harmonious world' that have been published since 2005 in any of the most influential Chinese journals in this debate, or authored by any of the 25 scholars identified as the most prominent Chinese IR scholars in a recent study. I identify the most influential journals by tracing the debates on harmonious world. The 14 journals that I have exhaustively studied include: *Shijie jingji yu zhengzhi*, *Guoji zhengzhi kexue*, *Liaowang*, *Xuezhi luntan*, *Dushu*, *Guoji jingji pinglun*, *Guoji zhengzhi yanjiu*, *Zhongguo fazhan guancha*, *Meiguo yanjiu*, *Jiaoxue yu yanjiu*, *Zhongguo yu shijie guancha*, *Zhanlue yu guanli*, *Xiandai guoji guanxi* and *Guoji zhonglie*. The list of most influential scholars is based on scholars' reputation among their peers, assessed through a survey distributed to 305 scholars at China's top universities (Kristensen and Nielsen, 2013: 5). I have also read additional books, articles and conference papers that appear particularly relevant because of a strong focus on the elaboration of 'harmonious world'. The literatures I examine are not exhaustive of things written on or referring to harmonious world, but they are numerous and influential enough to illustrate some general tendencies in academic imaginaries of China and the world.

2 For a theoretical challenge to such ways of periodizing history, and their implications for a future of open politics, see Davis (2008).

3 To the scholar who first used this term, Thongchai Winichakul, the geo-body is a discursive construct, an artefact that has come to seem natural: 'The geo-body of a nation is a man-made territorial definition which creates effects – by classifying, communicating, and enforcement – on people, things, and relationships' (Winichakul, 1994: 17). For its deployment in the Chinese case, see Callahan (2009, 2010: ch. 4).

4 For a few examples, see Liu Xinyu (2005: 41), Liu Dongjian (2006), Sow Keat Tok and Zheng Yongnian (2007), contributions in Guo Sujian and Blanchard (2008), Ding Sheng (2008), Shi Yinhong (2008b) and Hang Lihua (2010).

5 The term *minzu* can be variously translated as 'nation', 'ethnicity' or simply 'people', and *Zhonghua minzu* is used in the literatures to indicate a pan-Chineseness, as opposed to division among China's ethnic minorities and its Han majority.

6 The character *hou* (后) is a common component in words that designate being behind in space, in terms such as *houbian* (后边), and also being behind in time, in terms such as *youhou* (以后), *ranhou* (然后) or *houlai* (后来), meaning 'afterwards', as well as in some that are used to mark being behind in either time or space, such as *houmian* (后面).

7 For a 'hard-power' example, see State Council (2005a). The white papers on China's national defence that are published every two years begin in the foreword to reports on 2004, 2006, 2008 and 2010 by gesturing towards harmony and diversity (State Council, 2004, 2006, 2009b, 2011b). For 'soft-power' examples, see Wen Jiabao (2010a), Hu Jintao (2009) and Yang Jiechi (2010) on the Expo, and Wang Xuexian on the Beijing Olympics (2008).

3 Propaganda at the Shanghai Expo

Foreclosing futures and simulating Chinese world leadership

We have seen how China's harmonious rise is commonly described in terms of inevitable destiny because of history. Meanwhile, the People's Republic of China (PRC) leadership is strictly managing the imagined form and significance of such a rise. Since 2008 China has placed new focus on using mega events to shape the expectations of domestic and international audiences, and thus to shape the future. Such mega events included the 2008 Olympic Games, the 2009 sixtieth anniversary of the founding of the People's Republic of China, as well as 'Expo 2010 Shanghai China'.

The Shanghai Expo is significant because of the importance that the Chinese leadership attached to it. It is often understood as a tool of China's much-discussed 'soft power' (Blanchard and Lu Fujia, 2012). The Expo brought together various actors to negotiate ideas of China in the world, including governmental organizers, various local governments, foreign countries, enterprises and organizations that participated with pavilions, and of course the 73 million visitors that organizers say attended the Expo during the six months in which it was open (Expo Shanghai Online, 2010b). While it is less well documented than the prior mega event that was the 2008 Beijing Olympics, it was literally built as a Chinese image of world order, and therefore it provides an even richer case for the study of the way China's place in the world is imagined outside textual documents in the narrow sense. It shows how the ideas emanating from policy and academic discourse are communicated to, and negotiated in, different media and to different audiences (leisure, business, educational and so on). The analysis here pays particular attention to the official attempts at prescribing China's future relation to the world that went on at the Expo. For this reason, a majority of the data comes from the Expo organizers themselves in the form of books, pamphlets, news, the official Expo website and other media sources, as well as the images, structures, memorabilia, buildings and displays exhibited at the Expo. Although this data does not necessarily provide a coherent account of world-making, it nonetheless expresses a specific strategy linked to the party-state.[1]

Expo 2010 was seen by Chinese academics as an expression of, and tool for, the building of a harmonious world (for example Zou Keyuan, 2011: 11). For many, it symbolized the realization of an old Chinese dream of modernization and rejuvenation. The Expo was also associated with harmony by the party-state. Then Chinese Premier Wen Jiabao stuck closely to the official articulation of 'harmonious world' when he described the Shanghai Expo as:

> an encyclopedia lying open on the land and a magnificent painting showcasing the integration and harmony of diverse cultures.... The World Expo is a vivid demonstration of the diversity of human civilizations. The Shanghai Expo has offered a broad stage for inter-cultural exchanges and integration, reminding us that we live in a diverse and colorful world.
>
> (Wen Jiabao, 2010a)

He continued to argue that the Expo had fully demonstrated harmony to be the common aspiration of mankind, and that the Expo was above national, ethnic and religious boundaries. This, to Premier Wen, was why '[i]t is important that countries ... work together to build a harmonious world of lasting peace and common prosperity' (Wen Jiabao, 2010a).

The Expo was made possible by China's economic rise, but was also part of establishing the story of such a rise as true, and of narrating a future where China rises to be *the* benevolent leader of a new harmonious world order. This chapter examines the way ideas of China's role as leader of a harmonious world proliferated at Expo 2010. It goes about this examination in two parts. The first part traces the two cosmologies outlined in the academic literature in the previous chapter, 'unit-based' and 'holistic' spatial imaginaries. This chapter continues to argue, now in the context of Expo 2010, that the two cosmologies are not mutually exclusive. This chapter will show that the Expo worldview, like some of the academic literature examined in the previous chapter, portrays itself as 'from the world' or 'from everywhere', yet insists on 'specifically Chinese' terms and experience, and on the singular China's future as the (harmonious) world's future. On this view, there is only one future, and it does not welcome contestation. Having recognized this effect of harmony at the Expo, the second part of this chapter argues that scholars need to move beyond the reading of mega events as simple representation and ideology and read it also as simulation. Reading the Chinese world fair as a simulation of world order can provide different ways of relating 'the West' to its 'other country', China.

The two cosmologies and harmony at Expo 2010

Expo 2010 took place in the tradition of scientific and industrial world fairs following on from the Great Exhibition of Industries of All Nations that was held in London in 1851. Expo 2010 has been read in China to symbolize the greatness and international significance of China – indeed, it was the largest, most expensive and most visited of its kind (Barboza, 2010; Expo Shanghai Online, 2010b; *Xinhua*, 2010b, 2010c). The 73 million visitors who passed through the Expo in Shanghai during the six months it was officially open as a world fair would be even greater if one counted the subsequent visitors attracted to the site's permanent monuments

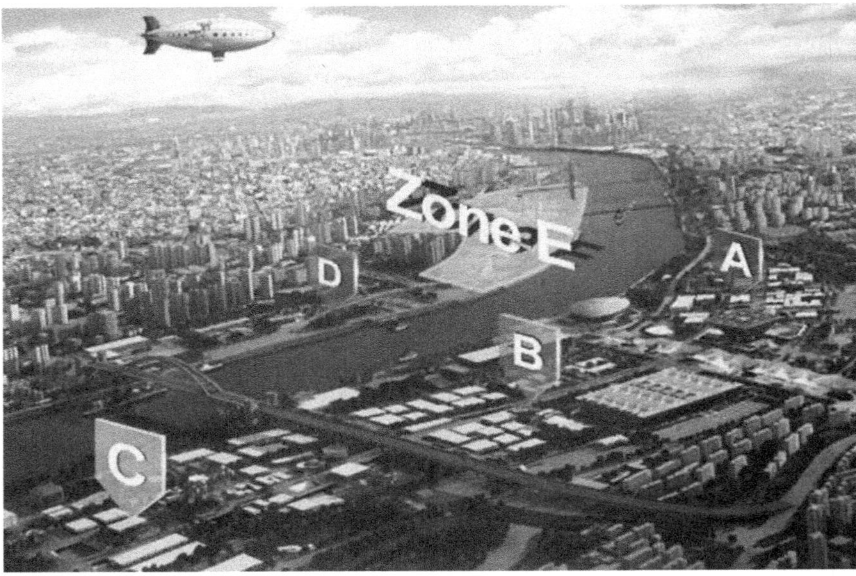

Figure 3.1 Map from online Expo (source: Expo Shanghai Online, 2010d).

(the Chinese national pavilion, for example, has been turned into a permanent museum). In addition, many visited the online version of Expo 2010, where one's avatar can stroll through a virtual 3D replica of the site, visit pavilions and partake in numerous exhibitions, as well as interact with other visitors.

The two cosmologies at the Expo

Unit-based spatial imaginaries are immediately obvious at the Expo. Space at the Expo is typically imagined in a modernist manner as a flat surface upon which humans act, as a 'stage' or 'platform'. As for the unit-based territorialization of this surface, the Expo site is organized as an imagined state system, divided into bounded continents of national pavilions. At the online Expo, visitors can take guided tours of pavilions and exhibitions and get a virtual passport in which visitors can collect visa stamps from the various territories visited.

Likewise, Expo visitors who may never have been abroad and may not own a passport in the outside world can get a multitude of visa stamps and 'play' at being well-travelled. It is an enactment of the world that pretends such international life is readily available and unrestricted. It draws up borders and barriers in order to let them be crossed, but by no means erased or blurred. Through turning visa collection into a game, border controls appear innocent at the same time as their indisputable 'natural existence' between states is reinforced. However, it becomes clear that partaking in this game of 'open borders' is conditional. At the Expo, I met a young travel guide who visited the Expo with 60 tourists from Beijing. While her group went into the *Pavilion of Future* (subtitled 'Dream Inspires the Future') and had their pretend passports stamped, she waited ticketless outside, stopped at the border because she did not have the right papers. Simultaneously, the 'external' nation-state system echoed in citizenship regimes inside the Expo when producing a 'real' passport meant one could jump pavilion queues for the pavilion of the country that had issued it.

This way of conceiving of space in terms of bordered units was marked throughout the Expo. China's own pavilion of regions was no exception, subdivided into regional containers of culture. Many even look like boxes with essentialized culture exhibited inside, like the virtual version of the Tibetan pavilion seen in Figure 3.2.

Although obviously steeped in a unit-based spatial imaginary, these bounded units are also enveloped in the holistic celestial order of one-worldness. The key terms in holistic imaginaries are 'all-encompassing' or 'all-inclusive', with 'no outside' or 'no exception', 'network' and of course *Tianxia*.

The holistic imagination of everything as always already connected to everything else appears in the room in *Urbanian Pavilion* themed 'Connection' (*jiaowang* 交往). This room is based on the 'scientific theory called six degrees spatial theory', which states that no two people are separated by more than six relationships (Xu Wei, 2010: 27). On the ceiling a film is projected showing selected people's movements on a map. Portraits of people appear in circles connected by lines to more and more other people/circles until they form a web or network on the round screen, bringing your mind to the Earth and thus the idea that all people of the world are connected (Xu Wei, 2010: 27). There is no one outside the network. Moreover, this claim is backed up by *science*, and thus requires no further explanation.

Figure 3.2 'Tibet in the heaven' (source: Expo Shanghai Online, 2010e).

The *Pavilion of City Being* describes the city as a living being or organism, focusing on the theme of *shengming* (生命), meaning life, being or bios. The holistic imagination implied in this idea of the city as one body or life is clear from slogans such as 'city being multiplies endlessly, held together by superseding cycles' and 'the unceasing adjustment between people and city maintains city life harmonious, healthy city life requires our common protection' (Xu Wei, 2010: 40).

The *Pavilion of Urban Planet* draws on a holistic spatial imaginary to tell us on the 'Road of Solutions' how the resolution to the world's problems can be found: '[t]he seasons change, settlement becomes cities and trading routes develop into a *completely networked world* ... Only with open mind and *all-inclusive view* can we bring the hope of sustainable growth to our planet Earth' (emphasis added).

These references to the organically connected single organism or body, the web of connections with no outside and the completely networked world with an all-inclusive view, all provide the basis of a holistic spatial imaginary. Moreover, the comments above indicate that this holistic imaginary is taken to demand the harmonious balance of all and 'our common protection'.

Classification in time and space

From the above we see that imaginations of China in the world at the Expo draw on both unit-based and holistic notions of space. This instance shows the two spatial imaginaries coexisting in contemporary China, and so refutes the idea that one would be superseding the other. We will now take a closer look at how they work in tandem at the Expo.

Throughout the Expo, classification of space is marked. We have seen it above in the unit-based form of mapping state units, as well as that of regions as containers of culture. The holistic *Tianxia* concept does not refer to the jigsaw-puzzled space of the unit-based imaginary, but nonetheless classifies and sequentializes through a centre/periphery, civilized/barbarian divide. *Tianxia* ordering is similar to the Expo site centred on the Chinese pavilion.

Similarly, the comparison and contrasting of 'East' and 'West' is ever-present. In a film screened at the *Pavilion of City Being* visitors are watched from the screen by 'the eyes of Eastern people, the eyes of Western people' (Xu Wei, 2010: 49). Likewise, 'Pre-show Hall' in the *Pavilion of Footprint* shows 'ideal cities' as they have been imagined in the East and in the West. Dreaming of a better future is described as universal, or eternal, but similarities end there and juxtaposition takes over.

The division of space into civilizational/regional/national units is aligned with division of time into eras, often in its ancient/modern guise. This is where, just as in much academic discourse, there is evidence of the alignment of dichotomized here/there, modern/ancient and subject/object (cf. Fabian, 1983). As a number of 'developing' countries could not fund their own participation in Expo 2010, Chinese subsidies to these countries ensured there were more state and organization pavilions, 246, than at any previous Expo (*Xinhua*, 2010c). The vastly different budgets and scales meant pavilions gave the impression of a developmental or aspirational classification, in a visual display of global inequality. As in global development, China financially supported 'less-developed' states in a way that visually emphasized the impressive scale and central location of the Chinese pavilion and reaffirmed China as a 'helper' and 'developer' ahead of the 'helped' and 'developing' states at the Expo site periphery, such as the African Joint and Pacific Joint pavilions.

This convening of others differentiated in space through time is crystallized in *Urbanian Pavilion*, which shows the morning rituals of families taken to represent five continents. It shows the similarities of getting up, washing, brushing teeth and so on of people from these different spatial/cultural units. However, the sequentialization in time is obvious. The man from Rotterdam has an electric toothbrush and the Chinese middle-class office worker wears new pyjamas in his modern bathroom, whereas the bathroom in Rio de Janeiro looks worn and dirty. In this way spatial difference is aligned in temporal sequence. We all do the same thing; it is just that some are a bit behind on the road to modernization and development.

Spatial division is thus not only conceived as classification of space, but also as classification in time. This classification is moreover conceived of in a time that runs towards a particular end. Clock-time running out, or towards the future, is emphasized at the Shanghai train station's Expo clock tower. Throughout the Expo itself, feature clocks, ticking pendula and hourglasses tell the same story.

The intertwining of temporal notions with strong assertions as to what Chinese identity is in world affairs is clear from an introduction to the Expo on its official website, ringing with familiarity with the official party line:

> [w]ith a long civilisation, China favours international exchange and loves world peace. China owes its successful bid for the World Exposition in 2010 to the international community's support for and confidence in its reform and opening-up. The Exposition will be the first registered World Exposition in a developing country, which gives expression to the expectations the world's people place on China's future development.... We count on the continuing attention, support and participation of all the peace-loving countries.
>
> (Expo 2010, 2008)

In this context, depicting China as 'original' confers on it a status as forerunner of developing countries, conveniently forgetting the 1949 Haiti Expo (Expo 2010, 2006a; Bureau International des Expositions, 2011).

China's present and future direction is frequently depicted in terms of a return to an original or always intended state. The Expo itself is typically portrayed as the fulfilment (led by the party-state) of an ancient Chinese dream. This portrayal appears in articles (Expo 2010, 2006b), in books such as *100 Years of Expo Dream* (*Bai Nian Shibo Meng* 百年世博梦) (Shanghai shibohui shiwu xietiaoju, 2009) and in the World Expo Museum that looks back at more than 150 years of historical preparation for the Shanghai Expo. Online commentators echo such narratives, and one commentator on the Expo online 'Dream Wall' comments that 'I believe in China's actual strength, a country that has 5000 years of civilization must be able to produce glory once more' (Expo Shanghai Online, 2010c).

Finally, the feature film of the Xinjiang regional pavilion demonstrates how classification of time and space come together into a particular, goal-oriented progress under PRC leadership:

> [Xinjiang is] the communication land of four great civilisations of the world.... It once was the road of bonze Xuanzang, the silk road, the road of western expedition and the road of eastern return.... The great transformation of 60 years is the evidence of our diligence and intelligence.... Today, the assistance from the motherland also lights up the passion in Xinjiang.[2]
>
> (Expo Shanghai Online, 2010g)

This quotation brings together the numerous elements that make possible the problematic imagination of self–other relations that is under discussion in this book. A separation between civilizations is posited. Xinjiang is subsequently conceived of as a place where these separate civilizations meet. Progress is imagined as a return to a state that *once* was, and that is now returning through Chinese diligence in its (re)civilizing mission. One can only wonder at the irony as the motherland's assistance 'lights up the passion' in Xinjiang after the brutal ethnic clashes in the years running up to the Expo (*Xinhua*, 2009d).

Metaphors of lines, circles, spirals and pendula may be used to describe this temporality, but may be misleading as they change significance in their *combined* use (cf. Gell, 1992). The point of China's progress/return (to its rightful place as world leader) is not whether it is described using the metaphor of the circle or the line. Of key importance is instead the way it operates through a classification of time and space: and there is no doubt as to where the world is/should be heading. The point is that these temporalities support each other and lead towards the same ultimate endpoint.

The future is one where China leads a new harmonious world order

Chinese discussions surrounding the Expo typically conferred on it one central meaning – it was a sign of China's legitimate rise to world leadership. Wishes for Chinese superiority similarly appeared in the online *Vanke Pavilion*, the corporate pavilion for a large Chinese property developer. One commentator wished that in 2049 'China is in leading position in the world' and another exclaimed that by then 'China has really changed into a great cultural country, ten thousand countries come to pay tribute!' (万邦来朝) (Expo Shanghai Online, 2010f). A majority of participants in the Expo's 'Dream Wall' expressed love for the motherland, the Expo and Shanghai, with one exclaiming, 'Go Expo, China is invincible!' (Go Expo 中国无敌) (Expo Shanghai Online, 2010c).

Key to justifying this Chinese world leadership is depicting such a world as 'harmonious', in accordance with the harmonious world discourse. The Expo is

Figure 3.3 Harmonious first-aid kit (source: Astrid H. M. Nordin).

steeped in this language of harmony. China's national pavilion begins with the film *Harmonious China* (*Hexie Zhongguo* 和谐中国) and concludes with telling us 'the lotus flowers blossom, symbolising the harmonious and glorious future of Chinese cities' (Expo Shanghai Online, 2010a). The Xinjiang pavilion is labelled 'Xinjiang – a harmonious land'. Visitors can go to the Expo on a harmonious train, to visit Harmony Tower, and if they hurt ourselves they can have a band-aid from the harmonious first-aid kit.

The language of harmony is also prevalent among the wishes of *Vanke Pavilion*. One participant wishes:

> 2010: A life at ease A peaceful and stable job Wishing the great motherland is increasingly thriving and prosperous My family is increasingly harmonious and happy.
>
> 2049: There is no war in any corner of the world There is no discrimination Peaceful getting along and also wish that when we reach that time people from every corner of the world can all profoundly understand China.
>
> (Expo Shanghai Online, 2010f)

We see here a mixing of ideas of harmony with notions of a good personal life, a thriving China and an image of peacefully connected world citizens who comprehend China. Again, there is an emphasis on making foreigners *understand* 'China'. A blurb for *Pavilion of Future*'s harmony sculpture similarly personalizes world harmony: 'core concept of traditional Chinese culture: only the harmony of the world and all things constitute the harmony of human's spirit'. Just as in Zhao's *Tianxia*, the harmony of all things is required. There can be no outside to the system, or it will fail. All things must be incorporated. The claim in both these contexts is that this is a distinctly Chinese idea of world order.

Throughout all of these imaginings of China in the (harmonious) world, the two spatial imaginaries combine in ways that repeat the problems outlined with regards to academic discourse, making it difficult to imagine others as coeval. The unit-based spatial imaginary provides a condition of possibility of Chinese particularism. Throughout the Chinese pavilions at the Expo, China is the very origin of civilization and of the world – it is where the first fire burnt, the first bird flew and the superior values of Confucian harmony originated. The holistic spatial imaginary becomes key to imagining the need for spreading this civilization, and for the Chinese civilizing mission currently observed around the world (Nyíri, 2006). The holistic idea of space is core to construing the rise of China to leadership of a harmonious world as peaceful and beneficial to all. On this view, there is no outside, everything is always already connected to everything else, and the view of the Chinese party elite is a 'view from nowhere', or a view 'from the world'.

Many of these themes are echoed through non-Chinese pavilions at the Expo, including the two spatial imaginaries, the goal-oriented notion of time, East–West juxtaposition and a reliance on blurry notions of civilization. Notably, many foreign states, organizations and enterprises used the Expo to exhibit their willingness to buy into the Chinese discourse on harmonious world, allowing it prominence of place in the way they name, speak of and write of their own pavilions. 'Harmony' in particular is given legitimacy through frequent use in foreign pavilions, such as 'Harmonious relations' (Pacific Joint Pavilion), 'Feel the harmony' (Austria), 'Harmony of the heart, harmony of the skills' (Japan) and so on. While some academic analyses of Chinese foreign policy argue that the PRC is being 'socialized' into values and norms of 'international society' (Johnston, 2008), the Expo showed the opposite: 'outsiders' competing to be most attentive to, and accommodating of, China's purported self-image.

Non-Chinese corporate pavilions too helped reinforce and legitimate this particular version of 'harmony' with reference to Chinese history. One example was the pavilion called *Tianxia yi jia* (天下一家): '*Tianxia* one family'. This pavilion was German multinational Siemens' corporate pavilion, showcasing its technology through the aspirational middle-class future of interactive games and wine coolers that would apparently be available to Chinese people in 2015. Entering Siemens' harmonious and commercialized rendition of *Tianxia*, visitors are photographed. As in a miracle of scientific development our faces appear on a film screen at the exit, manipulated to sing together in harmony with the Expo theme tune. The simulation is explained at a sign at the pavilion entrance:

> After scanning and capturing the user's facial features, the image will be recorded and transformed into an avatar allowing users to feel as if they are starring in a pre-programmed movie or video … How will this technology better our lives? Provides an entertaining experience for people to play a role in a movie or become a 'star.' Everyone has the chance to stand in the spotlight.

China's future, in this commercialized version as in its official one, provides the time and space for us all to be stars in the spotlight. It is worth recalling here the organizers' own claim that the Expo took place because of 'the international community's support for and confidence in [China's] reform and opening-up', expressing 'the expectations the world's people place on China's future development' with China sternly counting on 'the continuing attention, support and participation of all the peace-loving countries' (Expo 2010, 2008). In this version of the future world we are allowed into the spotlight on the condition that we become avatars that sing simultaneously in one voice to the Chinese melody.

Foreclosing futures at Expo 2010

Up to this point, this chapter has argued that the holistic and unit-based cosmologies, or spatial imaginaries, were prominent at Expo 2010, aligning classified units of time/space in sequence. They are simultaneously deployed in ways that support a particular discourse on China and the world, prescriptive of a particular future where China leads a new harmonious world order.

World fairs were from the outset an exercise where self/other relations were heavily tinted by imperialism (Rydell, 1984). Today, although the specific selves and others reproduced by the Expo may be somewhat different, their fundamental manoeuvre is the same. Despite its intentions, the articulation of time and space with the narrative of harmony is again problematic, because it marginalizes concepts of coeval multiplicities and difference. Others are not properly different, they are just behind. Just like Zhao's *Tianxia*, the Expo worldview portrays itself as 'from the world' or 'from everywhere', yet insists on 'specifically Chinese' terms and experience. This is reinforced as the Expo shows an already nationalistic domestic audience a China that rightfully rises to the place of world leader and the folly of anyone imagining that such a rise would be less than beneficial to all. This is buttressed by readings of foreign involvement and investment in the Expo as endorsements of the Chinese model for its rise, and is taken as a showcase for how harmonious the world is under Chinese leadership.

The Expo worldview portrays itself as 'from the world', yet insists on the singular China's future as the (harmonious) world's future. On this view, there is only one future, and it does not welcome contestation. This book proposes that we can refuse scripting our songs in the pre-programmed manner suggested by predominant imaginings at the Expo. It can indeed be possible to meet the challenge of coeval multiplicities that time and space should present us with. The next section begins to unsettle the dominant rendition of time, space and China in the world by way of reading it through the work of Jean Baudrillard.

Taking Baudrillard to the fair

This chapter has examined different ways in which China is imagined as *ahead* in the historical queue that is posited at Expo 2010. However, as explained in the Introduction to this book, a most common way of imagining China elsewhere in discourse on the country's relation to the world is as behind, or catching up. This way of understanding China's role in international politics has its roots in an imagination of Chinese experience as radically different from that of Western modernity – as the 'other country' (Chow, 1991: 81). In recent years a key Chinese strategy for negotiating both its claims to particularism and to being a modern great power has been through the public diplomacy of 'mega events', including Expo 2010. The success of Chinese mega events in altering international opinion is debatable (Manzenreiter, 2010: 29–48). As symbols of a changing Chinese identity and outlook they have nonetheless come to be understood as an important aspect of Chinese 'image management' (Xin Xu, 2006; Brownell, 2008; Price and Dayan, 2008). In what follows, this chapter argues that scholars need to take the next step and understand China's mega events not only on the level of representation and ideology, but also on the level of simulation.[3] It moreover argues that a consequence of such a reading is that scholars need to stop imagining China as the 'other country' (I make a similar argument, but for different reasons, in Nordin, 2014a, 2014b).

World fairs have been described as instrumental in creating the distinction between reality and representation, a dualism that has become central to contemporary ways of capturing the modern world (Mitchell, 1988; Harvey, 1996). The remainder of this chapter explores what happens when we read the world fair – symbol of modernity – through the work of Jean Baudrillard – symbol of postmodernity. I suggest that we read Expo 2010 not only as an exercise of nation-building, but as shaping also the imaginary of the world as a holistic unit. Expo 2010 could easily be read as a representation of the world, as mimicry or a fake version of the real world beyond its gates. In what follows, this chapter reads it instead as simulation.

The key claim it will make is that the world fair is everywhere, that in fact the world is a fair, and that this has serious consequences for the study thereof. The reading of the world fair as simulation shows how we may be mistaken to imagine Chinese experience as radically other to that of Western modernity, or postmodernity for that matter. It provides a different way of thinking about space, time and subjectivity. This chapter suggests that Baudrillard can help us think differently about intellectual strategy in our study of such a simulated harmonious world fair.

To be simulated, or where is the fair?

Baudrillard claims that the world has passed into the hyper-real, 'the generation by models of a real without origin or reality' (1994 [1981]: 1). What has been lost, he argues, is metaphysics: '[n]o more mirror of being and appearances, of the real and its concept' (1994 [1981]: 2). Crucially, this is not a question of imitation, duplication or even parody, but of substitution. As a consequence the real will never again have a chance to produce itself, but is replaced by a 'hyper-real' where there is no distinction between the real and the imaginary, 'leaving room only for the orbital recurrence of models and for the simulated generation of differences' (1994 [1981]: 3). What is at stake in Baudrillard's analysis, then, is the reality principle:

> [t]o dissimulate is to pretend not to have what one has. To simulate is to feign to have what one doesn't have. One implies a presence, the other an absence. But it is more complicated than that because simulating is not pretending.... Therefore, pretending, or dissimulating, leaves the principle of reality intact: the difference is always clear, it is simply masked, whereas simulation threatens the difference between the 'true' and the 'false,' the 'real' and the 'imaginary.'
>
> (Baudrillard, 1994 [1981]: 3)

There are few places where the question of the real and the imaginary, the true and the false, the original and the fake, is as pertinent and as sensitive as in contemporary China. The lack of respect in China for copyright is a frequent bone of contention in its foreign relations. Domestic relations have been shaken in recent years by the 'tainted milk' scandal, where a number of infants were killed and hundreds of thousands fell ill from ingesting 'fake' milk powder containing melamine (Barriaux, 2011). In International Relations (IR), voices are raised that worry about Westerners underestimating the 'China threat' because China may be faking it, 'a wolf in sheep's clothing' (Gang Lin, 2005: 1).

Expo 2010 was a highly controlled space, yet it too had its own associated scandals of fakery. Some suggested that Expo 2010's mascot, Haibao, was a resurrection of American cartoon character Gumby, dubbing it 'The Gumbygate scandal' (V. Saxena, 2010). The Chinese national pavilion was exposed to similar allegations of plagiarism, facing claims that it looked a lot like the Japanese pavilion from the 1992 Seville Expo, and equally similar to the Canadian pavilion at Montreal in 1967. The biggest diplomatic scandal, nonetheless, surrounded the promotional tune *Waiting for You* which was officially written for Expo 2010, its video featuring all-Chinese superstars like Jackie Chan and Yao Ming. A scandal erupted as it was revealed to bear an uncanny resemblance to Mayo Okamoto's 1997 Japanese hit *Stay the Way You Are*. The irony was not lost on foreign commentators, with one commentator noting that '[i]f the Shanghai Expo is the ultimate showcase of an economy roaring to world dominance, then the organizers have selected a theme song that perfectly captures China on the cusp of the twenty-first century: strident, stirring – and ripped off' (Lewis, 2010). The composer of the tune first strongly denied plagiarism allegations. Expo 2010 organizers thereafter suspended all use of the song citing 'copyright reasons', and after 'a flurry of face-saving efforts' Expo 2010 organizers, without admitting any problematic recycling, asked if they could please use Okamoto's work. The songwriter, whose practically forgotten tune had suddenly returned to the top of Japanese charts, selflessly acquiesced (Lewis, 2010).

These revelations of scandalous fakery, whether on the low level of song writing or the high level of lethal state violence, are typically understood as a form of resistance. They are taken to reveal the *real* state of affairs. Some commentators extrapolate fakery to a 'Chinese characteristic', portraying resistance to elite-led fakery as a resistance to power. In a short film on Chinese netizens and state power, blogger Wang Xiaofeng comments on Chinese fakes, with video shots of the Expo interspersed:

> China is a country who likes to make fake things. Lying is a virtue of the Chinese. This is evident in all kind of matters. Statistical numbers are fake (*jiade* 假的) and whatever we create, even the good things, are fake. They [the PRC government] must say that some other countries are worse than China, to make common people think that China is the best place to live in. The existence of mainstream media is based on this process of the never-ending creation of fake. And the government itself is constantly creating this 'fake'. If you go to remote places in China you discover very shocking realities, people can't even find something to eat, but you still think this country is a great country. So when you want to know the facts and get information you are actually challenging power. They are afraid of this.
>
> (Wang Xiaofeng in Marianini and Zdzarski, 2011)

The claim of the denouncers of scandalous fakery is that reality is being masked, and the purpose of denunciation is to reveal this reality through exposing fakery. The claim in the reminder of this chapter, and in this book, is that the distinction between the real and the fake of the harmonious world is disappearing in a system of self-referential signs.

In this respect, simulation is very different from representation. The way the latter is often used implies an equivalence of the sign and the real – even if it is a utopian equivalence. Where representation tries to absorb simulation by construing it as a false representation, simulation 'envelops the whole edifice of representation itself as a simulacrum' (Baudrillard, 1994 [1981]: 6). An interpretation through ideology may understand an image or sign as either reflecting or masking a profound reality. On such an ideological understanding, we might say that signs dissimulate something. In what follows, the focus will be instead on how images or signs might dissimulate that there is nothing. In other words, if they mask anything at all, it is not a profound reality, but the absence of a profound reality. At points, this logic might be pushed to its extreme, where the image has no relation to any reality whatsoever, but is 'its own pure simulacrum' (Baudrillard, 1994 [1981]: 6).

The shift 'from signs that dissimulate something to signs that dissimulate that there is nothing' is crucial because the real is no longer what it once was. This is the significance of simulation, and its key effect is that in place of 'the truth' we have myriad truths taking the shape of signs of reality and myths of origin (Baudrillard, 1994 [1981]: 6).

Baudrillard uses the example of Disneyland to model the 'entangled orders of simulacra' because he sees it primarily as a play of illusions and fantasy (Baudrillard, 1994 [1981]: 12). The adults' parallel to Disneyland in the contemporary era is the world fair, the most recent, the biggest, the most expensive and the most visited of which, again, was Expo 2010. Like Disneyland, Expo 2010 is built up of phantasm and '100 years of Expo dream' (Shanghai shibohui shiwu xietiaoju, 2009). At the same time, as will be seen in this chapter, Expo 2010 involved truth claims in an explicit way that Disneyland never has, which makes it pertinent to examining both its signs that dissimulate something (ideology) and signs that dissimulate that there is nothing or even let go of any relation to reality at all (simulation).

Expo 2010 was constructed as a simulation of the world in ways that mix dreams with truth claims (and, as argued above, the claims that the dreams are indeed the true dreams of humanity and that these dreams will come true). Just like Disneyland, the Expo is ideological: a digest of the Chinese way of life, a panegyric of Chinese values and an idealized transposition of a contradictory reality. Nonetheless, the 'Chineseness' of Expo 2010 can be overemphasized in a format that is all about recycling. As Penelope Harvey writes:

> [i]n many ways the form of the great exhibitions has been maintained despite the changing economic, social and political circumstances. Nation states displayed cultural artefacts and technological expertise in their individual pavilions, seeking to educate and entertain the visiting public. The obligations of the organizers of a fair with universal status are less concerned with the actual bringing together of exhibitors from all over the globe than with enacting a theme that simultaneously promotes the unity of mankind and the uniqueness of individual societies.
>
> (Harvey, 1996: 35)

The nation state has been the key cultural, political and economic unit through which both IR and world fairs have traditionally told the tale of global community, and Expo 2010 recycles this conceptualization. As argued above, the spatial organization of the Expo sites, in Shanghai and online, is a starkly visual simulation of the purported organization of the international state system. Essentialized culture is encapsulated in the spatial containers that are Expo pavilions, which in turn are encapsulated in continents or regions, which in turn are a subdivision of the neatly bounded and mapped world fair. These mappings are presented as neutral and innocent, helpful and real – some lines on a surface, fair and square (Expo Shanghai Online, 2010d).

This particular model depends on a metaphor of scale by which the international community reproduces the form of its constituent parts: '[b]oth part and whole function as self-contained, coherent, bounded entities which are mutual transformations of each other through simple principles of aggregation and disaggregation' (Harvey, 1996: 50). This imaginary reproduces units that differ from each other, but through a difference that is one of equivalence. Whether we think of these units as natural or culturally constructed, they are defined by precise boundaries in temporal, spatial and cultural terms, they are distinct but equivalent entities. This model of equivalence by difference was highly visible at Expo 2010 as at previous world fairs (Harvey, 1996: 51). The world fair appears as a taxonomization of equivalent national units with their own pavilion, listing in official guidebooks and dedicated day of cultural display. The official Opening Celebration of Expo 2010 saw the parading of national flags, carried by Chinese youth made up to appear as repetitions and copies of each other (CCTV Documentary, 2010).

In this way Expo 2010 recycled the form of Expo 1992 in Seville about which Harvey writes:

> [t]he Expo provided a concrete instance of endless replication, a cultural artefact built as if to demonstrate the possibilities and limitations of an entirely consumerist world. Thus there was the appearance of choice, of multiple perspectives, yet the cultural forms on show were nevertheless clearly reformulations and repetitions of each other and of previous events. Sameness and familiarity undermined the promise of difference.
>
> (Harvey, 1996)

What we learn from Baudrillard is that this ideology moreover functions as a cover for a simulation of a different order: 'Disneyland exists in order to hide that it is the "real" country, all of "real" America that is Disneyland' (1994 [1981]: 12). The world fair, in this vein, exists in order to hide that it is the 'real' world, all of the 'real' world that is the fair. The presentation of the Expo world as imaginary and as a dream functions to make us think that the rest is real. The world fair takes us further than Disneyland does, as it is not content with a country, but must simulate the world – always striving to be more inclusive, with Expo 2010 priding itself on including pavilions of more countries than ever before, an inclusion that cost the PRC government large sums in the form of subsidies (*Xinhua*, 2010c). In this way Expo 2010 marks a shift from ideological nation-building to worlding by simulation. Shanghai, China and the world that surrounds the Expo are no longer real, but hyper-real, belonging now to the order of simulation: '[i]t is no longer a question of a false representation of reality (ideology) but of concealing the fact that the real is no longer real, and thus of saving the reality principle' (Baudrillard, 1994 [1981]: 12–13).

The relation between Baudrillard's different orders – those that dissimulate something and those that dissimulate that there is nothing – comes to the fore in the hyper-awareness and self-reflexivity of Expo 2010, as it had begun to do in previous world fairs (Harvey, 1996). There were frequent references to the self-representations of previous world fairs, in TV programmes, books and in the 'Expo museum' at Expo 2010 (see for example Shanghai shibohui shiwu xie-tiaoju, 2009). In many instances of its replication, the world fair reflected on itself as the exhibition of the exhibition of the exhibition without end, as world fair exhibiting world fair. Key emblems, monuments and mascots of previous fairs were brought together with the effect of appearing as self-referential signs, as copies of copies, representations of representations without original, signifiers of signifiers without signifieds, ad infinitum. In this way, '[t]he exhibition represents the world, provides contexts and connections for an understanding of external realities, but its reflexivity simultaneously confuses or confounds the distinction of insider/outsider, representation and reality' (Harvey, 1996: 37).

The implication is one of implosion of the careful construct and of moving to the phase where 'it has no relation to any reality whatsoever: it is its own pure simulacrum' (Baudrillard, 1994 [1981]: 6). Therefore, scholars must take the step beyond understanding how the exhibition represents the world and grapple with how the harmonious exhibition *is* the world, and the harmonious world the exhibition.

Reading the Expo through Baudrillard thus turns the world into fair and the fair into the world. As this chapter will continue to show throughout, the distinction between one as real or original and the other as fake or copy can no longer be upheld (if it ever could). *All we have are versions or layers of the harmonious world/fair, all simulacra.* This is why this chapter argues that *we need to take the step and study it as such*, rather than limit ourselves to reading China's mega events purely on the level of representation and ideology, upholding the reality principle. The layers of simulacra are all world/fair, but cannot *be* the fair in a fully present way because Baudrillard, and others with him, have upset the dichotomization of presence and absence.[4] For this reason, the relation between the layers of simulacra is not that of a coherent system, of stable exchange or of dialectics. The world/fair is simultaneously nowhere and now here.

To be recycled, or when is the fair?

The previous section has asked *where* the fair is and argued that it is everywhere and anywhere – that the world/fair is simultaneously nowhere and now here. We turn next to the temporality of simulation in this formulation to ask *when* the fair is. Looking for the world/fair somewhere and some time beyond the dichotomization of presence and absence, this section argues that the fair works through recycling, revival and reuse, that as a rem(a)inder, it is not new.

What better place to start than with beginnings and origins? 'We require a visible past, a visible continuum, a visible myth of origin, which reassures us about our end. Because finally we have never believed in them' (Baudrillard, 1994 [1981]: 10). Beginnings were certainly important to displays of China at Expo 2010. Throughout the Chinese national pavilion and dozens of Chinese regional pavilions, China is described as the origin of the world, echoing wider media and academic discourse in China. Various Chinese regional pavilions also pride China for figuring as the origin of (Chinese) civilization. I use brackets here because there is some discrepancy or ambiguity in terms of communicating such messages to Chinese-speaking and English-speaking audiences. In the Gansu province case, for example, which circles around its 'long history' of more than 8,000 years of civilization, a sign that reads in English 'Dadiwan Site in Qin'an County Believed to Start the Chinese Civilization' in Chinese language simply reads 'Civilization begins – Qin'an Dadiwan' (*wenming zhaoqi* 文明肇启). This kind of slippage between these terms appears throughout Expo 2010 and makes Chinese civilization appear coterminous with civilization as such.

This exhuming of 'Chinese civilization' functioned as an ideological tool to make the '5000 years of uninterrupted Chinese civilization' appear real. This uninterrupted history of harmony is part of the shift in legitimization of the Chinese Communist Party (CCP) rule from socialism to nationalism and 'Chinese characteristics' (Cheung, 2012; Billioud, 2011). Most importantly, however, this exhumation took pride of place because of a dream, 'behind this defunct power that it tries to annex, of an order that would have had nothing to do with it, and it dreams of it because it exterminated it by exhuming it as its own past' (Baudrillard, 1994 [1981]: 10). IR scholars are performing this same exhuming ritual when we dream of the emerging 'Chinese school' of IR theory as a radical alternative to 'the West'.

The fascination with this Chinese school resembles that discussed by Baudrillard of 'Renaissance Christians' with 'American Indians'. At the beginning of the Christian colonizing movement existed an instance of bewilderment at 'the very possibility of escaping the universal law of the Gospel' (Baudrillard, 1994 [1981]: 10). In this bewilderment we could either admit to the lack of universality of the Law, or exterminate the evidence to the contrary. The conversion or simple discovery of these different beings is usually enough, for the Renaissance Christians as for scholars of IR, to slowly exterminate them.

This tactic of discovery and conversion as a form of extermination of others has been acknowledged elsewhere in IR scholarship (Inayatullah and Blaney, 2004) and it remains a tactic in PRC policy towards its 'internal others' in areas like Tibet and Xinjiang. Chinese policy towards its ethnic minorities is presented as proof of the superiority of Chinese civilization: it produces *more* ethnics than the ethnics themselves were able to do – since the PRC party-state provides modern health care and 'scientific development' and exempted ethnic minorities from the one child policy. Moreover the PRC state produces *more ethnic* ethnics than they themselves had mustered. This promotion of Chinese ethnic minorities through their regional pavilions lies at the heart of Expo 2010, a base from which the Chinese national pavilion rises. Everywhere, the ethnic is exotically reproduced, recycled and rescreened. Everywhere happy, colourful and anachronistic 'ethnics' sing, dance and rejoice in the greatness of the motherland, as in the Xinjiang pavilion ('a harmonious place'). If there were ever anybody 'ethnic' there, they have now been transformed into a caricature of themselves, and therefore vanished as such. This overproduction is a means of destruction, a 'promotion' and 'rescue' that forms another step to their symbolic disappearance.

Nonetheless, the Expo is highly self-aware in its use of time. As described above, it frequently uses clocks, hourglasses and pendula to mark the countdown to horror scenarios of planetary destruction in order to drum home its purported message of 'Better city, Better life'. In places it moreover explicitly favours 'recycling' over 'linearity'. The theme pavilion *City Being* uses similar metaphors to Baudrillard to conceive of time, that of biological life cycles, metabolism, circulation and recycling. These are said to be key to the proper functioning of the system. This pavilion is evocatively constructed as a sewerage system interspersed with circulating billboard messages of interconnection. It is explicit about its rejection of linear models, as in a pair of diagrammatical signs of which the first reads 'A linear model will result in excessive pollution and waste', and the second reads 'A cyclical model will feature greater recycling and less waste'.

Through these examples we can see the world/fair engaged in simultaneous attempts at both representation and simulation. It can therefore be understood as dissimulating something, but also as dissimulating that there is nothing. In places, the world/fair appears unreflexive, as attempting to reinstate the reality of its teleological progress. In other aspects, however, its reflexive hyper-aware recycling seems to show how 'it has no relation to any reality whatsoever: it is its own pure simulacrum' (Baudrillard, 1994 [1981]: 6). Not only, then, can the world no longer be represented by the fair, but more importantly it can no longer be re-presented, it can no longer be made present in time and space as some full or complete presence. As such, it is not enough to remain within a simple framework of representation and ideology in our analyses of the world/fair, but we need to take the next step and start analysing China's mega events also as simulation. The world/fair is simultaneously nowhere and now here. The world/fair is recycled.

To be screened, or who is the fair?

Having asked in previous sections *where* and *when* the fair is, this section turns to the question of *who* is the fair. What happens to subjectivity in the interactive technologies of the world/fair? This section argues that in an order of recycling, the technologies that make us simultaneously subjects and objects make the distinction between subject and object untenable with the effect of making these categories unworkable.

It is clear that our embodiment matters in the world fair as it differentiates between ways of being in the world/fair along lines of class, race, gender and so on. At the Shanghai Expo, where well over 90 per cent of visitors were Chinese, the ability to identify me as a fair-skinned visitor from the outside made me an immediate part of the exhibited exotica (my being fair made me the fair, so to speak. And simultaneously the reverse was true, it positioned me as though outside the fair, observing it/them). But Expo 2010 goes much further in making us part of the fair, through the layers of interactive technologies by which the fair itself emerges.

In the first instance, we are an active part of this emergence, we can plan, steer and shape the world/fair, we are the subjects of its emergence. Visitors are often asked to actively participate in Expo 2010. Indeed, interactivity is a key feature of many pavilions and different layers of the world/fair, and one pavilion is expressly dedicated to displaying it. Here, photographs from Expo 2010 and its preparation, submitted via the Expo 2010 website, are circulated on screens. Participants can also send 'blessings and wishes for Expo 2010' from various websites and have them screened in the pavilion, surrounded by cards with wishes and blessings written by its visitors. In a 'wishing tree' visitors are encouraged to write wishes on colourful paper, fold it into an aeroplane and throw it into an artificial tree. In parallel, the Online Expo 2010 has many venues where one's avatar can leave wishes, such as the *Vanke* pavilion or the *Expo Dream Home* discussed above. On a multimedia display stand visitors to Expo 2010 can arrange various building models and simultaneously a 3D image of its layout will appear on a background wall, surrounded by previous 'excellent works'. In this way, a sign for the multimedia display tells us, 'You could become one of the designers of a future city'. In Shanghai's own pavilion at Expo 2010 the 'Shanghai forever' image wall consists of revolving triangles and more than 15,000 photographs featuring Shanghai. It is a product of 'mass participation and joint creation' intended to expound the 'design conception of "New horizons forever"' (or in Chinese 'Shanghai eternally marches towards a new horizon'). Images of images are everywhere and we can be their creators.

Nonetheless, in subjecting the world/fair to our gaze and our actions, we are simultaneously subjected by it. Our bodies are not only *in* the world/fair, they *are* the world fair, as the fair is our bodies, simultaneously watching and watched, displaying and displayed. Often our recognition as participants rests on our willingness to take on specific subject positions – tellingly, the English title of the pavilion for popular participation is 'Citizens' initiative pavilion', interpellating us as citizens of the mapped state system on display. It is through such citizenship that we are allowed recognition in the world/fair. Indeed, the different layers of simulacra share citizenship regimes as a key feature, invoked through the passport. At previous world fairs, at the Shanghai Expo and at the online version of Expo 2010 visitors can have a passport in which we collect 'visa stamps' from the pavilions visited.

At points, we have to actively change ourselves to make us acceptable as subjects in order to have our fair share. Passing through the world/fair we are screened and tested. This screening echoes for the subject/object dichotomy (the who) the collapse we saw in previous sections of the here/there (the where) and the now/then (the when). As Richard Lane has observed with regard to Baudrillard:

> there is an interpenetration of the screen metaphor with the notion of everything being on the surface here, including the 'friendly' surveillance which simultaneously shows the people under surveillance on television screens, which leads to a collapsing of perspectival space (the removal of the 'gap' or distance both spatially and temporally between the viewer and the viewed).
>
> (Lane, 2000: 42)

Here interpenetration is total, including of architectural and geographical space. The layers of simulacra cannot be separated. All of Expo 2010, the Shanghai

Expo and its virtual replica, Shanghai, China, all of the world/fair are indistinguishable as a total functional screen of activities (cf. Baudrillard, 1994 [1981]: 76). In this way all of the world/fair operates through screening, in every sense of the word. The example above of the excluded tour guide moreover exemplifies how our participation in the citizenship regimes of the world/fair is conditional – she was stopped at the border because she had not paid the fee.

Indeed, the world/fair is most helpful in persuading us that we can (and should) adjust our selves to pass its screening. In a book dedicated to Expo etiquette prospective visitors to the world/fair are most helpfully taught how to modify their behaviour and their bodies (Xu Bo, 2009). Chinese readers can learn among other things how to greet, walk, shake hands, sit, queue and care for their personal hygiene in a polite manner. They can read about how to go to karaoke, drink coffee with foreigners and host them in their home according to global decorum. In an appendix we find a taxonomy of etiquette, outlining customs country by country, from the United States to Egypt (2009: 147–71). One drawn image, for example, shows one man (who we can presume, from the big nose in profile, is a Westerner) who sits nicely at his table with one glass and one plate on which he is attacking a square (perhaps a piece of toast) with his knife and fork. He looks with bewilderment and a hint of fear at another man or boy who smiles a big smile as he carries his second plate to the table, where he has already assembled two glasses, various fruits and one more plate overflowing with food (in the mish-mash of which we can identify various fruits, a whole fish, a crab and some shrimp). The picture's caption instructs its Chinese readers to eat moderately, with a rhyming line to the effect of 'don't have eyes bigger than your belly' (*yan da duzi xiao, meiwei chi bu liao* 眼大肚子小, 美味吃不了) (2009: 62).

The concluding chapter of the book, on 'how to be a refined and well mannered Expo person', clearly conceives of such politeness in terms of the *return* to an original state. Readers are encouraged to 'utilize the Shanghai Expo as a historical turning point, to make every one of us change into politely speaking Expo people' (2009: 141–6). Furthermore, readers are told about 'the Expo's demand on the etiquette of the people of the host country', through which the author hopes that the Expo will 'make elegant etiquette *return* to China' (2009: 141–6, emphasis added). Thus, being a civilized citizen of the world/fair is not about being more like somebody else, but about being more like your self; it is a question of recycling.

At other points, moving through the world/fair our bodies are more explicitly hijacked by screening, made to do things potentially against our will (and indeed through or in advance thereof), proliferated, taken apart. The Ningxia Hui Autonomous Region case for example shows visitors' images captured and repeatedly displayed on screens. As citizens of the world/fair our bodies are captured and displayed as copy upon copy throughout Expo 2010, media and academic work, including this book.

This hijacking technology is not simply in the hands of states. Siemens powerfully commoditized Chinese cultural heritage and the Chinese national

Figure 3.4 Screened in Ningxia autonomous region case (source: Astrid H. M. Nordin).

modernization project in its *Tianxia yi jia* pavilion discussed above. To English-language audiences the pavilion was marketed through the name *We Are the World*, a name that aptly brings out the recycling nature of the fair through reviving Michael Jackson's old hit song, but which also showcases the ambiguity of the question 'who is the world/fair?' The 'we' is ambiguous and inside the pavilion the capacity in which 'we' become the world/fair is telling – as described above, our faces pass through a computer program and are recycled on screen as avatars, transformed, singing along with the Expo 2010 theme tune. Our avatars in the virtual version of Expo 2010 are, to some extent at least, a consequence of our volition and choice, albeit screened and monitored with a mandatory Chinese ID number registration. In Siemens' corporate version of 'All-under-heaven' we are the world/fair without being told in what our stardom will consist. Our avatars are exposed as pre-programmed, as playing a prescribed role, and this play has only one script, one where we all sing along with the Chinese tune.

From these examples we can see two kinds of technologies operating in the world/fair: ones that represent the world and ones that operate through simulation, 'provoking a reflexive awareness of artificiality and simulacra':

> [t]he first of these conceives of technology as enabler, and is the concept that lies behind the notion of the Expo as a technology of nationhood. Technology enables a perspective that can produce wholeness from fragmentation. Expo enables the appearance of the world as a whole, through the revelation of the fragments that are cut from it and the apparent celebration of their differences.
>
> (Harvey, 1996: 123)

Expo 2010's use of interactive technologies moved away from 'representations' of the world as we know it to be. It celebrated instead the possibility of producing a simulated world, copies of copies (dis)interested in an original:

> a world of images more real than the real, a fascination with the hyper-real, pretensions to realities that were never there in the first place or at least not in such perfect form, concrete manifestations of abstract possibilities [that] produce the essence of life itself as outcome not origin.
>
> (Harvey, 1996: 123)

Through these technologies of the world/fair, not only our concepts of spatiality and temporality, but also our notions of subject and object, are displaced. Being in a simulated world/fair is simulated being. We are copies of copies without original, simulated avatars in virtual hyper-reality. The Expo is us: our bodies, our dreams, our future.

To be strategic, or how to be fair?

This chapter has asked where, when and who the world/fair is. It has argued that the world fair is not a fake copy of a 'real' world, but that as simulation it marks the breakdown of the distinctions of the copy from the original, of the fair from the world. The world/fair is everything and nothing, simultaneously nowhere and now here. This chapter has shown that the world/fair works through recycling, revival and reuse that, as a rem(a)inder, is not new. It has further argued that being in the world fair turns us all into simulated avatars without original, circulated in virtual hyper-reality. All these claims have serious consequences for the study of China in the harmonious world.

The reading here shows the problem of thinking of China as the 'other country' (Chow, 1991). Baudrillardian simulation has come to symbolize postmodernity, continental philosophy, late capitalism and an American way of life. All of these terms imply a *where*, *when* and *who*. A key finding of this chapter is that the implied answers to those questions are not as straightforward as may at first appear. Reading Expo 2010 as simulation shows that we cannot locate 'China' as an other, in another place and another time than that of our purported late capitalism or postmodern condition. Importantly, though, through focusing on simulation, we can see how this is not a case of 'catching up', of those behind (finally) becoming like us. The point is not that 'the others' have now become 'the same', so that scholars can happily apply our 'Western theories' and ignore difference. The point is, rather, that reading the world/fair as simulation messes with its notions of inside and outside, now and then, subject and object to the point where these terms are no longer workable. What we end up with is not the many turning into the one, with the convergence of others into the self. Instead, what remains is a fragmented plethora of truth, not the unreal but the hyper-real. The effect is our own disappearance. The object becomes us, sees us. We see ourselves through the harmonious Expo. The harmonious Expo is us. The reading here of Expo 2010 as simulation has examined some of the distinctions implied in the *where*, *when* and *who* of the world/fair. We need to make such distinctions, but given that they do not hold up, we might open up more space for different politics if we were to not take our distinctions so seriously.

But of course the study of the harmonious world/fair is serious, as is the challenge posed by its deconstruction. To return to the discussions in Chapter 1: in the simulated world/fair, can we still retain strategy? Already in his earlier work, Baudrillard had come to the conclusion that in a 'hyper-realist' system, '[s]trictly speaking, nothing remains for us to base anything on' (1993 [1976]: 4–5). In a hyper-real world of simulation, the weight of information makes modernity (and its space) fall apart. This has shattering implications for meaning: 'where we think that information produces meaning, the opposite occurs' (Baudrillard, 1994 [1981]: 80). Meaning, truth and the real are reversed, that is, they are divested of any universal meaning, which restricts them to local, partial objects (Baudrillard, 1994 [1981]: 180). In this age of simulation we have surpassed old versions of uncertainty and made our problem permanent (Baudrillard, 2002 [1997]: 90). Recycling and simulation, with what they do to reality, to time and space, demand something from us: we no longer have the choice of advancing, of persevering in the present destruction or of retreating – but only of facing up to this radical illusion (Baudrillard, 1994 [1992]: 122–3).

In this manner, the uncertainty of the simulated world/fair is not necessarily a cause for pessimism. Coulter has claimed:

> Baudrillard has long found a radically uncertain and ultimately unknowable world a far more comfortable place to live than one which is predictable. Baudrillard lives … in a world in a permanent state of reversibility, and he prefers it to a world that is accomplished.
>
> (Coulter, 2004)

The question this poses is most pertinent to the way we think about the Chinese dream of a harmonious world and our role in *doing* it, precisely:

> [d]oes the world have to have meaning, then? That is the real problem. If we could accept this meaninglessness of the world, then we could play with forms, appearances and our impulses, without worrying about their ultimate destination ... Do we absolutely have to choose between meaning and non-meaning? But the point is precisely that we do not want to. The absence of meaning is no doubt intolerable, but it would be just as intolerable to see the world assume a definitive meaning.
>
> (Baudrillard, 2001 [1999]: 128)

This implosion or disappearance of meaning, truth and the real, however, does not mean we cannot have strategy: '[t]heoretical violence, not truth, is the only resource we have left us' (Baudrillard, 1994 [1981]: 163). The strategy Baudrillard has developed is a 'fatal strategy', one that values uncertainty (Baudrillard, 1990 [1983]: 181). This is the type of strategy pursued in this chapter's engagement with the Expo and the harmonious world that it simulates. As explained in Chapter 1, this book pursues a form of theoretical violence against the Chinese dream of a harmonious world by tracing and accelerating its excessive proliferation. This chapter is part of that effort.

Conclusion

This chapter has argued that the 'holistic' and 'unit-based' cosmologies outlined in the previous chapter also appear to convey the Chinese dream of a harmonious world at the Shanghai Expo. It has shown how they are deployed at the Expo in ways that reinforce one another by ordering spatial difference through teleological time. This has the effect of disallowing coeval multiplicities and prescribing a particular future where China leads a new harmonious world order. Like the academic literature examined in the previous chapter, the Expo worldview portrays itself as 'from the world' or 'from everywhere', yet insists on 'specifically Chinese' terms and experience, and on the singular China's future as the (harmonious) world's future. This chapter has also argued that we need to move beyond the reading of these types of propaganda events as simple representation and ideology and read it also as simulation. Reading the Chinese world fair as a simulation of world order can provide different ways of relating 'the West' to its 'other country', China. Through asking where, when and who the world/fair is, reading it as simulation disrupts the fair's notions of inside and outside, now and then, subject and object to the point where these terms are no longer workable. What we end up with is not the turning of others into sameness, but a fragmented multitude of reality, the hyper-real. Through examining some of the boundaries drawn to delineate the *where*, *when* and *who* of the world/fair, this chapter has argued that we may be better off not taking these so seriously. In contrast to the teleological narratives on China in the harmonious world – in policy discourse under Hu, in the academic literature that analyses it and in the conceptualizations of time and space at Expo 2010 – the world described by Baudrillard is not determined. In this world 'everything is antagonistic' rather than harmonious, and good will not necessarily triumph over evil (Baudrillard, 1990 [1983]: 162, 182).

The strategy, then, is not for theory to reflect the real, but instead to work as a challenge. The world/fair is not compatible with the 'real' that is imposed upon it. Importantly though: 'the function of theory is certainly not to reconcile it, but on the contrary, to seduce, to wrest things from their condition, to force them into an over-existence which is incompatible with that of the real' (Baudrillard, 1988 [1987]). The purpose then of theory is to s(t)imulate the (im)possible in the Chinese dream of a harmonious world/fair. The aim of this chapter has been to take one step in such a direction and provoke us into thinking of China's harmonious 'mega events' beyond representation, reality and ideology – to think of them also in terms of simulation. It is to further challenges to 'harmonious world', to the question of the antagonistic, that we turn in the next chapter.

Notes

1 To collect data I deployed a number of methods in the various 'sites' that constituted the Expo. A first form of data collection was the assembling of commentary on the Expo in Chinese official news media, blogs and secondary literature on the Expo. Another crucial method was participant observation at the physical Expo, where I visited numerous pavilions, queued, collected pamphlets and memorabilia, and photographed buildings, exhibitions and signs in June 2010. There was also a virtual replica of the Expo, a detailed online landscape simulating the Expo site and Expo experience (Expo Shanghai Online, 2010). After visiting the physical Expo I spent several months at its virtual counterpart in the autumn of 2010, visiting pavilions and exhibitions, playing Expo games, reading other visitors' messages on its notice boards and interacting with visitors in this virtual environment. I also conducted semi-structured interviews with participants during my visit to the physical and virtual Expo.

2 Bonze Xuan Zang is a Buddhist sage from Chinese literary classic, *Journey to the West*.

3 Penelope Harvey has begun the work of reading world fairs as simulation in *Hybrids of Modernity: Anthropology, the Nation State and the Universal Exhibition* (1996). Recent publications have hinted at the possibility of such a reading of Chinese mega events. Most notably, Price and Dayan's *Owning the Olympics* takes off in an imaginary of the Beijing Olympics as 'spectacle, festival, ritual, and finally as access to truth' and concludes: 'Or should we rewrite MacAloon's sequence in a style inspired by Baudrillard: "spectacle, festival, ritual, and finally … simulacrum?" ' (Dayan, 2008: 400). To my knowledge none have followed through with an empirical analysis of what such a reading may look like in the Chinese case.

4 This problematique has been discussed by, among others, Jean-Luc Nancy (1991 [1983]), Giles Deleuze and Felix Guattari (1988 [1980]) and Derrida (1976 [1967]).

4 Online spoofs under harmonization

Complicating cooperation and resistance

In previous chapters we have seen how Hu's 'harmonious' policies have come to involve increasing 'harmonization' of one form of difference or different voices through addressing them in an allochronic manner. This chapter looks at another form of difference, which is found on (and off) the Chinese Internet, and which is critical of harmony itself. This critique of harmony takes shape through a creative form of discursive negotiation that has grown in popularity as a way of simultaneously avoiding and criticizing harmonization.[1] Through this online discourse, this chapter examines instances of what may be called a 'deconstructive close reading' of the harmony character, a reiterative and playful practice. This playful reading of the harmony concept can work to expose some of the discursive exclusions of Hu's dream of a harmonious world. It simultaneously opens the term up to readings that can be more conducive to thinking the 'heterotemporalities' in the fragmented present that we saw Hutchings calling for in the Introduction to this book. In this way, it is a step towards thinking differently about coeval multiplicities.

Reiteration and language play: negotiating harmonization

Previous chapters of this book have examined how the Chinese discourse on 'harmony' operates by way of exclusion of discord, and through the spatio-temporal double-move of inclusion into sameness and exclusion as 'behind'. If such attempts at harmonization of others have been traced in various times and spaces, this is not to imply that they are not crucially linked to the sovereign power of the policy discourse, by way of which we began the exploration of harmony in this book: Hu's Chinese dream of harmony. This version of harmony has bordered its national space in many ways, including by the insistence on territorial sovereignty so closely associated with Hu's harmonious world policy. This insistence on sovereignty and non-interference has been deployed precisely to legitimate in the international arena the various forms of harmonization that have come to be associated with harmonious world's policy twin, 'harmonious society'.

Being harmonized online

One key tactic employed by the party-state for containing dissidence and making resistance more difficult has been to harmonize expression on the Internet. Where some may initially have imagined the Internet to provide the space for near-unlimited freedom of expression and provide a tool to hold government accountable, more empirical studies soon resulted in more sober analyses (Chase and Mulvenon, 2002; Kurlantzick, 2004; Lagerkvist, 2005).

On the one hand, the party-state has been active in trying to *include* the public through e-governance and 'guidance' (*daoxiang* 导向), and by shaping opinion through overt or covert propaganda online (Lagerkvist, 2005: 206). Officials have portrayed the implementation of information and communications technologies in police and security organs as a 'necessary strategic choice', echoing Hu's view of the future in terms of an 'inevitable choice' (Minister of Public Security, Jia Chunwang, in *Huliang zhoukan*, 2002, cited in Lagerkvist, 2005). One example of such propaganda is the anonymous participation in online fora by what netizens call the '50 cent party', individuals paid to toe the party line and steer online discussion so as to be favourable to the party.[2] Another example is the increasing amount of what Johan Lagerkvist has called 'ideotainment'. This term denotes 'the juxtaposition of images, symbolic representations, and sounds of popular Web and mobile phone culture together with both subtle and overt ideological constructs and nationalistic propaganda', which may be exemplified by the Online Expo examined in the previous chapter (Lagerkvist, 2008: 121). Even a decade ago, the desired outcome of such e-governance, according to Lagerkvist, was 'installing a machine' that can provide '"scientific and correct" knowledge among citizens and state officials' (2005: 197). The success of the party-state in achieving the goals of its inclusionary 'thought work' (*sixiang gongzuo* 思想工作) has nonetheless been questionable (Lynch, 1999).

On the other hand, the party-state has simultaneously been active in trying to *exclude* the public, through deleting posts and blocking the Internet. Border regions like Xinjiang have been without Internet access for long periods, as a way to hinder communication and spread of information about the work of the government's military 'harmony makers', and to pre-empt the spread of 'splittism'.[3] A parallel strategy deployed to keep the flow of information harmonious and pure throughout China has been to surround Chinese virtual space by a 'Great Firewall'. This consists of layers of blocks that prevent many sites based outside China from being accessed from within China (including Google+, Facebook, Twitter and other social media), and to simultaneously demand extensive policing and censorship of sites located 'inside' this walled space. An important part of this exclusionary censorship practice has been the widespread blocking of specific words in online communication. A message that includes one of the thousands of characters that at any particular moment is deemed 'sensitive' can be instantly deleted by censorship software. The line between acceptable and unacceptable expression remains elusive and shifting (Breslin and Shen, 2010: 266). In drawing it, however, explanatory emphasis is on a language of 'health', with censorship purported to cleanse 'pollution' and 'unhealthy' elements in favour of 'health' and 'hygiene' (Lagerkvist, 2008: 123, 134).

In response to the governmental policing of the Internet, and to its 'harmony makers' in offline conflicts, the notion of having 'been harmonized' (*bei hexie le* 被和谐了) has become popular as a way of expressing discontent. The use of this passive grammatical voice (*bei* 被), dubbed by one commentator the 'passive subversive' (Kuhn, 2010), came to indicate that one had been coercively made to (appear to) do something (a conversation extract where the term is used in this sense can be found in Nordin and Richaud, 2014: 57). The term gained such popularity that the 'passive tense era' (*beishidai* 被时代) made the top of the list of *Southern Metropolis Weekly*'s 2009 list of most popular neologisms (Southern Metropolis Weekly, 2009), and *bei* was made quasi-official when an arm of the Education Ministry elected it the Chinese character of the year in 2009. Lei Yi, one judge of the event and a historian of CASS, said the term won by a landslide by popular Internet vote: '[w]e felt we should recognize this result … so we named "bei" as the character most representative of China's situation last year' (in Kuhn, 2010). Doubleleaf, a Beijing-based blogger who had his blog 'harmonized', meaning shut down, emphasized in an interview the subversive nature of *bei*:

> [f]or centuries we've been told that the emperor represented the people's interests … or that some organization or some leader represented our interests. People did not realize that they had 'been represented'. This word of the year signals the awakening of citizens' consciousness.
>
> (in Kuhn, 2010)

Chinese netizens have made use of this language in particular to criticize the Chinese censorship of the Internet to shut down any uncomfortable discussion. For example, one Flash animation, found at an online competition to raise awareness about scientific development and harmonious society, features a Bulletin Board System (BBS) comment thread that gets 'harmonized'. It shows the BBS thread of net jargon, discussions of a famous person, people trading insults and the posts being suddenly deleted. When one netizen asks what happened the answer is 'they have been harmonized'. Finally, a smiling Hu Jintao appears alongside the slogan 'Everyone is responsible for a harmonious society' (*renren you ze, hexie shehui* 人人有责，和谐社会) (Martinsen, 2007; Zhuru cilei, 2007).

Egao*: resistance in the sphere of politics and the political?*

The Flash animation that has 'been harmonized' is part of a wider form of online culture known as *egao* (恶搞), which has become popular since the launch of the harmonious policies and received international attention since around 2006. The term is made up of characters *e* (恶), which means bad or evil, and *gao* (搞), which means to change or deal with, leading to translations of the word as 'evil jokes' (Li Hongmei, 2011: 71), 'reckless doings' (Meng Bingchun, 2009: 52), or simply 'spoofing' (Lagerkvist, 2010: 150). This spoofing culture uses irony and satire to mock power holders as well as government policies and practices.

Scholars have almost universally described *egao* as a form of 'resistance', 'subversion' or 'contestation' (Arsène, 2010; Diamond, 2010: 74; Inkster, 2010: 7.2; Tang Lijun and Yang Peidong, 2011: 680, 682, 687; Wiener, 2011: 156; Xiao Qiang, 2011a: 52). Many base their claim on George Orwell's comment that '[e]very joke is a tiny revolution' (Li Hongmei, 2011: 72; Tang Lijun and Bhattacharya, 2011: 2.4). To a number of commentators, it is moreover based on an understanding of a discrepancy between on the one hand, the People's Republic of China (PRC) party-state language, including set phrases like 'harmonious world' and 'harmonious society', and on the other hand an 'alternative political discourse' (Meng Bingchun, 2009: 39) or 'hidden transcript' (Perry, 2007: 10; Esarey and Xiao Qiang, 2008: 752; Meng Bingchun, 2009: 39), including expressions like having 'been harmonized'.[4]

The most pervasive scholarly interpretation of this relation between official and unofficial discourse has been in terms of Bakhtinian carnival – an unruly and fantastic time and space in medieval and Renaissance Europe. One volume characterizes the entire Chinese cyberspace as a quasi-separate space of the carnivalesque (Herold and Marolt, 2011). On this understanding, the carnival is an event in a time and space where rules are suspended, separate from normal constraints (Herold, 2011: 11, 12). It is the antithesis of normal life, 'free and unrestricted' (Bakhtin cited in Herold, 2011: 12). Similarly, to Li Hongmei, this space 'marked the suspension of all hierarchical rank, privileges, norms, and prohibitions' (Bakhtin, 1984 [1965]: 10, cited in Li Hongmei, 2011: 72). Meng Bingchun reads a 'collective attempt at resistance' (2011: 44) in the *egao* 'virtual carnival' (2011: 45, 46). This resistance is said to be directed against the 'official' (Meng Bingchun, 2011: 46) or 'established' (Li Hongmei, 2011: 71) order. Tang Lijun and Syamantak Bhattacharya, despite reading *egao* as carnivalesque, take it to reveal a 'widespread feeling of powerlessness, rather than offering the general public any political power' (2011). Nonetheless, they see in such online spoofs 'the potential to generate a chain of related satirical work, which can create a satire movement and subject power to sustained shame and ridicule' (Tang Lijun and Bhattacharya, 2011).

Some scholars, however, have expressed scepticism about this interpretation of *egao* as resistance. These scholars have cautioned against fetishizing anything that can be considered resistance in authoritarian regimes (Wallis, 2015; Nordin, forthcoming b). One of the reasons for this caution has been the reactionary gender politics of much *egao*, which inadvertently supports both state and market in China (Wallis, 2015: 2; Nordin, forthcoming b). Another reason has been that young Chinese people who deploy this type of wordplay in their daily lives do not themselves tend to understand this practice in terms of resistance (Nordin and Richaud, 2014: 58–9; see also Lagerkvist, 2010: 159). A third reason has been the intricacy of *egao*, leading some to question 'what larger influence you have on politics … if your critique is too subtle' (Lagerkvist,

2010: 146). Accordingly, Johan Lagerkvist suggests that *egao* may not have an immediate effect on politics, but is better understood as venting anger and stimulating 'the growth of an alternate civility' that can build up pressure against the political system over time (Lagerkvist, 2010: 158).

Lagerkvist rightly makes the point that irony is not *by definition* radical or revolutionary. This claim in itself, however, says little about what it *does* do (or undo). In previous analyses of *egao*, the focus is clearly on potential for changing politics, but few sustain any discussion about what they mean by this 'politics'. In order to understand their disagreement, we can benefit from returning to the distinction made at the outset of this book between politics in the narrow sense, or *politics*, and politics in the wider sense, or *the political*. This book has taken the latter to be concerned with 'the establishment of that very social order which sets out a particular, historically specific account of what counts as politics and defines other areas of social life as *not* politics' (Edkins, 1999: 2). On such a reading, 'depoliticization' is equal to 'a reduction to calculability' or the application of rules (Edkins, 1999: 1, 11). To *repoliticize*, again, is instead 'to interrupt discourse, to challenge what have, through discursive practices, been constituted as normal, natural, and accepted ways of carrying on' (Edkins, 1999: 12).

In view of this differentiation between politics and the political, Lagerkvist's evaluation of *egao* with regard to what larger influence it has on politics seems to refer to politics in the narrow sense, rather than to the political. Tang and Bhattacharya's judgement of *egao* with reference to its potential to 'create a satire movement' seems to be concerned with the same narrow politics. These accounts, then, dismiss *egao* as not political *unless* it can achieve some movement or influence with regard to politics (in the narrow sense). This makes the scholars' readings of *egao* themselves depoliticizing, because it shifts *egao* into the realm of politics in the narrow sense (Nordin and Richaud, 2014: 52). The concern here, by contrast, is rather with the question of the political, and I will comment on this in more detail at the end of this chapter.[5]

It is in this realm of discourse and the political that I ground an understanding of a strategy that is not based on the a priori assumption that *egao* constitutes a form of resistance, or that effective intervention in *politics* would make it more relevant to *the political*. The previous chapter pointed to the problems of conceptualizing resistance as revealing 'realities' or 'the facts', when what we are dealing with is a hyper-real system. Rather, it argued, we need to think about strategy and theory as a challenge. What does this mean? Roland Bleiker has written about the type of negotiation that occurs in this realm of the discursive, a negotiation that revolves around interactions between different types of speech. To him:

> [o]vertly committed art forms often do no more than promote a particular position.... Aesthetic politics, by contrast, has to do with the ability of artistic engagements to challenge, in a more fundamental way, how we think about and represent the political. Here the political content lies in the

> aesthetic form itself, which often is not political in an explicit and immediately recognisable manner.
>
> (Bleiker, 2009: 8)

On this understanding, Bleiker has shown that engaging with language is engaging in social struggle (2000: 43). Alternative forms of language, he argues, can challenge 'the state's promotion of a black-and-white, one-dimensional and teleological approach to history' by celebrating multiplicity and making ambivalence part of language (2000: 43). Moreover, he shows that this is part of global politics through drawing on David Campbell to the effect that the everyday life in which these forms of linguistic negotiation are deployed is not 'a synonym for the local level, for in it global interconnections, local resistances, transterritorial flows, state politics, regional dilemmas, identity formations, and so on are always already present' (Campbell, 1996: 23, cited in Bleiker, 2000: 44). Alternative forms of speech and writing, then, show how political change can be brought about by forms of expression that 'deliberately and self-consciously stretch, even violate existing linguistic rules' because in doing so they can provide us 'with different eyes, with the opportunity to reassess anew the spatial and political [and, I would add, temporal] dimensions of global life' (Bleiker, 2000: 45). Rather than seeking a quick fix by revealing the scandalous 'truth', or forming a mass movement explicitly aimed at intervening in narrow politics, this discursive strategy works through pushing gradually at the terms in which the world is conceived. It thereby 'resists the temptation to provide "concrete" answers to "concrete" questions' (Bleiker, 2000: 45). The rest of this chapter examines *egao* as one particular instance that can help us think further about such linguistic strategy, negotiation and perhaps even resistance in/to 'harmonious world'.

Negotiating harmonization and deconstructive reading

The above example of the BBS that has 'been harmonized' shows how Chinese netizens are 'being harmonized' by the government. However, it also shows how they are negotiating such 'harmonization' through language and grammar. By re-citing official language and reinscribing it in other chains of meaning, Chinese netizens are turning its purported message against itself. Where Hu's harmony purports to be inclusive, peaceful and open, its reiteration with a simple grammatical modifier, *bei*, reads this official take on harmony as being exclusive, violent and working to close down possibilities for difference. This shows us that language is indeed a crucial part not only for the government to try to harmonize dissidents, but also for these to negotiate such harmonization.

This language play is thus made possible because we can remove the repeatable meaning of a term like 'harmony' from the specific context in which it was first deployed and 'recognize other possibilities in it by inscribing it or grafting it onto other chains', as discussed in Chapter 1 of this book (Derrida, 1988: 9; cf. Massey, 2005: 19). For this reason 'harmony' does not have one fixed meaning, but we can play with it, graft it into other chains of signification that can reveal meanings that were always already there in harmony in the first place. This possibility is exploited by netizens. We can read deconstruction taking place in the term 'harmony' in many places. What dissident use does is precisely shake it loose from its intended meaning in Hu's policy documents, reversing and displacing its meaning, without therefore separating it from that policy discourse. This chapter illustrates how this takes place in various tactics of negotiating harmonization in China. The point is to not simply accept 'harmony' as having one straightforward meaning, to obey, avoid or bin the term. Instead, we can, as Baudrillard would have it, 'recycle' it in potentially subversive ways.

Recycling harmony (和谐) 1: close reading of the radicals that make up a character

Derrida's way of reading a text is often termed 'close reading', which involves paying attention to the details of structure, grammar and etymology of a term or text. This is a tactic often used in academia when scholars discuss the meaning of Chinese terms through a close reading of the 'radicals' that make up a character. This is also a common practice among netizens, in online discussions and in other media, like the logo seen in Figure 4.1 (which was used by the *Economic Observer* for its feature section on the 2006 National People's Congress (NPC) and Chinese

Figure 4.1 Close reading the radicals of 'harmony' (source: Danwei.org).

People's Political Consultative Conference (CPPCC) Sessions; Martinsen, 2006). All Chinese characters consist of one or more 'radicals', the simple characters that are combined to indicate the sound and meaning of a given word. The logo reproduced here separates each of the two characters of 'harmony' (*hexie* 和谐) into the two radicals of which each consists (禾, 口 and 讠, 皆). This makes visible the etymological roots or range of associations that are embedded in the Chinese pictographic script.

The English term 'harmony' comes from Greek *harmos* or *harmonía*, meaning 'joint, agreement, concord' (Hoad, 1993; Oxford Dictionaries, 2011c). *Hexie* 和谐 is usually translated as 'harmonious' or 'concordant', the individual characters carrying the same meaning. 谐 is composed of radicals 讠 (言) 'words' and 皆 'all' (Karlgren, 1974 [1923]: 364; *Hanyu da zidian*, 1995). With the 口 'mouth' radical the 和 character, pronounced *hé*, can signify singing in harmony, or talking together (Wieger, 1965 [1915]: Lesson 121a; Karlgren, 1974 [1923]: 70; Lindqvist, 1991: 187; *Hanyu da zidian*, 1995: 1.602.601). If what is seen in China's current 'harmonizing' of dissidents is a harmonious society or harmonious world, harmony here retains only its meaning of 'singing in harmony' (as we saw through the example of Expo avatars singing the Expo song in harmony), its 'talking together' is only in 'agreement' or 'concord'.

Recycling harmony (和谐) 2: different pronunciations of Chinese characters give alternative meanings

This brings us to another tactic of bringing out and playing with the differently *pronounced* alternative meanings that Chinese characters often have. This is

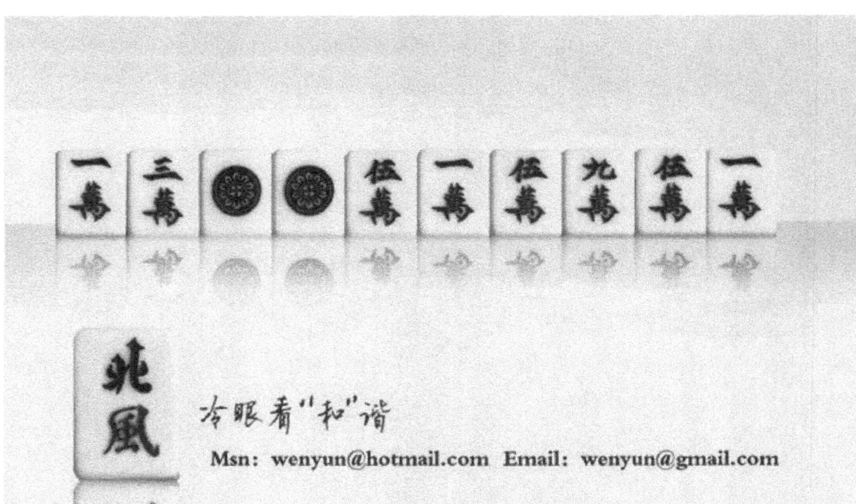

Figure 4.2 和 pronounced *hú* is the battle cry when winning a game of mah-jong (source: Zhang Facai, 2008).

what graphic designer Zhang Facai plays on in the business card seen in Figure 4.2. 和 can also be pronounced *hú*, a battle cry of victory when completing a game of mah-jong. Through this battle cry competition or conflict returns to visibility in harmony, as the excluded term on which it relies. This disruption acknowledges the antagonism involved in play, unsettling the notion of permanent harmonious 'win–win' purported by the party-state. It reminds us of the violence we have traced in previous chapters of a dominant China's turning other into self.

What goes on in this reading is in a sense the first of the two moves of Derrida's deconstructive double gesture. We have read Hu's Chinese dream of harmony in a way that is faithful to its purported meaning, where the end-state of 'harmony' rests on the exclusion of violence, discord and conflict. His harmonious world, as we saw in Chapter 1 of this book, is one that has done away with misgivings and estrangement, where everyone wins and no one loses. The 'inevitable choice' (or what, if we were cynical, we could call 'the single prescribed future without responsibility of choosing') is a future harmonious world order where *China* will always stand for 'fairness and justice'. Anyone who disagrees with this sense of justice is simply wrong and irrational, euphemized as 'unscientific'.

What the pronunciation *hú* does is acknowledge the excluded other of Hu's 'harmony', namely discord and competition. *Hú* can only be achieved after vanquishing the opponent, there is no win–win here.[6] The *hú* of mah-jong, just like the harmonious *Tianxia* utopia, is premised on the superiority of the self to the other. Only this hierarchy can establish order, harmony or *hú*. Acknowledging that competition is always already there in harmony, implied in the alternative pronunciation *hú*, we can acknowledge a third tactic of negotiation, the play with homonymous characters.

*Recycling harmony (*和谐*) 3: 'rivercrab' (*héxiè*) as a near-homonym for 'harmony' (*héxié*)*

Derrida's first deconstructive move is reversal, identifying an operational binary – such as harmony/discord – and showing how the exclusion of the second term from the first is artificial and that in fact the first is reliant on the second. An equally important move is displacement, the creation of a term that is not fully contained within the old order. We can get at such a displacement through paying attention to 'rivercrabs' (*héxiè* 河蟹), a near-homonym for 'harmony' (*héxié* 和谐). Before I go on to discuss these rivercrabs in more detail, I should point out that these two deconstructive moves are not separate, chronologically or otherwise. The discussion of them here in turn is for the benefit of my reader, in order to illustrate more clearly what this language play can do for us.

Similar-sounding characters are often used to replace sensitive words as a way to get through the keyword searches of censorship software that has been bolstered as a way to simultaneously avoid and criticize 'being harmonized'. When netizens are blocked by harmonizing government software from writing 'harmony' (*héxié* 和谐), they can replace the term by the similar sounding characters for 'rivercrabs' (*héxiè* 河蟹). In popular Chinese language a 'crab' is a violent bully, making its image a new playful and satirical, but heavily political, way of criticizing the harmonizing 'rivercrab society' (Xiao Qiang, 2007).

One popular satire on it can be seen in the rivercrab with three watches seen in Figure 4.3. The caption overhead reads: 'insist on three watches, establish rivercrab society' (*jianchi san ge daibiao, chuangjian hexie shehui* 坚持三个戴表，创建河蟹社会). The first phrase is a nonsensical mockery of the party slogan 'insist on the three represents' (*jianchi san ge daibiao* 坚持三个代表) and the second is a mockery of the slogan 'establish harmonious society' (*chuangjian hexie shehui* 创建和谐社会).[7] The political tactic here is one of intentional (mis)reading of official discourse, a reiteration of party-state language against itself in order to reveal aspects of harmony that remain hidden from view in official discourse. Again, the acknowledgement of the purported message and its hierarchical binary as well as the first deconstructive move of reversing that hierarchy are here in this picture, this is not a separate stand-alone symbol or event. However, the rivercrab also displaces this binary and functions as a new term that does not obey that order in any simple manner, but rather shakes it up and brings to the fore the irresolvable contradiction between these terms.[8]

This mockingly reiterative form of negotiation is not confined to Internet *egao* culture, but has spread beyond its online origins to impact both on official media and on offline responses. Artist Ai Weiwei staged one such example some time before his infamous detention. When his newly built Shanghai studio was to be demolished by the authorities, Ai threw a grand farewell party in November 2010, to which he invited several hundred friends, bands and other supporters to feast on a banquet consisting of rivercrabs. Ai was placed under house

Figure 4.3 Insist on three watches, establish rivercrab society (source: Xuanlv, 2010).

arrest in Beijing to prevent him from attending the banquet, but the event took place nonetheless with supporters chanting: 'in a harmonious society, we eat rivercrabs' (Branigan, 2010).

Party-state response

The official party-state strategies of responding to such negotiation take the form of harmonizing it, ignoring it or, on occasion, acknowledging its presence while attempting to again re-read its meaning, significance and implications in an effort to downplay its critical potential. With respect to the 'passive subversive' *bei* making the top of the list of neologisms in 2009, a *Xinhua* article displays the latter tactic. The article stresses state tolerance through emphasizing that the poll, which resulted in *bei* being elected character of the year, was 'jointly conducted by a linguistic research centre under the Ministry of Education and the state-run Commercial Press'. The tense was said 'to convey a sense of helplessness in deciding one's own fate' and to reflect 'dissatisfaction over the abuse of official power' (*Xinhua*, 2010a). The example of 'being suicided' (*bei zisha* 被自杀) was discussed, explaining that the abuse of official power concerned was perpetrated by a *local* official, who was duly sentenced to death by higher authorities. Other examples were 'being volunteered' (*bei ziyuan* 被自愿) and 'being found a job' (*bei jiuye* 被就业). From the 'passive subversive' *bei* the article turns into proof of how good and improving the government is:

> '[b]ei' was not censored in the government-run poll of buzzwords, and grassroots' voices are finally being heard and even recognized by the government.... The government is beginning to respond to inquiries from the public, instead of 'dodging' them as it did before.
>
> (*Xinhua*, 2010a)

Yet much negotiation is still treated with violence or silence by Chinese official sources. According to interviews by Tessa Thorniley at Ai Weiwei's rivercrab banquet, over 40 domestic media sources were invited and none showed up, and among the over 50 media outlets that interviewed Ai in house arrest regarding the event, the only domestic media that spoke to him was the English-language edition of conservative paper *Global Times* (Goldkorn, 2010). Within half a year of the rivercrab banquet, Ai had been detained by Chinese police, accused of a number of crimes. After 81 days in detention he was released on bail, on the condition that he did 'not speak' (Branigan, 2011; Committee to Protect Journalists, 2011; US Asia Law NYU, 2011). During his disappearance Chinese Internet sites such as Sina Weibo blocked searches on Ai Weiwei (艾未未), a number of his nicknames and puns on his name including '艾未' (Ai Wei), '未未' (Wei Wei), '艾' (Ai), '未' (Wei), '艾胖子' (Fatty Ai), '胖子' (Fatty) and '月半子' (Moon Half Son). They also blocked writing including the term *weilai* '未来', meaning 'future', which is built up of characters similar to 'Weiwei' (Xiao Qiang, 2011b).

Harmony as cancer and autoimmunity

From the above analysis we see that there are similarities between Derridean approaches to reading deconstruction in academia and practices of (subversive) reiteration of 'harmony' among netizens in contemporary China. The possibilities for alliances that reside within such shared tactics are potentially valuable to both parties and may help us here to bridge the theory/practice divide (see also Nordin, forthcoming b). Derrida and Baudrillard were both masters of language play, frequently building on the various meanings that can be drawn out of words by way of their etymological roots, their different pronunciations, by playing with homonyms and near-homonyms and by combining words into new ones to reverse and displace previous binaries. Such techniques pervade the writing of both thinkers.[9]

However, this is not to say that the similar practice of Chinese language outlined above is an entirely new phenomenon created by recent practices of Internet censorship and/or influences from some 'Western postmodernity'. On the contrary, the struggles and practices outlined are genuinely innovative while they also draw on a long and rich history in China (Nordin, 2014c). Linguistic play with characters and homonyms has been a sensitive topic in China for millennia. Such practices have also been known to academics in the anglophone world for decades. For example, a 1938 article argues that literary persecution was especially cruel during the Qing dynasty (1644–1911 AD), and continues with a description that could just as well be of contemporary Chinese censorship regimes on the Internet:

> under the circumstances they [Chinese scholars, artists, intellectuals and others] could do nothing but resort to veiled satire. This being the situation, their words and writings were spied on and scrutinized; if they did not use every care they suffered the severest punishments.[10]
>
> (Ku Chieh-Kang, 1938 [1935]: 254)

The author then discusses how similar practices of harsh censorship had taken place since the first two dynasties of what is typically considered imperial China, the Qin (361–206 BC) and Han (206 BC–8 AD). It lists a quantity of death sentences based on the 'homophonic nature of certain words employed' during the Ming dynasty (1368–1644 AD) (Ku Chieh-Kang, 1938 [1935]: 262). As in the contemporary PRC, although 'misreading' set texts could be very dangerous (1938 [1935]: 296–301), the attempt to provide set phrases and pre-structured models for expression could not prevent such double meanings from seeping through text (1938 [1935]: 263). There is thus Chinese historical precedent of interplay between violent oppression of speech and the kind of linguistic negotiation that builds on reiterative, mocking punnery in ways similar to the contemporary deployment of rivercrabs.[11]

Crabs as cancerous disease

Where associations emerging from the Chinese language align crabs with harmony, bullies and competition, most European languages associate it with the disharmony of the body that shares its name: cancer.[12] The following section introduces the European roots of this term in order to foreground the subsequent analysis of the above 'harmony/rivercrabs', which argues that these 'rivercrabs' operate precisely according to a cancerous logic.

The term 'cancer' is originally Latin, meaning 'crab or creeping ulcer', with its etymological roots in Greek *karkinos*, said to have been applied to such tumours because they were surrounded by swollen veins that looked like the limbs of a crab (Demaitre, 1998: 620–6; Oxford Dictionaries, 2011b). Although the European term, like the Chinese one, has mythological connotations,[13] a contemporary dictionary entry for 'cancer' describes it as 'a malignant growth or tumour resulting from an uncontrolled division of cells', but also as 'an evil or destructive practice or phenomenon that is hard to contain or eradicate' (Oxford Dictionaries, 2011b).

In this second capacity, cancer is not separate from contemporary understandings of international politics and the Chinese dream of a harmonious world. Rather, the language of cancer and tumours has long been common in International Relations (IR) and politics, and cancer is frequently used as a metaphor for moral and political ills on the body politic to be cured or removed.[14] At the same time, descriptions of biomedical cancer often resort to metaphors or similes borrowed from societal relations[15] and from military conflict and battle.[16] In the Chinese language, the close link between security in the medical and political realms is explicit in the character *zhi* (治), which refers to both therapy (*zhi liao* 治療) and governance (*zhi li* 治理) (Unschuld, 2010: xxvi; Cheung, 2011: 7). Many studies have shown how the knowledge systems of Western biomedicine and Traditional Chinese Medicine (TCM) reflect the intellectual and political landscape in which they respectively developed.[17]

As such, many have understood the spatial distance between China and Europe as a foundation for an epistemological difference in understanding of their medical bodies, which directly parallels that which is claimed to underpin the understanding of the Chinese geo-body, examined in previous chapters.[18] Western biomedicine, it is thus said, follows Descartes and builds on the idea that parts of the body are discrete and can be calculated, measured and cured in isolation (Have, 1987; Kaptchuk, 2000). Chinese medicine is said to build instead on a 'holistic' idea of the body where illness is explained in terms of a 'pattern of disharmony' (Kaptchuk, 2000: 4). Just as a bounded notion of space is typically portrayed in terms of an imposition on China by Western imperialism, so too is a biomedical imaginary and representation of discrete body parts portrayed as an imposition by the West and a catching-up by a China that had fallen behind (Cheung, 2011: 9; Gilman, 1988: 149, 151, 154).

With regards to the geo-body, previous chapters have argued that its two spatial imaginaries (that of discrete units and that of a holistic system) are not mutually exclusive, but rather coexist in practices in contemporary China. The scope of this book does not allow for a thorough deconstruction of the parallel epistemology that is applied to debates over the medical body.[19] Suffice it to say at this point that contemporary literature on Chinese medicine typically reflects on how biomedicine and TCM are complementary.[20] Most importantly for the argument here, and as this chapter will explain in what follows, TCM and biomedicine have produced strikingly similar responses to the appearance of cancer: to cleanse and purge in conjunction with studied manipulation of the immune system.

Reading cancer and the autoimmune through social theory

The previous chapter drew on Baudrillard's interest in the pre-programmed character of contemporary culture to examine the (re)production of human bodies as computer coded avatars on the Expo screen. His interest in the coding of the human body also extended to the replication and transmission of data on the micro level, in the form of genetic code and cellular regeneration. As pure information, the human body is not understood as the source of selfhood, but rather as an effect produced by the code (Baudrillard, 1994 [1981]: 98; see also Toffoletti in Smith, 2010: 28). Embedded in this code is the potential for cancer and autoimmune disease (Baudrillard, 2002 [2000]: 98, 207).[21]

According to Baudrillard, consumer society or European democracy is driven by a 'perverse' logic (2002 [2000]: 97, 207), where a range of phenomena – terrorism, fascism, violence, depression and so on – are the outcome of 'an excess of organization, regulation and rationalization within a system' (2002 [2000]: 97). These societies tend to suffer from an excess of rationality and logic, surveillance and control, which in turn leads to the emergence for no apparent reason of 'internal pathologies ... strange dysfunctions ... unforeseeable, incurable accidents ... anomalies', which disrupt the system's capacity for totality, perfection and reality invention (Baudrillard, 2002 [2000]: 97). This is the logic that Baudrillard reads of an excessive system that fuels the growth of anomalies – just like cancer and autoimmune disease (2002 [2000]).

What characterizes these anomalies in Baudrillard's theorizing is that 'they have not come from elsewhere, from "outside" or from afar, but are rather a product of the "over-protection" of the body – be it social or individual' (Smith, 2010: 59):

> [e]very structure, system or social body which ferrets out its negative, critical elements to expel them or exorcise them runs the risk of catastrophe by total implosion and reversion, just as every biological body which hunts down and eliminates all its germs, bacillae and parasites – in short, all its biological enemies – runs the risk of cancer or, in other words, of a positivity devouring its own cells. It runs the risk of being devoured by its own anti-bodies.
>
> (Baudrillard, 2002 [1997]: 3)

On this reading, 'the system's overcapacity to protect, normalise and integrate' (Smith, 2010: 60) (we could say 'harmonize') is shown throughout society as natural immunity is replaced by artificial systems of immunity – like pre-programmed firewalls (Baudrillard, 2002 [2000]: 98). This replacement happens in the name of science and progress (or perhaps a 'scientific outlook on development').

Derrida developed a strikingly similar deployment of the autoimmune, where for example the West since 9/11 is 'producing, reproducing, and regenerating the very thing it seeks to disarm' (2003: 99).[22] Derrida analyses this 'perverse' logic in terms of an autoimmune process (2003: 99); 'that strange behaviour where a living being, in quasi-suicidal fashion, "itself" works to destroy its own protection, to immunise itself against its "own" immunity' (2003: 94). This term recalls previous Derridean terms,[23] but particularly reinforces Baudrillard's claim about cancer and immunity: '[i]n an over-protected space, the body loses all its defences' (Baudrillard, 2002 [1997]: 3). In this way, to Baudrillard and Derrida, in cancer and autoimmunity it is the system's own logic that turns it against itself; the code works too well in its overzealous cleansing, integrating, normalizing logic.

Derrida reads in this process a double and contradictory discourse of concurrent immunity and autoimmunity in endless circulation, where the system 'conducts a terrible war against that which protects it only by threatening it' (1998: 46).[24] The immune and the autoimmune may not, then, be easily distinguishable: 'murder was already turning into suicide, and the suicide, as always, let itself be translated into murder' (Derrida, 2005 [2003]-a: 59).

Derrida and Baudrillard – and others who have since deployed this aspect of their analyses – tend to describe autoimmunity as generated by the current Western system, although they sometimes indicate the more general nature of such praxis (Thomson, 2005).[25] I have argued in previous chapters that other phenomena they bring to our attention (such as the deconstructibility of language, or simulation) cannot be confined in time and space to a bounded notion of 'the West', 'late capitalism', 'postmodernity' or some other unit to which we posit China as the 'other country'. In the same way, the observed 'unfettered process of a techno-metastatic production of value, the hyperinflation of meaning and signs' is not confined to democracy/capitalism/the West/America that they take as the primary focus of their analyses (I. C. R., 2007). Rather, this cancer has its parallel in contemporary China, precisely in the form of rivercrabs.

Reading cancer and the (auto)immune through biomedicine and Traditional Chinese Medicine

To explain this point, and to dispel any understanding of my argument in terms of a Chinese 'catching up', let me elaborate slightly on how biomedicine and TCM have understood cancer.

The disease that in English is called cancer is called *ai* (癌) in modern TCM terminology, and tumours (whether cancerous or not) can also be referred to as *liu* (瘤).[26] The philosophy of TCM is based on the idea that a body is healthy when it is in harmony, and illness and pain occur when harmony fails to be achieved, manifest in a 'pattern of disharmony' (Bao Ting *et al.*, 2010: 171).[27] Cancer/*ai*/*liu* is on this view 'a systemic disease from the start' (Schipper *et al.*, 1995; Wong and Sagar, 2010: 3). Cancer and tumours are understood as the manifestation of disharmony (Bao Ting *et al.*, 2010: 170; Chiaramonte and Lao Lixing, 2010: 344), and more specifically of the relative lack of *Zhengqi* (正气), a concept analogous to the biomedical notion of immune system competency/strength (Abbate, 2006; Dorsher and Peng Zengfu, 2010: 57). The understanding of TCM's potential to aid the body in restoring harmony is similarly centred on immunity.[28]

Biomedicine, which has been associated with the West and with the imagination of body parts as discrete and calculable, explains cancer in a very similar way, emphasizing the role of immunity. In this school of thought, cancer is a development where transformed cells 'acquire the ability to disregard the constraints of its environment and the body normal control mechanisms [*sic*]' (Wong and Sagar, 2010: 3), or 'the abnormal and uncontrollable proliferation of cells which have the potential to spread to distant sites' (Chiaramonte and Lao Lixing, 2010: 343). Like TCM, biomedicine thus understands cancer as immune system failure (Chiaramonte and Lao Lixing, 2010: 349). Microscopically, cancer cells display features indicative of a faster proliferative rate and disorganized alignment in relation to other cells, and differences between cancer cells and normal cells are increasingly understood at the level of genetic code (Marcovitch, 2005: 111). The very code that is pre-programmed in the system thus has the capacity to produce the cells that threaten it, and the spread of malignancy in the system is a result of its failed attempts at 'regulation' and cleansing.

Like cancer/*ai*/*liu*, the Chinese crab has early associations with cleaning and purification of spaces, with one legend having the emperor using the crab to rid his palace of the scorpions, fleas, mosquitoes and mice that disturbed his harmony and caused dis-ease.[29] In Europe, like in China, cancer has a long history of association with insufficient cleansing, since its description in premodern pathologies that attributed it to insufficient purging of black bile.[30] One contemporary cancer self-help book likewise describes cancer in terms of societal disorder strikingly reminiscent of disruptions to the harmony conveyed by Hu Jintao and Zhao Tingyang respectively: '[c]ancer growths are made up of cells which belong to our body but which have stopped behaving in a co-operative and orderly fashion' (Reynolds, 1987: 26, cited in Lupton, 2003: 71). It further observes that the multiplication of cancer cells 'has no purpose … unlike normal body cells we can think of cancer cells as unco-operative, disobedient, and independent … [n]ormal cells exist peacefully side by side with their neighbours' (Reynolds, 1987: 27, cited in Lupton, 2003: 71).

This description is certainly fitting to characterize the Chinese 'rivercrabs' described above. Crabs/cancer disturb and threaten the harmony of the system. They are truly 'malignant' in the sense that they disregard normal mechanisms of control and cleansing (they are uncooperative), and they are capable of spatio-temporal spread into secondary deposits or 'metastases'. As such, we may understand crabs/cancer in terms of the European medieval rendition as a parasitic animal (Pouchelle, 1990: 169; Demaitre, 1998: 624), pervasive also in contemporary society (Herzlich and Pierret, 1987).

Yet, crabs/cancer are indeed 'a systemic disease from the start' (Wong and Sagar, 2010: 3), their malignancy is a direct product of the code. The possibility for drawing out the various meanings of *hexie* 和谐 explored at the outset of this chapter was always already there in the character – through its pictographic make-up, its alternative pronunciation as *hú* and through its homonym the river-crab. Moreover, the ironic critique displayed by these reiterations was provoked by Hu's policy of overzealous 'harmonization', and the online deployment of rivercrabs came about as a way to simultaneously avoid and criticize 'being harmonized' by the Great Firewall and other government censorship software. In this way, it is the harmonious system itself that produces that which leads to dis-harmony. As such, rivercrabs are not simply unco-operative, but onco-operative: they operate like cancerous metastases that derive from the code of the system itself to cause dis-harmony and dis-ease.

The coeval multiplicities of (auto)immune harmony

The claim made up to this point of the chapter is that the Chinese 'harmonious' system is not so different from what Derrida and Baudrillard describe in contemporary 'Western democracy' or late capitalist 'consumer society'.[31] Although China is often recast as the opposite of these systems and their logic – the 'other country' – it seems to suffer from the same autoimmune problems. Its symptoms may be different, but the cancerous character of its dis-ease is the same. What, then, are the implications of such an illness – and how do we deal with it?

Looking for cures in a cancerous system

Biomedical and TCM treatments of cancer/*ai*/*liu* do, as indicated above, follow a similar pattern to those commonly prescribed for dealing with uncooperative elements of the geo-body. Biomedicine typically resorts to screening, 'surgical strikes', chemo- and radiotherapies (Marcovitch, 2005: 112). The lack of precision of these therapies give them a quasi-suicidal nature through which the parts of the body deemed 'healthy' or 'normal' become collateral damage. This in turn often further endangers the system through weakening its immune system. The alternative approach, of strengthening the system's own immune capacity or *zhengqi*, urges the system to auto-harmonize, to turn the bad *qi* into the good – another form of cleansing, or 'purging the excessive' and ousting 'evil Qi' (Liu Zhanwen and Liu Liang, 2009: 30). Both these ways of dealing with uncooperative elements of the medical body thus echo the problems seen in relating to 'others' in the geo-body: we eliminate through radical separation (cutting off) or through radical harmonization (turning the bad into the good).

In this way, the cancerous character of the system means its over-zealous attempts at cleansing – through therapy (*zhi liao* 治疗) and governance (*zhi li* 治理)

– actually come to threaten the system itself. This, in turn, exposes an aporia at the very heart of the system, in that the dis-ease must be cured, but cannot be cured without sacrificing the system itself: 'there is no effective prevention or therapy; the metastases invade the whole network "virtually".... He who lives by the same will die by the same' (Baudrillard, 2002 [1997]: 2). Or, in Derrida's words: 'there is no absolutely reliable prophylaxis against the autoimmune. By definition' (2005 [2003]-b: 150–1). To Baudrillard, the fact that cancer is a reflection of the body's victimization by the disruption of its genetic formula is thus what makes it impossible for conventional medicine to cure it: '[t]he current pathology of the body is now beyond the reach of conventional medicine, since it affects the body not as *form*, but as *formula*' (2002 [1997]: 1). To put it a different way, the fact that the system itself produces, through its own code, that which threatens it means there is little use looking to the rationality of the system to combat its excrescences: '[i]t is a total delusion to think extreme phenomena can be abolished. They will, rather, become increasingly extreme as our systems become increasingly sophisticated' (Baudrillard, 2002 [1997]: 7).

On Baudrillard's reading, spontaneous self-regulation of systems is something well known: systems produce accidents or glitches in their own programme, interfering with their own operation (2002 [1997]: 5). This enables systems to survive on a basis contrary to their own principles, against their own value systems:

> they have to have such a system, but they also have to deny it and operate in opposition to it.... But it is entirely as though the species were ... producing ... through cancer, which is a disruption of the genetic code and therefore a pathology of information, a resistance to the all-powerful principle of cybernetic control.... With ... cancer, we might be said to be paying the price for our own system: we are exorcising its *banal* virulence in a *fatal* form.
>
> (Baudrillard, 2002 [1997]: 5, emphasis in original)

Again, this is precisely how rivercrabs operate: they metastasize and spread through a disruption of the code that lets them slip through its pre-programmed screening/firewall/censorship. This is indeed a 'resistance' to cybernetic control, but one generated by the system itself.

If we bring this analysis back to the discipline of IR, this way of understanding cancer complicates things. Within Chinese IR, Wang Yizhou has argued that analysing terrorism in terms of cancer calls for the question of how cancer comes into being. He reads it as a symptom of structural imbalance (Wang Yizhou, 2010: 11). Where military action can only 'cure the symptom but not the source', harmonization or rebalancing of the system will prevent radicalism from breeding (2010: 16). In view of the above explanation of cancer, we may concur with both him and Baudrillard that traditional treatment may only serve to aggravate the problem through weakening the system and causing collateral damage. However, having excavated the forms of therapy suggested by the 'alternative' of 'harmonization' by TCM or Chinese IR, it appears that it stands equally powerless. Increasing harmonization is unlikely to curb cancer/crabs, but may rather contribute to spurring them on. There is no use looking to the system's own rationality to combat the crabs it produces.

Spatio-temporal bordering in a cancerous system

What, then, are the spatio-temporal implications of these crabs, as metastases of an (auto)immune and cancerous system? Nick Vaughan-Williams (2007) has productively drawn on Derrida's notion of autoimmunity to discuss spatial and temporal bordering. The temporal bordering he discusses draws on Brian Massumi's description of 'flashes of . . . sovereign power' as a particular form of pre-programmed decision making in the 'space of a moment' (Massumi, 2005: 6; Vaughan-Williams, 2007: 187–8; see also Nordin 2014a for a discussion related to the Chinese Internet). This parallels what Baudrillard thinks of as a pre-programmed instantaneous operation. Understanding borders in terms of this decisionist ontology highlights the specificity of contemporary wordplay and rivercrabs, in relation to previous historical deployment of homonyms to avoid censorship in China, as described earlier in this chapter. Previous forms of bordering decisions with regards to such homonymous wordplay involved a deliberative process of human interpretation. In this era of the virtual and the hyper-real, the bordering decision is pre-programmed and instantaneous.

Vaughan-Williams, following Massumi, argues that this approach is the temporal equivalent of a tautology: '[t]he time form of the decision that strikes like lightning is the foregone conclusion. When it arrives, it always seems to have preceded itself. Where there is a sign of it, it has always already hit' (Massumi, 2005: 6, cited in Vaughan-Williams, 2007: 188). This form of decision is accordingly a foregone conclusion (or, following Hu, perhaps an 'inevitable choice') 'because it sidesteps or effaces the blurriness of the present in favor of a perceived need to act on the future without delay', in the face of a threat of an indefinite future yet to come (Vaughan-Williams, 2007: 188; Massumi, 2005: 4–5).

Both authors read this as a temporal shift, from 'prevention' to 'pre-emption', from the temporal register of the indefinite future tense to the future perfect tense: the 'always-will-have-been-already' (Massumi, 2005: 6–10; Vaughan-Williams, 2007: 188). In parallel to the autoimmune, this politics induces rather than responds to events:

> [r]ather than acting in the present to avoid an occurrence in the future, pre-emption brings the future into the present. It makes present the future consequences of an eventuality that may or may not occur, indifferent to its actual occurrence. The event's consequences precede it, as if it had already occurred.
>
> (Massumi, 2005: 7–8, cited in Vaughan-Williams, 2007: 188)

The Chinese practice of censoring/harmonizing specific terms through its Great Firewall works through this form of pre-programmed code, which sensors in a 'flash of sovereign power'. Terms are censored pre-emptively to harmonize some not-yet-existing but possible future dissident deployment of a once-unthreatening term (such as the term 'future' 未来 itself, as seen earlier in this chapter in relation to Ai Weiwei's detention). In this manner, PRC Internet censorship policy acts as a temporal bordering process: it pre-empts threats to the government's version of 'harmonious world/society' that come from the future, thus securing time and the future as something that belongs to the party-state and not to the crabs or dissidents (cf. Vaughan-Williams, 2007: 189).

As a wall, the form of electronic bordering that is exercised by the Great Firewall is also a form of spatial bordering, in that it is intimately connected to questions of sovereignty, territory and governmental power. Vaughan-Williams draws on William Walters' work to refer to this spatial bordering as 'firewalling' – in contemporary China another term for having 'been harmonized' by the Great Firewall is having 'been GFWed' (Walters, 2006; for examples see Calon, 2007; Chow, 2010).

The self-attacking or autoimmune logic of such GFW-ing is clear in the 'blocking' of Internet and telephone access that was used for example in attempts to harmonize Xinjiang during the 2009 riots. This firewalling was intended to prevent 'splittism' from spreading, yet could only do so by splitting Xinjiang as a spatial unit off from the rest of China, in virtual/physical space. This, too, is the exclusion by which the Great Firewall operates – to maintain a harmonious space, that space must be sealed off as a (virtual) geo-body from the rest of the world. Again, what is described by Vaughan-Williams as 'innovations in the ways sovereign power attempts to secure the temporal and spatial borders of political community' could refer to something less localized in time and space than may at first appear (Vaughan-Williams, 2007: 191; see also Nordin, 2014a).

The practices of Internet 'harmonization' in China can thus be described in terms of a bordering of time and space that has parallels in contemporary expressions of (auto)immunity in the European system. Having said this, the particular practice of using homonymous characters like the rivercrab, to simultaneously criticize and avoid 'being harmonized' on the Chinese Internet, is a locally specific way of negotiating this particular kind of virtual bordering in time and space. This particular form and double function differentiates it from other forms of satire or political irony that can be found in other systems around the world (Nordin, 2014c). Moreover, in attempting to secure time and space as belonging to the party-state, these harmonizing Chinese censorship regimes effectively provoke the kind of critical wordplay that is exemplified here through rivercrabs. In this way, cancer/crabs work within the system and yet repeatedly escape it: where 'harmonization' may be understood as an attempt at temporal bordering, the experience of cancer has been described as a disturbance to such temporality, a 'falling out of time' (Stacey, 1997: 10). The more the Chinese government attempts to secure, cleanse and harmonize, the more creative and subversive are the iterations that use its language against itself.

Rivercrab metastases and heterotemporalities

As a consequence of this (auto)immune logic of the system, rivercrabs, like cancer cells, increasingly display features indicative of a faster proliferative rate and disorganized alignment in relation to other cells (Marcovitch, 2005: 111). In the here and now, crabs, like cancer, are marked by the way they spread and metastasize through mutation of the code. In this way, we can understand how Chinese crabs similarly migrate, multiply and change in a (re)iterative manner. Every crab draws on previous reiterations of harmony and crabs, but also mutates into something different.

One example of such a 'metastasis' can be seen in Figure 4.4. It shows a replica of the logo for the computer game 'World of Warcraft', saying instead 'Rivercrab World' (*hexie shijie* 河蟹世界), which sounds the same as Hu Jintao's slogan 'harmonious world' (*hexie shijie* 和谐世界). The text at the top means 'do things others could never do' (*zuo bieren yongyuan zuobudao de shi* 做别人永远做不到的事). The text below means 'the late arrival of the battle expedition' (*chidao de yuanzheng* 迟到的远征). The links to themes discussed throughout this book are marked, including the direct link to Hu's 'harmonious world' policy, the competition inherent in games and play and the violent military underpinning of harmonious world.

The rivercrab metastasizes in similar ways into numerous constellations – some very close copies, some with more creative distance. The rivercrab recurrently appears on blogs and can be found in an online dictionary compiled by *China Digital Times* (Xiao Qiang, 2010; China Digital Space, 2011a), where it appears together with dozens of other characters and expressions that have metastasized from similar homonymic wordplay and in reaction to governmental harmonization. It also appears as a permanent feature on the cap of another Internet meme, the 'Green Dam Girl' (*lübaniang* 绿坝娘). The Green Dam Girl is an anthropomorphism of the 'Green Dam Youth Escort' software (*lüba huaji huhang* 绿坝·花季护航) that was developed under the direction of the Chinese government to filter Internet content on individual computers.[32] The Green Dam Girl and rivercrab also appear in merchandise (Xu Yuting, 2009; Gaofudev,

Figure 4.4 Rivercrab world of warcraft (source: Heifenbrug, 2008).

2011; Lotahk, 2011), numerous cartoons (Hecaitou, 2009a; Hexie Farm, 2011) and music videos (Hrehnr 2009a, 2009b; Stchi, 2009; Tutuwan, 2009; DZS manyin, 2010) that typically work through copies of copies, interweaving the themes and symbols discussed throughout this book.

This mixing of online lingo and symbols is reiterated also in art offline. For example, Ai Weiwei's world-famous art has included the *Hexie* installation, where 3,500 porcelain crabs crawl and spread, as menacing copies of one another. The work is a reference to the party held when the Shanghai studio he was asked to build for the 2010 Expo was demolished (Fuchs, 2014). In 2013, he released a metal music video that depicted his time in prison, with lyrics and imagery reflecting *egao* culture, including river crabs in a dirty prison toilet (Ai Weiwei, 2013).

With a similar set of references, in a 2011 art exhibition at the Postmaster Gallery in New York, Kenneth Tin-Kin Hung exhibited his mixed media installation, *The Travelogue of Dr. Brain Damages* (Hung, 2011). The installation was a response to the increasing harmonization of artistic and netizen expression in China, and explored the role of the Internet in facilitating 'both freedom and suppression' (Hung, 2011). The Chinese title *Naocan youji* (脑残游记) is a wordplay on *Lao Can youji* (老残游记), 'The Travelogue of Lao Can', a late Qing dynasty novel attacking the injustice and hypocrisy of government officials at the time. The project thus questioned whether the Internet in China is an effective tool for social change, through remixing Chinese netizens' meme languages with Western icons.

The installation consisted of ten framed digital prints, a six-minute-long video and a ping-pong table sculpture, seen in Figure 4.5. Several of the prints in the

Figure 4.5 'Ping, ping, no pong' (source: Kenneth Tin-King Hung).

installation include replicas of one or more rivercrabs, often copied from images circulated on blogs. For example, in the piece titled *Justice Bao Faces the Red Sun Everyday* (*tiantian jian hongri* 天天见红日), Bao Zheng (包拯), a Song dynasty judge who is a symbol of justice in China, is holding a laptop of the 'Great Firewall' brand displaying a copy of the rivercrab with three watches that was discussed at the beginning of this chapter (Hung, 2011).

On the walls behind the prints were written in large red characters: 'You are not a real man until you have leaped the Great Wall of China' (*Bu fan changcheng fei haohan* 不翻长城非好汉), which is one character from the original quotation from Mao: 'You are not a real man until you have been to the Great Wall of China' (*Bu dao changcheng fei haohan* 不到长城非好汉). The calligraphic style recalls the hand-painted signs that forbid uncivilized behaviour (like spitting) and promote harmonization in Chinese cities, but also the 'harmonious demolition' signs that appear on walls to be torn down.

The central sculpture of the installation (Figure 4.5) was titled 'Ping, ping, no pong' (*Ping, ping, wu pang* 乒乒无乓) and consisted of a ping-pong table with a hole cut out in the shape of a rivercrab on the Chinese side panel. The net was replaced by a sculptured wall, symbolizing the Great Firewall of China, and accompanied by a ping-pong ball to symbolize the exchange of information (Hung, 2011). On one reading, the sculpture highlights how the purported harmonious 'win–win' of mutuality is undermined by harmonization, in the form of the rivercrab. The ball of 'communication' simply disappears into a hole on the Chinese side (it is harmonized), and the intended Chinese recipient never gets a chance to participate in the exchange. On another reading, the rivercrab hole can also be understood as 'protecting' the intended recipient from a hard serve. After all, ping pong is also a competitive zero-sum game, where the opponent's chances of winning over you must be significantly reduced if their serve cannot bounce off your side of the table, no matter how hard or skilful their hand is. Through depicting the rivercrab as a clearly visible and distinct hole or void, this installation also highlighted the undecidable nature of rivercrabs as neither present nor absent, but simultaneously both.

The metastasizing, hybridizing, prostheticizing, mutating displacement of harmony 和谐/rivercrabs 河蟹 goes so far as to penetrate and reformulate the very characters themselves, as can be seen in Figures 4.6 and 4.7. The mutating of characters into new ones became popular after China's Ministry of Education unveiled a list of standardized Chinese characters in common usage, including 44 characters that were slightly revised in their print formats in the Song style, a popular Chinese character style in book printing format (Jiang Aitao, 2009). This re-formation of characters has grown in popularity since 2009, and can be seen in offline art such as Hung's (on the ping-pong racket, see Figure 4.5) and on blogs and webpages on the Internet.[33]

The image in Figure 4.6 shows a t-shirt printed by critical blogger Keso. The print displays a rearrangement of the classical Chinese characters, used in Hong Kong and Taiwan, for 'rivercrab society' (*hexie shehui* 河蟹社会). The characters in Figure 4.7 similarly display an amalgamation of the characters for 'harmony' (*hexie* 和谐) and 'rivercrab' (*hexie* 河蟹).

Figure 4.6 Hybrid *hexie shehui*, rearranging the characters for 河蟹社會 (source: Keso).

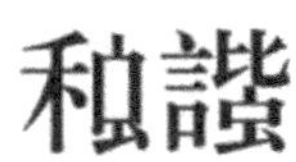

Figure 4.7 Hybrid *hexie*, combining the characters 和谐 and 河蟹 (source: Alison, 2010).

This hybridization of crabs has clear parallels to Baudrillard's alignment of metastases and prostheses, where the fractal (geo-)body,

> fated to see its own external functions multiply, is at the same time doomed to unstoppable internal division among its own cells. It metastasizes: the internal, biological metastases are in a way symmetrical with those external metastases, the prostheses, the networks, the connections.
>
> (Baudrillard, 2002 [2000]: 3)

In this way rivercrabs, too, metastasize in time and space.

Heterotemporalities and the undecidability of rivercrabs

Having examined the hybrid nature of the metastasizing crabs, the final point of this chapter is that this hybridity, in combination with the autoimmune logics of which they are part, imbues them with a radical undecidability. Derrida too emphasizes this link between the autoimmunitary and undecidability: suppression in the name of the (harmonious) system may be legitimate in protecting it from those who threaten it, but is simultaneously autoimmunitary in exposing the immune system by which the system defends itself as an '*a priori* abusive use of force' (Derrida, 2005 [2003]-a). This final section thus emphasizes the links between cancer/crabs and undecidability of the future against which harmonization attempts to secure the Chinese dream of a harmonious society and world.

The undecidable nature of cancer/crabs is visible in an aspect of the lore surrounding them, which refers to the way the crab moves in time and space, in a sideways or 'back and forth' motion that has been connected to threatening dishonesty, but also to the inability to decide something one way or the other, or to predict where it is going (Demaitre, 1998). This undecidability embodied in the crab is also emphasized by the Chinese interpretation of harmony that sees its roots in cooking. The crab can at times be poisonous, and as a bottom-feeder it often includes contaminated substances. At the same time, however, it is considered a delicacy and is believed to nourish the marrow and semen, making it a symbol of male potency and virility (Vanishing Tattoo, 2011). As crabs are considered exemplary 'salty', they can in the logic of TCM either disturb or restore harmony of the body through their effect on the kidneys, and can thus cause or treat cancer (Lu, 1986: 52, 125–6; Wong and Sagar, 2010: 16).[34] Like Derrida's reading of the *pharmakon* in 'Plato's Pharmacy', the crab, then, is simultaneously potential poison and potential cure – indeed Derrida says that '[t]he *pharmakon* is another name, an old name, for this autoimmunitary logic' (Derrida, 2003: 124).[35]

Again, the interpretation of the crab as alimentary poison/cure as always already central to the concept of harmony can be seen in the building blocks of the harmony concept itself. An alternative explanation of the character 和 reads the radical to the left 禾, which depicts standing grain, with the radical to the right 口, which depicts an opening or mouth (*Hanyu da zidian*, 1995: 4.2588.1, 1.566.14). Together they link harmony to eating, or having plenty of grain 禾 to eat 口.[36] David Hall and Roger Ames accordingly argue that 'harmony is the art of combining and blending two or more foodstuffs so they come together with mutual benefit and enhancement without losing their separate and particular identities, and yet with the effect of constituting a frictionless whole' (Hall and Ames, 1998: 181, cited in Callahan, 2011: 259). Callahan also draws on this metaphor in a famous passage from the *Spring and Autumn Annals* (*Lüshi chunqiu* 吕氏春秋), where a minister uses it to explain to his king the art of empire building: '[y]our state is too small and is inadequate to have the full complement of the necessary ingredients. It is only once you are the Emperor that you would have the full complement' (*Lüshi chunqiu*, 1996, cited in Callahan, 2011: 260). To Callahan, this shows the constructed nature of harmony, built through 'an active political process, and judged from a particular perspective – in this case the king's perspective' (Callahan, 2011: 260).

In Chinese mythology, the crab is similarly associated with sovereign power and violent might, as well as with guarding and screening the passage into secured spaces. For example, in Chinese mythology and popular fiction, the Crystal Palaces of the Dragon Kings of the Four Seas are guarded by shrimp soldiers and crab generals (Mythical Realm, 2011). This stands as a parallel to the guarding of Chinese sovereign space by the Great Firewall, and the Green Dam Girl with her crab sign of repressive authority. At the same time, however, this crustacean army is parodied in the Chinese idiom of 'shrimp soldiers and crab generals' (*xiabing xiejiang* 虾兵蟹将), which is used to denote useless troops, a connotation that remains with contemporary Internet users, as can be seen in one online spoof which depicts shrimp soldiers and crab generals as precisely 'ineffective troops' (Lee, 2011).

What is clear from these metastases and their association is the undecidability of these crabs of the (auto)immune Chinese system. They are simultaneously poison and cure, effective harmonizers and useless troops, a consequence of sovereign bordering of time and space and that which 'falls through' or escapes such confines. This undecidability is inseparable from the 'mutual contamination' seen above in the crabs' interaction with their environment and with other species of the zoology that has emerged as part of netizens' play with humorous homonyms in the face of Internet harmonization.

It is this 'mutual contamination' that I think makes these rivercrabs and their peers step up to the challenge of coeval multiplicities that was outlined at the outset of this book. We can recall that Hutchings referred to the notion of 'heterotemporality' as 'ultimately neither one present nor many presents, but a mutual contamination of "nows" that participate in a variety of temporal trajectories, and which do not derive their significance from the one meta-narrative about how they all fit together' (2008: 166). These metastases, differentiated and deferred, are of the system yet fall through the cracks of its time and space to engage in a 'mutual contamination of "nows"' that each incorporates undecidable futures in the here and now. Their very undecidability means that we have to take responsibility in the here and now for which of their possible readings, or temporal trajectories, we choose to put across. In this chapter I have chosen to put across one such narrative, of crabs as (auto)immune metastases of a cancerous harmony. Their significance, however, cannot be ultimately decided or locked in by this narrative – it is not a meta-narrative from which we can judge how they all fit together. It is indeed impossible to do justice to the excess of meaning embodied in these crabs. Nonetheless, I have traced some of them here and pointed to some of their significance, in a way that I believe can emphasize their radical undecidability as a 'plurality of trajectories' or 'simultaneity of stories-so-far'.

Conclusion

This chapter has explored how Hu's version of a harmonious world is being challenged and reproduced by a particular form of Chinese *egao* wordplay that works through deploying official language against itself. These redeployments make visible how Hu's Chinese dream of harmony has come to work through violent 'harmonization' of others. The chapter has argued that these forms of wordplay draw on tactics similar to Derrida's in particular, but also to Baudrillard's, thus providing for a resonance here between academic scholarship and popular practices in China. It has moreover argued that these forms of negotiation are inherently linked to Hu's Chinese dream of a harmonious society and world through the autoimmune logic of a system that in seeking to protect and cleanse itself actually violates itself as the consequence of a violent non-recognition of the 'other' in the self.

In exploring this quasi-suicidal interplay of harmony and rivercrabs, it has shown how they are intimately linked to party-state attempts at spatial and temporal bordering as a means to maintain a cleansed/harmonious timespace. Deconstruction highlights the impossibility of ever making a clear-cut division between inside and outside, self and other and thus brings out a key feature of the logics of 'harmonious world' (or perhaps any system). Resistance *to* harmony/harmonization can in this way not be thought outside the resistance *of* harmony/harmonization, the resistance of the system itself to itself, of and to its 'self' as 'other', a resistance of the 'other' of itself to itself. For this reason, it is impossible for harmony to acquire the conceptual unity or self-identity that would be needed in order for it to be placed as a secure 'object' to be straightforwardly resisted, critiqued or condemned.

In this manner, this chapter has insisted on the impossibility of succeeding in creating such a purified space or object, and on the undecidability of both harmony and crabs: like harmony, the crabs are simultaneously poison and cure, they are intimately linked to the possibility of the system in the first place, yet threaten it with murder/suicide. The tendency of any community to close in on itself, and to exclude the outside on which it relies for survival, works according to an autoimmune logic. Therefore, '[t]his tendency is not a perversion of proper community (whether inoperative, unavowable, or coming, as for Blanchot, Nancy, Agamben), but the condition of its existence' (Thomson, 2005). This is certainly the case for Hu's dream of a harmonious world. In this way '[t]his self-contesting attestation keeps the auto-immune community alive, which is to say, open to something other and more than itself' (Derrida, 1998: 51). Finally, then, this chapter has argued that this undecidability is what makes it possible to think of this autoimmune system of metastases in terms of 'heterotemporalities' or 'coeval multiplicities'.

Returning to the question of the political in harmony/rivercrabs, it seems the claim that the online world of *egao* offers a 'free and unrestricted' time and space of Bakhtinian carnival is premature. Rivercrabs are used to circumvent constraints, not abolish them, and constraints are certainly still in place. The descriptions of this culture as a separate sphere or 'the antithesis of normal life' seem similarly exaggerated. However, Lagerkvist's idea that *egao* is for venting anger *as opposed to* offering the public political power hinges on a focus on politics in the narrow sense, which is seen throughout prior analyses of *egao*. Much previous scholarship rests on the assumption that *egao* should be judged on its potential to influence politics, to contest the legitimacy, accountability or policy of the PRC government. Others imply that it should be measured against its potential to cultivate collective resistance, collective empowerment or grassroots communities. If measured against such standards, rivercrabs certainly appear as 'ineffective troops' in battling out Chinese politics. They make us laugh, but offer no way out, no alternative telos or endpoint towards which a movement of mass resistance can be directed. They even refuse to adapt a single meaning and always oscillate – they are simultaneously harmony and rivercrab, resisting and perpetuating the proliferation of harmony.

Precisely herein lies the political potential of rivercrabs. Previous scholarship has aimed to understand the *meaning* of *egao*, to pin down its potential significance in terms of a resistance/not resistance divide of *politics*. This chapter has suggested instead that we approach such phenomena by way of interrogating *the political*, where 'repoliticization' involves a disruption of the regular proliferation of allochronically organized harmony, a 'challenge' to 'what have, through discursive practices, been constituted as normal, natural, and accepted ways of carrying on' (Edkins, 1999: 12). Through repeatedly deploying expressions like having 'been harmonized' or 'rivercrab world', the meaning of the official 'harmonious world' discourse is 'hollowed out' or 'disrupted', rather than contested head on. The point is not necessarily to resist or not resist, but to 'make strange' (see also Nordin, forthcoming b; Nordin and Richaud, 2014). This is what pushes rivercrabs into the political, where multiple meanings or doings – of words and purported significance – leads to instances of openness where we need to make 'impossible decisions' with regard to their use and interpretation. It is only if we shift the focus from politics to the political that it makes sense to conceive of this language play as 'alternative political discourse' (Meng Bingchun, 2011: 39) or 'alternate civility' (Lagerkvist, 2010: 158).

With this said, repoliticization is not stable, but *egao* too is repeatedly depoliticized, by being designated as unimportant or as meaning only one thing (*only* revolution, *only* apolitical escapism, *only* a potential to become a *proper* political movement). The point of this chapter is not to designate to *egao* another *correct meaning*, but to indicate the undecidability of this meaning-making process. The point is to open back up the question of *egao* as potentially *political* even if it does not lead to a revolutionary *politics* (cf. Nordin and Richaud, 2014: 63).

The cancerous logic of the system means that 'our solutions to problems, our attempts to perfect the world ... are but a step on the way to worse viruses developing' (Coulter, 2004). The question, then, has to be asked: '[w]hat is cancer a resistance to, what even worse eventuality is it saving us from?' (Baudrillard, 1993 [1990]: 10). It is thus to the question of eventualities of harmony that the next chapter turns, before we return in the Conclusion to the (im)possibility of openness to harmony's other 'to come'.

Notes

1 The form of online expression that I discuss is important because it is widespread in China, and has come to be understood as an important form of resistance by international scholars and Chinese dissident groups. In my discussion of this playful and critical reference to 'harmonious world' I draw on a quantity of blog posts, images, music videos, songs, design items, arts exhibitions and photography that have appeared online since 2005. I focus on examples that have reached a relatively wide audience inside and outside China.

2 Chinese 'netizens' (*wangyou* 网友), or online activists, are increasingly understood as a force of change in Chinese society and politics. Studies of Chinese online discourse has tended to focus on online nationalism and xenophobia (Qiu, 2006). Recently, however, scholars have shown how, since the mid-1990s, the Internet has revolutionized popular expression and provided unprecedented means for users to organize, protest, influence public opinion and even bring down corrupt officials, at least at a local level. Some argue that these netizens are laying the groundwork for the eventual realization of 'institutionalized democracy' (Yang Guobin, 2009), although others argue that there is no strong evidence to date of such a development (Shen and Breslin, 2010: 264).

3 The blackouts were noted in the Western mainstream press (Blanchard, 2009; AFP, 2011). For a fuller explanation of exactly what this blockage entailed in terms of access, see Summers (2009).

4 Scholars have discussed this discrepancy in various contexts. See for examples Link *et al.* (2001), Thornton (2002), Esarey and Xiao Qiang (2008), He Zhou (2008).

5 My discussion of the literature on *egao* in relation to politics and the political here draws on Nordin and Richaud (2014), where we discuss the distinction as perceived by the young netizens who produce and consume it, based on ethnographic fieldwork and interviews. In Nordin (forthcoming b), I also suggest we approach the study of *egao* through a methodology that refuses the resistance/not resistance binary.

6 Indeed, the very game of mah-jong is itself involved in contestation as a battleground for politics, where popular practice has been shown to resist official campaigns to regulate and 'sanitize' a 'popular mah-jong' and promote 'healthy mah-jong' (*jiankang majiang* 健康麻将 or *weisheng majiang* 卫生麻将, meaning no gambling) as 'a competitive national sport and a symbol of China's distinctive cultural legacy' (Festa, 2006: 9).

7 The 'three represents' is previous General Secretary Jiang Zemin's legacy set phrase, which became a guiding ideology of the Chinese Communist Party (CCP) at its Sixteenth Party Congress in 2002, together with Marxism-Leninism, Mao Zedong Thought and Deng Xiaoping Theory. It stipulates that the CCP should be representative to advanced social productive forces, advanced culture and the interests of the overwhelming majority. The slogan was part of the shift to Chineseness as a legitimizing force of the CCP as a ruling party representative of the majority of Chinese people as opposed to its original legitimization as a vanguard revolutionary party driven by the 'proletariat'. It also helped legitimize the inclusion of capitalist business elites into the party.

8 To clarify the position of the analysis here in relation to Derrida's, I write of the river-crab as a 'second term' that displaces the harmony/discord binary implied in Hu's harmonious world and society. As such, it does not obey the order of that binary in a simple manner. However, it also does not necessarily function as a new 'master term' in the way Derrida often seems to understand the role of a new term.

9 In Derrida's work, one such term is *différance*, which combines the two meanings of French *différence*, difference and deferral, 'changing an "e" to an "a" adds time to space' (Massey, 2005: 49). It also includes terms such as iterability, artifactuality, activirtuality, circonfession, *avenir/à venir*, *hauntologie* and so on. Despite what may

be interpreted as a dismissal at points of Derrida's deployment of wordplay (Baudrillard, 1996 [1990]: 25), Baudrillard uses very similar tactics in his deployment of terms such as seduction, drawing on the original Latin sense of *seducere*, 'to lead away', and semiorrhage, semiotic haemorrhage (Baudrillard, 2002 [2000]: 208).

10 It should be noted that this article was written by a Chinese author at a time when the 1911 nationalist revolution had recently removed the Qing dynasty from power, which may have affected this commentary.

11 Elsewhere, I argue that *egao* is a distinctly innovative practice, as opposed to the censorship practices that are marked by copying from abroad and remarkable continuity with Chinese historical practice (Nordin, 2014c).

12 Scandinavian languages have interpreted cancer to equate a crayfish, rather than a crab, to give the Swedish *kräfta*, Norwegian *kreft* and Danish *kræft*.

13 In astronomy, the 'cancer' constellation represents Hercules crushing a crab with his foot. This tale derives from Greek mythology, where the crab nipped Heracles when he was battling the monster Hydra and was crushed. The mother deity Hera, who was at odds with Hercules at the time, honoured the crab's courageous efforts by placing it in the heavens. In astrology, the cancer/crab is the fourth sign of the zodiac, which the sun enters at the northern summer solstice, about 21 June (Oxford Dictionaries, 2011a). The term also has spatial connotations, indicating the direction south, as in the tropic of cancer.

14 Hobbes (1996: 221–30) gave a detailed analysis of dangers to the state as illnesses to the body politic, building on an established metaphor of societies as bodies (Hale, 1971). For another example of early European use, Italian thinker Francesco Guicciardini, writing in the sixteenth century, constantly repeats the metaphors of medicine and cure. Guicciardini identifies the disease with the Italian city-states' willingness to ally with outside states that are more powerful than themselves, and cautions against ignoring 'how dangerous it is to use medicine which is stronger than the nature of the disease' (Guicciardini, 1984: 20–1). The French Revolution saw the use of illness/therapy metaphors to justify the *terreur* as a cure for societal illness (Musolff, 2003: 328). In contemporary scholarship, Susan Sontag in her famous *Illness as Metaphor* singled out cancer as a type of 'master illness' that is 'implicitly genocidal' (Sontag, 1991: 73–4, 84). Otto Santa Anna describes how the American civil rights movement used cancer as a metaphor for racism in the 1960s (Santa Anna, 2003: 215–16, 222). In contemporary IR, Kevin Dunn has written at length about how Mobutu's cancer-ridden body led to a recasting of him as a cancer on the body politic of the Republic of Zaire, and Zaire in turn as a tumour on the region (Dunn, 2003: especially 139–42). See also Deborah Wills (2009) for recent use of 'cancer' terminology in English-language IR, and Wang Yizhou (2010: 11) for similar use in Chinese-language IR.

15 For a good overview of such metaphorical use in patients and media, see Lupton (2003). For a good overview of other forms of cultural and artistic expression relating to the narrativization of cancer, see Stacey (1997).

16 For such military metaphors, see for example Annas (1995: 745), Clarke (1996: 188), Stibbe (1997), Clarke and Robinson (1999: 273–4), Lupton (2003: 72), Reisfield and Wilson (2004) and Williams Camus (2009).

17 For its treatment in recently discovered Chinese medical literature, see Lo and Cullen (2005). For commentary on the parallel emergence of political and medical epistemologies in imperial China, see Unschuld (2010). For commentary on parallel developments of political and medical knowledge in Europe, see Have (1987) and Stibbe (1997).

18 This imagination of the human body is particularly clear in writing on pictorial representations thereof. The negotiation of Chinese–Western power relations and self/other hierarchization through modes of pictorial representation has been traced in the mid-nineteenth-century medical paintings of Lam Qua, who focused on depicting tumours

on Chinese bodies for Western consumption. Discussions of these can be found in Gilman (1988) and Heinrich (2008), as can some of Lam Qua's pictures of tumours and abscesses (Gilman, 1988: 150; Heinrich, 2008: 50, 54, 55, 81, 82, 83, 84, 86, 87), as well as earlier and later Chinese images of such growths (Heinrich, 2008: 57, 91, 92; see also Barnes, 2005: 292).

19 Such an endeavour might point to the early exchange and hybrid nature of information, and to similarities of TCM and early forms of European medicine: the inner body as masculine (or *Yang*) and the outer body as feminine (or *Yin*) (for expression in European tradition, see Erickson, 1997: 10; for expression in Chinese tradition, see Liu Zhanwen and Liu Liang, 2009: 12); the focus on balance of a holistic system (for expression in European tradition, see Turner, 2003: 2; for expression in Chinese tradition, see Unschuld, 2010: xxvi); the focus on bodily flows and the understanding of blockage of flows as cause for disease (for expression in European tradition, see Turner, 2003: 2; for expression in Chinese tradition, see Liu Zhanwen and Liu Liang, 2009: 28); the discursive parallels to the societal body and the need for governance of both societal and medical body (for expression in European tradition, see Porter, 1997: 158; Turner, 2003: 2; for expression in Chinese tradition, see Unschuld, 2010) and so on.

20 There are many examples of this (for example Cui Yong *et al*., 2004; Bao Ting *et al*., 2010; Chiaramonte and Lao Lixing, 2010; Dorsher and Peng Zengfu, 2010; Wong and Sagar, 2010).

21 Like cancer, the question of immunity reinforces the close link between the governance of the socio-political and the biomedical body, as 'immunity' was originally a legal concept in Ancient Rome (Cohen, 2009: 3). For my analysis of cancer and autoimmunity in Baudrillard's work, I focus on the various articles collected in *Screened out* (2002 [2000]), and particularly the essay 'Aids: Virulence or Prophylaxis?' (2002 [1997]).

22 For Derrida, I draw mostly on his reading in 'Autoimmunity: Real and Symbolic Suicides' on 9/11 (2003) and in *Rogues: Two Essays on Reason* (2005 [2003]-a, 2005 [2003]-b), rather than on earlier mention of autoimmunity in texts such as 'Faith and Knowledge' (1998) or *Resistances of Psychoanalysis* (1998 [1996]; for some comments on the use of the 'autoimmune' in this volume, see Wortham, 2010: 160).

23 As expressed by one commentator: '[u]ndecideability, aporia, antinomy, double bind: autoimmunity is explicitly inscribed in *Rogues* into a veritable "best of collection" of Derrideo-phemes or deconstructo-nyms' (Naas, 2006: 29).

24 Derrida sometimes takes the term to denote a specific targeting of a body's defence mechanisms, its 'protecting itself against its self-protection' (1998: 73, note 27), which is closer to the biomedical definition of autoimmunity and further from its description of certain forms of cancer. At other times, the autoimmune involves an attack against any part of the body, 'in short against its own' (*son propre tout court*) (Derrida, 1998: 44). We note here the numerous meanings of French '*propre*', translated here as 'own', but which also means self-possession, propriety, property and importantly cleanliness, stressing again the cleansing that I emphasize in this chapter (cf. Spivak's translation in Derrida, 1976 [1967]: 26). Where some have found this ambiguity problematic (Haddad, 2004: 39–41), I think it points to an important aspect of autoimmunity that is the impossibility of separating a part that 'defends' a (geo) body from one that simply 'is'. It acknowledges the malleability of the system. For this reason I also allow for (auto)immunity and cancer to denote the same process, as they do to Baudrillard.

25 In particular, a literature has emerged that draws on Derrida's concept of autoimmunity in IR to discuss 'Western' practices, for example Bulley (2009: 12, 25–9), Vaughan-Williams (2007: 183–92), Osuri (2006: 500), Thomson (2005) and Haddad (2004: 30). I discuss these literatures in relation to the policy and academic discourse of harmonism in Nordin (2016).

26 The first known description of *ai* comes from *Wei Ji Bao Shu c.*1171 AD, in the Song dynasty (Pan Mingji, 1992, in Bao Ting *et al.*, 2010: 57). Tumours were also referred to as *liu* in inscriptions on oracle bones over 3,500 years old (Pan Mingji, 1992, in Bao Ting *et al.*, 2010: 57).

27 For a more thorough explanation for the layperson of the philosophical foundations of TCM as well as an outline of its foundational texts, see Liu Zhanwen and Liu Liang (2009).

28 This is a marked trait throughout contemporary TCM literatures (Abbate, 2006; Lahans, 2008; Chiaramonte and Lao Lixing, 2010: 342, 349; Dorsher and Peng Zengfu, 2010: 57; Wong and Sagar, 2010: 3, 4, 15). TCM scepticism of biomedical forms of treatment – such as radiotherapy and chemotherapy – stems from their 'collateral damage', the killing of normal cells along with the malign cancer cells, which leads to further immune suppression and hence further reduction of *zhengqi*. TCM treatment focuses on strengthening *zhengqi* in order to maximize the immunity of the system beset by cancer. Herbal medicines used to treat cancer are thus (partly) focused on strengthening the body's general immunity (*fuzheng*) (Lahans, 2008; Dorsher and Peng Zengfu, 2010: 57).

29 Renditions of this lore can also be found online (Vanishing Tattoo, 2011).

30 On this understanding, breast cancer for example was caused by insufficient cleansing by menstruation of the blood from the dregs of spoiled black bile (Caulhiaco and McVaugh, 1997: n. 9, 94; see also Demaitre, 1998: 618 and nn. 37, 38). An overview of the development of European ideas of cancer can be found in Demaitre (1998).

31 Elsewhere, I have shown how the discourse of harmony undermines such Western-centrism in writing by Derrida (Nordin, forthcoming a) and Baudrillard (Nordin, 2014b), respectively.

32 According to China Digital Space:

> Pre-installation of Green Dam software was originally intended for all new computers; however, because the proposed policy proved deeply unpopular, mandatory pre-installation has been delayed to an undetermined date. Green Dam girl first appeared sporadically in June 2009 on Baidu's online encyclopaedia.
>
> (China Digital Space, 2011b)

Some, however, suggested that the actual reason for the government's about-face was the many security flaws within the software that allowed hackers to take over computers (jozjozjoz, 2009), and that it was built on copyright and open source code violations (Koman, 2009). Popular Chinese blogger Hecaitou (和菜头) says the Green Dam Girl shows the creativity of the post-1980s generation in resisting Internet regulation (Hecaitou, 2009a). For an analysis of the Green Dam Girl, see Wallis (2015).

33 The first instance of this trend may be when on 31 August 2009, netizens created three new Chinese characters together with other digital artwork within 12 hours. These new characters can be seen on Hecaitou's blog and include a character pronounced 'nan', which combines the characters for 'brain damage' (*naocan* 脑残), which is online lingo used to describe someone incapable of thinking straight because they have been crippled by party ideology; 'wao' combining the characters for 'fifty cents' (*wumao* 五毛) in a reference to the 'Fifty cent party', which is an online term for online commentators paid and trained by the government to anonymously spin online debate in favour of the Party Line; and 'diang', combining the characters for the CCP Central Committee (*dangzhongyang* 党中央), interpreted to mean 'the ultimate, sacred, absolutely correct, cannot be questioned; you get the shit beaten out of you but cannot say a word' (Hecaitou, 2009b; for English-language commentary at *China Digital Times*, see Xiao Qiang, 2009).

34 One example of such a cure: 'Bake one male crab and one female crab and grind into powder, take the powder with wine all at once to facilitate healing of breast cancer' (Lu, 1986: 126).

35 See also Derrida (1976 [1967]: 292, 1981 [1972], 1995 [1989]-a: 233, 2005 [2003]-a: 52, 82, 157). This is also how Chinese lore traditionally conceives of poisons/cures more generally, as is clear from the 'Five Poisons' (*wu du* 五毒), incidentally near-homonymous with 'no poison' (*wu du* 无毒). These are, like the crab, actually several (five) animals that have traditionally been held to counteract harmful influences through counteracting poison with poison. They also had corresponding medicines made from five animals or corresponding herbs, used to treat ulcers and abscesses, probably through active ingredients such as mercury and arsenic (Yetts, 1923: 2; Williams, 1976).

36 This etymology can be found in a number of dictionaries and books on Chinese characters (Wieger, 1965 [1915]: 121a; Karlgren, 1974 [1923]: 70; Lindqvist, 1991: 187; *Hanyu da zidian*, 1995: 1.602.1).

5 Xi Jinping's Chinese dream

Dreaming away the harmonious world

Every generation of Chinese leadership uses set phrases to stamp their mark on Chinese politics – and 'harmonious world' was Hu Jintao's legacy. Previous chapters have shown Hu's dream of a harmonious world to be riddled with problematic contradictions. By the end of his tenure these had become so overexposed that the harmony that may once have appeared attractive had collapsed into a joke. There seemed to be good reason to dream of something else.

And indeed, after taking over as leader of the Chinese Communist Party (CCP) in November 2012, Xi Jinping proceeded like previous leaders and launched his own set phrase: the Chinese dream (*Zhongguo meng* 中国梦). On 29 November 2012, two weeks after he was appointed as CCP general secretary, Xi stood at the National Museum next to Tiananmen Square and declared that the greatest Chinese dream was the 'great rejuvenation of the Chinese nation' (*Zhongguo weida fuxing* 中国伟大复兴). When he was confirmed as state president and chairman of the State Central Military Commission by the first plenary session of the Twelfth National People's Congress (NPC) in March 2013, he closed the session by vowing to press ahead with this Chinese dream (*Xinhua*, 2013b).

Xi's proposal of the Chinese dream appears as a timely boon to Chinese politics, with the potential to generate unity and fill a space left by the disappearance of harmony. Yet, this chapter will show that Xi's Chinese dream has suffered the same fate as Hu's harmonious world.[1] Xi had used the language of harmony in the run-up to his takeover,[2] and his new slogan has continued to build on the idea of harmony in terms of time, space and multiplicity. With it came the same kinds of allochronic thinking, and the same contradictions, that made harmony impossible under Hu's leadership. What is more, the 'Chinese dream' has proliferated in as exponential a manner as 'harmonious world'. This excess of communication has continued to accelerate the disappearance of harmony, and has ultimately made the Chinese dream itself disappear.

The structure of this chapter mirrors previous chapters in this book. It discusses in turn the Chinese dream in policy discourse, academic discourse, public propaganda and online spoofing culture. Through an examination of these contexts, this chapter will suggest that although the terminology of the 'Chinese dream' and 'harmony' are still heavily promoted and reiterated by the party-state, they are the empty terms that remain after the underlying principle of the Chinese dream of a harmonious world has disappeared (cf. Öberg, 2013). If 'harmonious world' and the 'Chinese dream' ever had the capacity to pose as ideals in or for China, that capacity has now been destroyed by excessive visibility, transparency and proliferation. This in turn raises the question of why the party-state continues to promote and police the Chinese dream of harmony so forcefully. This chapter will suggest that the proliferation of the Chinese dream may serve as a cover-up for the disappearance of any 'real' Chinese power, values or spirit of harmony behind it. This in turn reinforces the point made in the previous chapter that 'resistance' to harmony and the Chinese dream may not be possible in the way we are used to imagining it.

The Chinese dream in policy discourse

Although Xi turned the 'Chinese dream' into a set policy phrase, discussion in terms of a Chinese dream had been widespread in wider popular and intellectual circles for several years before 2012, and had already shaped and been shaped by the wider 'discourse of harmonism' (see Callahan, 2013). Part of the trajectory of the Chinese dream can be seen in the large-scale mega events that were staged under Hu Jintao's presidency, but under Xi's direction, including the 2008 Beijing Olympics and the 2010 Shanghai Expo. The terms and imagery of these events foreshadowed the dream motif, in the Olympic 'One World, One Dream' slogan, and in the Expo's '100 years of Expo dream'. The harmony that is envisaged by Xi's Chinese dream circles around the notion of a 'great rejuvenation of the Chinese nation'. This had also been an explicit goal of Chinese leaderships at least as far back as Sun Yat-Sen, invoked by almost every Chinese leader since, including nationalist Chiang Kai-Chek, reformist Jiang Zemin and harmony-promoter Hu Jintao. Against this background, researchers have argued that '[h]armony, peace, stability as well as wealth and power – elements developed in the political harmony debate under the fourth generation [of People's Republic of China (PRC) leadership under Hu Jintao] – serve now as corner stones of the "Chinese dream" ', without major changes in China's international posture (Noesselt, 2015a: 24; see also Zhao Suisheng, 2015: 962). Party outlets unequivocally establish that the Chinese dream is to work for a harmonious world (Qiushi, 2013; see Teufel Dreyer, 2015).

In the context of this existing diversity of Chinese dreams, Xi and the Central Propaganda Department of the CCP (2013) set out to make sure the Chinese dream was correctly understood, and have worked hard to guide and inform public opinion through a wide range of public campaigns and a dozen books elaborating on the concept (for example Wang Yingmei and Wang Pujing, 2013). Through these, we get a relatively clear idea of how the current PRC leadership imagines time, space and multiplicity in its dream of a harmonious world.

Time, space and multiplicity in Xi's Chinese dream of harmony

The key unit that determines the organization of difference in Xi's Chinese dream is the PRC state – it is an unashamedly nationalist dream. Xi's Chinese dream is often described as including four parts: Strong China (economically, politically, diplomatically, scientifically, militarily); Civilized China (equity and fairness, rich culture, high morals); Harmonious China (amity among social classes); and Beautiful China (healthy environment, low pollution) (see for example Kuhn, 2013). This list of dream ingredients carries forward harmony within China as a key element of the Chinese dream. It also focuses more broadly, though not exclusively, on the areas of development and modernization that Xi wants to accomplish *in* the PRC state. In this manner, two key goals of Xi's Chinese dream are said to be the 'Two 100s': the PRC becoming a 'moderately well-off society' by 2021, the 100th anniversary of the CCP, and a 'modern socialist country that is prosperous, strong, democratic, culturally advanced and harmonious' by 2049, the 100th anniversary of the founding of the PRC (State Council, 2014b: conclusion). These are aims inherited from Hu's vision of a harmonious society. They mean that what may be considered internal metrics, such as gross domestic product (GDP), are key to measuring the rejuvenation of the Chinese nation. At the same time, and despite the ever-present win–win rhetoric, it is measured against other states – power, influence and strength are understood, to some extent at least, as relative on a global playing field. This raises the question of how Xi's Chinese dream may relate to other national dreams.

Seen from one perspective, it appears that a diversity of 'dreams' can coexist harmoniously, just as civilizations did in Hu's rhetoric. In a June 2013 meeting with US President Barack Obama in California, Xi emphasized that '[t]he Chinese dream … is a dream of peace, development, cooperation and win-win. It includes every country's people's fine dreams, including the American dream' (Xi Jinping in Chen Zhi and Qian Tong, 2013).

In September 2013, Consul General Li Huaxin expressed this stance quite clearly in a speech at the University of Sydney:

> It is natural that different countries have different opinions on different issues because of totally different history, culture, traditions and national conditions.… The 'Chinese Dream' and the dreams of other countries in the world are different but they can coexist harmoniously and advance together. Only by living in harmony can those dreams complement each other compatibly; only by allowing differences can those dreams learn from each other.
>
> (Li Huaxin, 2013)

Elsewhere, government white papers have also outlined such a harmonious coexistence of separate dreams, for example in suggesting that win–win trade cooperation between China and Africa can 'help both sides make their respective dreams come true' (State Council, 2013a). In these examples, themes are repeated from Hu's harmonious world rhetoric, including the focus on mutual respect and win–win cooperation – a benevolent reading might even read into this a nod at genuine 'harmony with difference' (*he'er butong* 和而不同).

However, there is also another way of looking at things. We have seen in previous chapters how 'harmonious coexistence' in much official rhetoric tends towards a particular organization of time, space and difference – and this pattern is repeated in Xi's Chinese dream. There are three aspects to this. First, the 'respective dreams' that are recognized clearly align with predefined units, in the jigsaw-puzzled imaginary of mutually exclusive states, nations or civilizations. There is no room for groups within China to dream differently, or share dreams of other civilizations if they are different from Xi's Chinese dream. Although Xi's rhetoric pays significant attention to individuals' aspirations, it is unambiguous that these should be subordinated to and made to serve the national dream as defined by the party-state. For example, in May 2013, Xi addressed an elite group of 'model youth', making clear that he expected young people to 'contribute their wisdom and energy to the realization of the Chinese dream', but that '[o]nly by integrating individual dreams to the national cause can one finally make great achievement' (*Xinhua*, 2013d). As Li Huaxin went on to explain: 'The path of socialism with Chinese characteristics is the answer to the question after Chinese people summarized historical experience and lessons. It's also the only path we should take to realize the "Chinese Dream" ' (Li Huaxin, 2013).

Second, when Xi and his officials speak of a single right road for China in this way, it is commonly accompanied by comments that it can only be achieved by spreading 'the Chinese spirit' (*Xinhua*, 2013b). As under Hu, 'China advocates a new type of international relations built around win–win cooperation', described in deterministic terms of 'common destiny' where China's choice and dream is 'inevitable' (Liu Xiaoming, 2015). The strong notion of linear development that underpinned Hu's harmonious world is also very much present in Xi's Chinese dream. When Li Huaxin reiterates that '[t]he aims of the "Chinese Dream" are not to conquer, exceed or replace anyone', he nonetheless replicates the imagery of a movement of a new and better world from inside the PRC to its outside: 'The "Chinese Dream" will bring to the world new hope, new opportunities and new driving forces' (Li Huaxin, 2013). In this way, Xi's Chinese dream combines a unit-based nationalist cosmology with a more holistic imagination of a harmonious world through the now familiar alignment of space in time.[3] The Chinese dream is *one* concept that breaks with the purportedly clear-cut inside/outside division of 'harmonious society' for domestic policy and 'harmonious world' for foreign policy. The explicit implication is that there can be no contradiction between the party-state's dream of China's internal development and others' dreams for the world. Rather, on this logic, '[t]he "Chinese Dream" is an inseparable part of the dream of the world' (Li Huaxin, 2013).

Third, as in policy discourse under Hu Jintao, it is again claimed that Chinese (elites) have privileged access to these better ideas and seeds of destiny. As Ambassador Liu Xiaoming summarizes Xi's Chinese dream: 'These new ideas and new initiatives reflect centuries-old Chinese wisdom … As we can see from

President Xi's diplomatic philosophy and practice, they embody a distinct Chinese characteristic, Chinese touch and Chinese style' (Liu Xiaoming, 2015). In exchange, the PRC needs 'more understanding, support and assistance from the world' and those who disagree with it have simply failed to understand (Li Huaxin, 2013).

Promoting the Chinese dream with hard and soft power

How, then, is this support to be achieved from a world that frequently 'misunderstands' the Chinese dream? It is clear that Xi considers what some call 'soft power tools' to be key in globally spreading the Chinese dream as the harmonious world dream (Xi Jinping, 2014a). As scholar Xie Lei argues, the 'beautiful China' that is envisaged through both Hu's 'harmonious world' and Xi's 'Chinese dream' also lies in the eyes of the beholder, and China will be truly 'beautiful' only once it is universally recognized as such by other countries (Xie Lei, 2014: 483). In policy, this emphasis goes so far that a 2013 white paper on *The Diversified Employment of China's Armed Forces* focused on the People's Liberation Army's (PLA) role in maintaining national harmony and stability, also highlighting its provision of medical care and aid to developing countries, most notably through the hospital ship *Peace Ark*'s 'Harmonious Mission' to provide a humanitarian medical service (State Council, 2013b).

Nonetheless, many commentators have worried about increased Chinese military assertiveness after Xi spoke of a 'strong-army dream' (*qiangjun meng* 强军梦) during an inspection tour of the navy in southern China in December 2012, part of which was a prominent visit to the destroyer *Haikou*. He said that resolutely obeying the party's orders was the 'spirit of a strong army', thus rebutting those who would see it removed from direct party control (*Xinhua*, 2012f). In March 2013 the PLA issued a circular to troops saying that the 'strong-nation dream of a great revival of the Chinese people' was in effect a 'strong-army dream' (see *The Economist*, 2013). Vice-chairman of the Central Military Commission Xu Qiliang has explained that 'the Chinese dream explicitly set forth the Party's goal of strengthening the military' (*Xinhua*, 2013e).

This strong army dream is said by some to rely on technological advancement. So, for example, General Armament Department chief Zhang Youxia has argued '[w]e must lose no time preparing the necessary equipment for military struggle, accelerate the promotion of high-tech equipment projects ... and make our due contributions to the realization of the "China Dream" and "dream of a strong army"' (cited in Cao Zhi and Li Xuanliang, 2013: as translated in Miller, 2013). Technological advancement has also been taken by some to involve continued development of military power projection capabilities that were already under way under Hu's leadership. This idea has been reinforced by Xi's other early visits to naval installations.[4] Understandably, some of the PRC's neighbours worry that the Chinese dream will look an awful lot like their nightmares.

Exclusion and incorrect understanding in Xi's Chinese dream

This build-up of power-projection capabilities and the 'strong army dream' may be one reason why Xi Jinping has found it so important to continue stressing harmony, peacefulness and win–win cooperation. Perhaps the uneasiness it has elicited among neighbours is also one of the reasons why we so frequently hear PRC officials reiterate that anyone who perceives such military build-up as threatening has simply misunderstood. As Li Huaxin concludes:

> as long as one put aside his prejudice, he can view China more objectively and rationally and understand that the 'Chinese Dream' is by no means a threat to the world.... For a long time, China has been endeavouring to explain its commitment to pursue peaceful development. But it's not easy to dispel long existing misunderstandings.
>
> (Li Huaxin, 2013)

Though it may not be easy, the PRC leadership has certainly tried hard to stamp out alternative interpretations of the Chinese dream. As in its incarnation under Hu, the harmony envisaged through Xi's Chinese dream can only be achieved by way of exclusion of dreams that do not align with the aims of a China dreamed up by the PRC leadership.

One incorrect dream that has needed stamping out is the dream of independence or increased autonomy for Xinjiang. In the midst of violent clashes and suppression in the region in 2014, the PRC government published a white paper that explained that 'all Chinese people are striving to realize the Chinese Dream of the great rejuvenation of the Chinese nation', and that as part of that dream 'the XPCC [the Xinjiang Production and Construction Corps] lives in harmony with all ethnic groups ... promotes religious harmony [and] ... advocates harmonious development' (State Council, 2014a: IV). Clearly, there are Chinese citizens in Xinjiang who do not share this view of the state of affairs, or the aims of the party-state, but there can be no room for their dreams in Xi's dream of harmony.

Another incorrect dream is that of democratic reform in Hong Kong, which culminated in the 'umbrella revolution' in 2014. In the build-up to that conflict, the PRC government published a white paper which explained that 'confused or lopsided ... understanding of "one country, two systems"' failed to see it as a 'holistic concept' under the 'unitary state' of China's central government (State Council, 2014b: V). Only by learning, it said, 'can the "two systems" in the "one country" coexist harmoniously' (State Council, 2014b: V). It called on the people of Hong Kong to 'achieve the broadest unity under the banner of loving the country and Hong Kong with strengthened social harmony' as an 'integral part of the Chinese dream' (State Council, 2014b: V, conclusion). Harmony, in this vision, means submission to the central government and renunciation of the dream of a democratic Hong Kong.

The most widely debated 'incorrect' dream has been the dream of constitutionalism. In January 2013 the state-controlled newspaper *Southern Weekend*

(*Nanfang Zhoumo*) tried to publish a new year message entitled 'The Chinese Dream: A Dream of Constitutionalism'. The message called for legal limits to party-state power, and suggested that 'the real "Chinese dream" is a dream for freedom and constitutional government' (Nanfang Zhoumo quoted in Callahan, 2015b: 222; Bandurski, 2013a). Only with a division of powers, said one passage, could China become a free and strong country. The editorial was censored by the provincial propaganda chief, and replaced by a version titled 'The Chinese Dream is Nearer to Us Than Ever Before', which endorsed the national dream of strong state power. Several journalists went on strike in protest against this censorship, and the incident sparked a long discussion in China about the relationship between the state and its citizens (*The Economist*, 2013). This period of protest and heated debate demonstrates that a significant number of Chinese people still harbour strong attachment to their dreams of constitutionalism and media freedom. Despite its best efforts, the party-state is struggling to confine a multiplicity of actually existing dreams within the parameters of national rejuvenation as prescribed by the CCP.

The Chinese dream in academic discourse

As noted above, the Chinese dream was already widely discussed among academics and public intellectuals before Xi launched it as an official slogan.[5] Nevertheless, this launch soon led to a burgeoning literature on the concept, which elaborated on its significance to International Relations (IR) scholarship.[6] In contrast to academic literature on the 'harmonious world' policy term, scholarly analyses of the 'Chinese dream' slogan have paid considerable attention to its multiple simultaneous meanings, including its deployment as a critical tool.[7] Encouraging as this diversity is, many scholars followed Xi in striving to elucidate the one true meaning of the Chinese dream and dispel alleged 'misunderstandings', just as they had done with Hu's 'harmonious world'. For example, Wang Zheng, a prominent scholar of Chinese historical memory and foreign policy, noted that while this dream was 'applauded enthusiastically at home, people outside of China have struggled to ascertain the precise meaning of Xi's statement' (Wang Zheng, 2013). A number of media sources outside mainland China also tapped into this idea and asked 'What does the "Chinese dream" really mean?' (Mendis, 2013; Patience, 2013; Yoon, 2013; Grammaticas, 2013). Accordingly, Wang called for Chinese elites to 'work on helping the outside world understand what exactly the Chinese Dream is. Only by doing this can the Chinese Dream be comprehended and blessed by China's neighbours and the international community' (Wang Zheng, 2013). As in previous instances of the discourse of harmonism, correct understanding is said to be something that the Chinese elites naturally have and that non-Chinese outsiders need to be taught.[8]

If one looks to Chinese-language publications, however, it quickly becomes clear that academic advocates of the Chinese dream have had their work cut out also in correcting 'misunderstandings' within the PRC and its academic community.

Accordingly, Han Qingxiang from the CCP's Central Party School has urged Chinese scholars to:

> supply the 'Chinese dream' with scholarly elucidation and scholarly support, deeply excavate and bring to light the content possessed, the political wisdom contained, and the new thinking embodied in the 'Chinese dream', as quickly as possible eliminate the divergence and misconceptions of some people based on scholarly principles.[9]
>
> (Han Qingxiang, 2013)

In such a context, most Chinese-language texts on the Chinese dream play it safe and take it to build on or include the established idea of a harmonious world. For example, Mu Ren explains that 'harmonious society' is the fundamental essence of the Chinese dream, and 'harmonious world' is its projection to the outside (2014: 28, 31–2).[10] A vast majority also repeat the underpinning assumptions about time, space and difference seen in previous articulations of 'harmonious world' and in government discourse on the Chinese dream. This is what one would expect – after all, scholars do not invent completely new research agendas with every new slogan, but often pursue pre-existing interests with some modification. In addition, many Chinese scholars write closely to the official government take on international affairs – partly because of the opportunities offered and penalties avoided by such an approach, partly perhaps as a symptom of 'patriotic worrying'.

The harmonious Chinese dream of surpassing the West and the United States

At the same time as most scholars write closely to party-state rhetoric on the Chinese dream, the academic process of elucidation inevitably pushes researchers to comment on areas of international politics that Xi himself has largely ignored or actively avoided in public. A most notable difference between official and academic discourse has been comparisons of the Chinese dream with other national dreams, and in particular the American dream.[11] The key message that comes out of these comparisons aligns with the dichotomizing academic discourse seen under Hu Jintao: China is the good, moral and rising leader of 'the Global South'; the United States is the bad, immoral and declining leader of 'the Global North' or 'the West'.[12]

One of the most vocal commentators on the Chinese dream, and its relation to America, has been Professor Hu Angang. Hu sits on the committee that works out China's five-year plans on social and economic development, and leads a research centre at the prestigious Tsinghua University. He wrote before Xi's deployment of the Chinese dream about the need for a new 'great leap forward' that would enable China to economically surpass the United States by 2020, in order not only to rejuvenate China but to replace the current US-led world order with a world of Great Harmony (*Datong shijie* 大同世界) led by China and the

Global South (Hu Angang and Yan Yilong, 2010; Hu Angang *et al*., 2011; Hu Angang, 2011, 2013a, 2013b).

Like many in Chinese academia, Hu Angang dreams of a future that mixes socialism with Confucianism in selective ways, projecting back to claim that Great Harmony was Confucius' own Chinese dream (Hu Angang *et al*., 2011: 4, Hu Angang, 2013a).[13] Based on this legacy:

> The Chinese people … not only untiringly seeks the 'Chinese dream', she also unceasingly pursues the 'World dream', that is the dream of the 'Great Peace of All-under-heaven' (*Tianxia taiping* 天下太平), 'All-under-heaven held in common' (*Tianxia weigong* 天下为公), the 'World of Great Harmony' (*shijie Datong* 世界大同).
>
> (Hu Angang, 2013a)

Here, the harmonious world of which the Chinese people and the world are said to dream is framed in the holistic terms of *Tianxia* and *Datong*. As we have seen in previous chapters, both of these terms emphasize all-encompassing hierarchy in harmony. Although Hu Angang also refers to harmony with diversity (*he'er butong* 和而不同), he strongly emphasizes harmony as unity. 'Harmonism' or 'harmony thought' (*hehe sixiang* 和合思想) are the 'fountainhead' of the great rejuvenation of Chinese civilization (Hu Angang, 2013a). In order for this World of Great Harmony to exist, he writes, we need to abolish borders and gaps between peoples and between countries, and 'merge civilizations' into a world characterized by the 'symbiosis' of an all-encompassing and integrated community of destiny and benefit (Hu Angang *et al*., 2011: 193, 216; Hu Angang, 2013a). On our way to such a goal, Hu Angang thinks China will lead the Global South in competition against the Global North, in a hierarchy that will only be positive when China has reached its top position and broken the cultural hegemony of the North (Hu Angang, 2013a).[14]

Another scholar who was an important part of debates surrounding the Chinese dream even before Xi made it an official slogan is Colonel Liu Mingfu. Liu's 2010 book *The Chinese Dream* (*Zhongguomeng* 中国梦) was widely discussed in debates about 'harmonious world', and became even more influential after the Chinese dream became official policy.[15] Some suggest that Liu's discussions of the Chinese dream are especially important because many of his recommendations have been taken up by the Xi leadership (Callahan, 2015a: 988).

If the PRC's political leadership has tended to emphasize what it considers win–win situations, Liu is unabashed in his zero-sum understanding of power. Like Hu Angang, he draws on Mao's discussion of China surpassing America, arguing that this should be China's great contribution to humanity as well as the key aim of the Chinese dream. Liu explicitly falls back on the same framework of spatial units in historical sequence that we have seen underpin both government rhetoric and much previous scholarship. 'If China cannot become the world number one in the twenty-first century', he proclaims, 'if it cannot become the top power, then it will inevitably become a straggler that is cast aside' (Liu

Mingfu, 2010: 9). In order to avoid falling behind in this way, Liu advocates rebalancing the PRC from civil to military power with the clear goal of making the PRC the world's number one power in a racial struggle between 'yellows' and 'whites' where China needs to destroy the old order and win over the United States (Liu Mingfu, 2010: 22).[16] Accordingly, in a recent discussion of the Chinese dream, Liu conjures the 'moral lesson' of China's 'century of calamity' to urge China to be a heroic nation, as opposed to a mediocre nation that loses battles (Liu Mingfu, 2014). The lesson he learns is that a prerequisite for China's peaceful rise is the courage and physical strength of its 'combat rise' (*zhandou jueqi* 战斗崛起). Liu warns with Marx that 'those who are content with things as they are, are doomed to be defeated', with Roosevelt that 'nations without a martial spirit are sure to decline', and with Stalin that 'the one who is happy can be trampled over' (Liu Mingfu, 2014). He wants the Chinese to be more proactive, more martial and more assertive in countering American power, and ends his book by calling for Chinese actors to be more alert to 'China collapse' arguments in order to prevent their predictions from coming true (Liu Mingfu, 2010: 290; see Callahan, 2014: 155, for a discussion). With its focus on destroying its challengers, this imagination is clearly not one of 'harmony with difference', but a struggle for civilizational survival where the only option for China is to struggle its way to the top through military might.

Zhao Tingyang, whose work on a renewed 'All-under-heaven' system (*Tianxia*) has remained influential in recent Chinese dream talk, had compared 'the American dream, the European dream and the Chinese dream' already in 2006 (Zhao Tingyang, 2006b). Returning to the comparison in 2014, Zhao still advocates relational rationality and *Tianxia*, presented as the holistic, all-encompassing and good alternative to a contemporary Western-led modernity that is competitive, divisive and bad. He draws these notions from Chinese history, but hopes that they will one day be realized as a 'world dream' (Zhao Tingyang, 2014: 141). However, Zhao suggests that the competition of values and systems in global times will not pit East against West, socialism against liberalism, or democracy against authoritarianism. Instead, the competition will be between 'the modernity of exclusive subjectivity' and 'the globality of coexistential trans-subjectivity' (Zhao Tingyang, 2014: 140). Most interestingly, although the modernity that Zhao criticizes is led by 'the West', it also includes the Chinese dream.

To Zhao, the Chinese dream is a dream of Westernization, because the challenge of modern Western powers made it necessary for China to adapt modernization in order to survive (Zhao Tingyang, 2014: 129). Zhao recognizes that the turn he laments, from a universalist *Tianxia* ideal to Chinese exceptionalism, had begun already in 221 BC, when the Zhou Dynasty's 'netlike world system' was eclipsed by the establishment of a Chinese empire that reduced it 'from an ideal for the world to a dream for China' (Zhao Tingyang, 2014: 129). With the Marxist dream of modernization China further transformed into 'a nation dependent on the Western system and game' of antagonistic competition (Zhao Tingyang, 2014: 130). On this view, this may have been necessary, but resulted in 'a paradoxical dream of the revival of China by the simultaneous devaluation of China' (Zhao Tingyang, 2014: 130). Chinese leaders try to evade this paradox through the awkward notion of 'modernization with Chinese characteristics' (Zhao Tingyang, 2014: 130, 134), but where Marxist doctrine 'is essentially a doctrine of revolution and liberation in the framework of antagonistic struggle', Zhao suggests that 'almost all traditional Chinese political and ethical theories advocate peace, harmony and compatibility' (Zhao Tingyang, 2014: 137–8). The real 'Chinese characteristics' are not the values of Marxism or even Confucianism, but a methodology of flexibility that finds its roots in Daoism and the *Book of Changes* (*I-Ching*), and that emphasizes changeability, prudence and 'the natural approach to understand and accept the future of unpredictable possibilities' (Zhao Tingyang, 2014: 135–6). Against this background, Zhao dreams of a non-fundamentalist ideal where 'every concept or principle can be reinterpreted or redefined to fit the conditions' (Zhao Tingyang, 2014: 136).

Zhao's emphasis on trans-subjectivity, change, anti-fundamentalism and unpredictable futures here certainly gestures towards the kinds of multiplicities that are of concern in this book. At the same time, it raises the question of who gets to redefine our concepts, in order to fit what conditions. To Zhao's mind, the methodology of flexibility demands that 'everything should be changed to be good in order to be for good' (Zhao Tingyang, 2014: 136). As in previous articulations of *Tianxia* harmony, there is no recognition in Zhao's discussion of the Chinese dream that different views on what is methodologically 'good' may exist and be valid.

On the one hand, Zhao is sceptical of American, European and modern Chinese dreams alike, because they are unlikely to be universalized without disastrous consequences (Zhao Tingyang, 2014: 139). On the other hand, he is clear that the methodology of flexibility that he describes as the 'essence' of Chineseness is where the future lies. Some modern powers, especially America, are 'still trying to spoil others' dreams by the never updated modern strategies' of containment, deterrence, sanction and war (Zhao Tingyang, 2014: 139). This approach is outdated because globalization has brought about total inevitable interdependence and a 'new ontological condition of coexistence' (Zhao Tingyang, 2014: 139). This condition requires that the rules of the game change and the dream of modernity transform into a dream of establishing globality as envisaged in *Tianxia*. In other words, America is not only bad, it is behind the times. Or, as Zhao puts it: '[i]t is impossible to foresee what the future will be, but I believe the future has sent us a message about what should not be' (2014: 140). Zhao is being deceptively humble here about his own ambitions at fortune-telling: he is clear that the vision imagined based on Chinese historical thought is 'the only way' to development, and 'the next mission of the methodological China must be to develop the ideal of China so as to establish the order for the globalized world' (Zhao Tingyang, 2014: 140).

The Chinese dreams of Hu Angang, Liu Mingfu and Zhao Tingyang show the diversity of economic, military and moral Chinese dreams. They also show how anti-Americanism has become part and parcel of the debate surrounding the articulation of harmony through the Chinese dream (for other influential examples, see

Zhang Weiwei, 2014; Yue Daiyun, 2013). They claim that the Chinese dream is the world dream, including a retrospective ideal of harmony to which the Chinese have privileged access. This view is reinforced by Chinese diplomats and official media (Hua Shiping, 2013; Tian Wenlin, 2013). Much of these debates bring together apparently contradictory texts in 'a new form of statism that is involved in a global competition of social models: the China dream versus the American dream' (Callahan, 2015a: 986). What they have in common, on this understanding, is not so much a positive vision as a common opposition to the United States and the West.

The harmonious Chinese dream of overcoming Western IR theory

Scholars like Hu Angang emphasize the need for knowledge to serve the Chinese party-state, where young people in particular 'should strive to achieve the "Chinese Dream" and learn knowledge for the people, for our country' (Hu Angang, 2014: 5, 13). It is similarly commonplace for scholars to link the Chinese dream to notions of soft power and knowledge production (Cai Mingzhao, 2013; Wang Yiwei, 2013; Zhang Weiwei, 2014; Han Qingxiang, 2013; Zeng Xiangming, 2014). It is of little surprise, then, that some prominent proponents of the 'Chinese school' idea proclaimed a 'Chinese dream' in IR theory soon after Xi came to power. The suggestion came from Professor Wang Yiwei and colleague Han Xueqing (2013). In Chapter 2, we saw Wang point to the alignment of spatial difference in time as a problem of 'Western thought', and offer 'harmonious world' as a Chinese and better alternative. Now Wang and Han put forward a 'Chinese dream' that the emerging Chinese paradigm will overcome the pitfalls of Western IR theory in order to replace it as the dominant school of IR theory. On this view, Chinese approaches to IR can form the integrative framework within which Western IR theory sits:

> Encouraged by Chinese inclusiveness of Indian Buddhism into Chinese Zen, China can also include Western universalism into a Chinese theoretical framework. As a consequence, the Chinese dream in IR will turn into reality with the full shaping of global China.
>
> (Wang Yiwei and Han Xueqing, 2013: 38)

Here, diversity is subsumed under the Chinese dream of IR theory, which goes hand in hand with China's rise more widely. China will surpass Western IR theory because it has three things that Western IR does not: ethical idealism (*daode lixiang* 道德理想), Tianxiaism (*Tianxia zhuyi* 天下主义) and harmonious ideas (*hexie linian* 和谐理念) (Wang Yiwei and Han Xueqing, 2013: 32–7). As in policy discourse, we see the theme of harmony (and the notion of *Tianxia* that has become integral to it) as a core component of the new Chinese dream idea in IR theory.

Wang and Han point out that Chinese IR theory harbours 'harmony with difference', but this harmony is negated because it is then used to support the same linear notion of time and space that we have seen in previous accounts. Harbouring 'harmony with difference' is what differentiates the Chinese dream from the universalist American dream – and what therefore makes it a model for Americans and all others to follow. They can (and will) be subsumed under this Chinese dream. For this reason, the posited future Chinese IR theory will contribute to making not only the discipline of IR, but also the 'real world' out there 'a better place' than that which Western IR theory has to offer (Wang Yiwei and Han Xueqing, 2013: 39).

In the spirit of eliminating 'misunderstandings' discussed above, and in parallel with his call for a displacement of Western IR theory, Wang Yiwei also published an essay with nationalist outlet *Global Times*, called 'Debunking Ten Misconceptions of the Ideal of the Chinese Dream' (Wang Yiwei, 2013). The ten misconceptions, according to Wang, are that the Chinese dream: (1) is equal to China's dream; (2) will replace the American dream; (3) is just a new form of utopia; (4) signifies China's abandonment of the communist ideal; (5) does not include reform through trial and error; (6) is just a dream of constitutionalism, of human rights or of democracy; (7) is just a dream of modernization; (8) is just a dream of rejuvenation; (9) is just a dream of China's rise; and (10) is the incarnation of Chinese liberal nationalism.[17] The most interesting thing about Wang's list of misconceptions is the simple fact that he felt compelled to write it. This compulsion is surely an indication of the de facto diversity of interpretations that the Chinese dream has conjured up. It also demonstrates again the simultaneous claim to accommodate such multiplicity and the perceived need to 'debunk' and 'eliminate' it. Another interesting aspect is Wang's compulsion to blame misunderstandings on 'foreigners', some of whom are allegedly 'trying to slander the Chinese dream as spiritual opium, which will cover social conflicts and hypnotize Chinese people to be less reform-minded' (Wang Yiwei, 2013).

Through these arguments, Wang taps into a common line of reasoning in discussions of the Chinese dream, which begins by asserting the need for harmonious pluralism and exalting the Chinese nation for upholding it, only to then dismiss divergent understandings as 'misunderstandings' that are typically blamed on 'foreign' or 'Western' politicians, media or thought (for other examples, see Zhou Junjun, 2014: 1; Zhang Xiaoming, 2014: 17). Wang's academic intervention into debates over the Chinese dream rings familiarly with imaginations of time, space and multiplicity that we now recognize from the party-state discourse of harmonism under both Hu Jintao and Xi Jinping, as well as academic discussions of it by thinkers like Hu Angang, Liu Mingfu and Zhao Tingyang. Callahan also suggests that the rhetoric of 'harmony with difference' that arguably dominated Hu Jintao's early leadership has decreased in popularity since the mid-2000s, while positioning Great Harmony as China's long-term goal has become very popular in the last few years (Callahan, 2015a: 996). We can observe a parallel shift in the gradual linguistic displacement of 'harmonious world' by the 'Chinese dream'. Indeed, by early 2015 a scholarly article reached publication which discussed the thought of scholars like Zhao Tingyang and Wang Yiwei – and what had a few years earlier been referred to as 'harmonist discourses' (Son, 2012) – in terms of an emerging '"Chinese dream" in international relations theory' (Do, 2015: 21).

Wang and Han suggest that their Chinese dream in IR theory can be realized in three ways: by reviving Chinese cultural tradition; by de-Westernizing (and de-Americanizing in particular); and by constructing IR theory that 'originates in China and belongs to the world' (Wang Yiwei and Han Xueqing, 2013: 38–9). As in the imagination of time and space discussed in this and previous chapters, this claim builds on a separation between 'China' and 'the West', where 'China' is constructed as superior, and 'the West' as something that should be contained, assimilated or exterminated (as we may put it with reference to Inayatullah and Blaney, 2004). In this story, the dream of a better and more harmonious world spreads in an inside-to-outside movement from China to the rest of the world. Others' dreams may or may not be within the realm of the acceptable, but they are certainly *particular* dreams aligned with particular interests, as opposed to the *universal* world dream that comes from Chinese thought but that is in everyone's interest.[18] Internationally, there is recognition that this ethno-nationalist Chinese dream needs to accommodate other countries' legitimate, reasonable or fair interests – but little recognition that opinions may diverge as to what constitutes a legitimate interest or demand (for other examples, see Zhou Junjun, 2014: 1). Such a judgement is not recognized as political, and so the opening of the Chinese dream to a politicized view of harmony and of the world's futures remains elusive.

To tie this back to our discussion in previous chapters, those chapters showed how policy and academic discussions of the Chinese dream of a harmonious world under Hu Jintao tended towards an imagination of others as 'behind' China. Time, space and multiplicity were organized in an allochronic manner that placed China at the head of a historical queue, where Chinese leadership appeared natural because of the alleged historic predisposition to harmony of the Chinese state or culture. We have seen here that this alignment of spatial units in temporal sequence reappears together with the language of harmony in discussions of the Chinese dream. Although the new slogan has begun to replace 'harmonious world', it repeats the same tropes and incorporates the same language of world harmonization. As in previous incarnations, this is a depoliticizing move, which makes it hard to imagine multiplicity in the here and now, and open futures for China and the world. By negating the possibilities of genuine multiplicity in the here and now in this way, it also negates the possibility of harmony, since diversity in the here and now is its precondition. In this way, the Chinese dream continues to make the possibility of a harmonious world disappear.

The Chinese dream in propaganda

Given its track record in the sphere of 'thought management' (Brady, 2011), and the concern over misunderstandings of the Chinese dream, it is unsurprising that the party-state launched a massive public education effort to secure its impact. In the context of what has been described as 'the re-birth and modernization of the

Chinese propaganda state', plans for propaganda work at local levels were published (Brady, 2008: 200).[19] As with 'harmony' after 2004–5, the Chinese dream became a topic for speaking competitions and flower displays at schools. It was propagated on Sina Weibo, WeChat and other social media platforms. It was given its own pages by government-run media outlets. Party officials selected model dreamers to give inspirational speeches in workplaces. The Chinese dream was given voice by the *X-Factor*-style television programme *The Voice of the Chinese Dream* (*Zhongguo meng zhi sheng* 中国梦之声), as well as by Chen Sisi, star of a song-and-dance group run by China's nuclear-missile corps, in a ballad dedicated to the slogan that topped folk-song charts in early 2013. In December the same year, *Xinhua* declared the 'Chinese dream' the 'most popular word' of that year (The China Story, 2013; *Xinhua*, 2013a). By 2015, it was decided that the Chinese dream should be worked into Chinese school textbooks, at the same time as universities are reportedly told to limit the use of foreign textbooks in order to stem infiltration of 'Western values' (Chen and Zhuang Pinghui, 2015). In what follows, we will trace parts of this mass proliferation through propaganda in the form of a poster campaign themed on the 'Chinese dream'. We will do so by first looking at some of this poster campaign itself, and then at how its proliferation has been re-rendered in independent artistic form.

The Chinese dream poster campaign

A particularly visible part of the public education effort has been the use of propaganda posters in primarily urban space. As Mike Gow describes it:

> Go to any major city in China, walk down any street and I guarantee you will be within 50 m of a poster listing the 12 core principles of socialism that have become the central pillars of president Xi Jinping's 'China Dream'.
>
> (Gow, 2015)

Indeed, mass propaganda on notice boards, billboards and bus stops have become a staple of Chinese urban scenery.[20] The 12 core principles of socialism to which Gow refers were proposed by the Eighteenth National Congress, and include prosperity, democracy, civility, harmony, freedom, equality, justice, rule of law, patriotism, dedication, integrity and friendship (*People's Daily*, 2014). These values had been propagated in artistic form since Xi's early days in power, including by an extensive series of posters that were designed under the Public Service Advertising Art Committee (PSAAC) and published by China Internet Television Station. They first went up around July 2013, and have been ubiquitous ever since. The posters are interesting because they clearly visualize the ideological shift that took place under Hu Jintao and has continued under Xi Jinping and his Chinese dream, which no longer focuses only on socialism and modernization, but increasingly also on the 'Chinese characteristics' of premodern traditions like Confucianism and harmony.

A key poster in the campaign shows a clay figure of a young, fair-skinned and plump girl – a Chinese model child embodied in a traditional figurine seen in Figure 5.1 (see also PSAAC, 2015e). Beside her, big characters announce 'the Chinese dream, my dream'. The message echoes Xi's insistence that individual dreams coincide with the national purpose. In smaller characters beside her, a poem portrays a 'dream-eyed' girl, and concludes: 'Ah China, my dream, a truly fragrant dream.' The poem is written by pro-government blogger Xie Shaoqing, who writes under the pen name Yi Qing. His writings are extensively reprinted on posters, mostly in the form of homilies and party slogans – a complement to the new-left material he publishes on his blog, including attacks on the *Southern Weekend* paper that got in trouble for suggesting that the Chinese dream may be a dream of constitutionalism (Johnson, 2013).

The Chinese dream of a harmonious world is integral to this propaganda effort, and the language of harmony features prominently within the posters' depictions of the Chinese dream. A range of harmony-themed posters advertise slogans like 'the Chinese dream, treasuring harmony' (*Zhongguo meng, he wei gui* 中国梦 和为贵); 'heart of China: harmony' (*Zhongguo xin, he* 中国心·和); 'China full of harmony' (*heman Zhonghua* 和满中华); and 'harmony, the most beautiful poem' (*he, zuimei de shipian* 和 最美的诗篇) (PSAAC, 2015a, 2015b, 2015c, 2015d, 2015f). The illustrations of these posters do not feature the hi-tech

Figure 5.1 'The Chinese dream, my dream', Beijing 2013 (source: Astrid H. M. Nordin).

futures of the Shanghai Expo or the Olympic dream, but romanticized versions of a rural life full of fat geese, golden fields, pristine villages and lively ducklings. Accompanying poems describe singing children and lotus ponds, moonlight and white feathers, and conclude with lines such as 'Chinese dream, wish for peace' (*Zhongguo mengxiang, heping xiwang* 中国梦乡，和平希望) and 'China joy of all ages, people's hearts carry harmony at their centre!' (*Zhonghua fu wandai, renxin zaizhong he* 中华福万代，人心载中和!). Traditional symbols of purity, joy and health populate the posters in the form of pairs of fish, lotus flowers and the five bats that symbolize the five traditional blessings of a long life, wealth, health, love of virtue and a peaceful death. This symbolism of the bat (*fu* 蝠) stems from its pronunciation, which sound like the word for good fortune (*fu* 福). The bats can be seen in the poster in Figure 5.2, with the title, 'harmony, flourishing national destiny' (*he guoyunchang* 和 国运昌).

The medium is clearly part of the message of these posters. Where the Shanghai Expo's aesthetics relied on interactive digital hi-tech for blurring the lines between subject and object, this campaign relies most heavily on the traditional medium of paper posters. Propaganda posters of this kind have a long tradition in China, where they were a key feature under Mao (Landsberger and van der Heijden, 2008; Barmé, 2012). Xi's Chinese dream poster campaign flirts by its choice of medium and aesthetics with this Maoist tradition. However, where

Figure 5.2 'Harmony, flourishing national destiny', Beijing 2013 (source: Astrid H. M. Nordin).

campaigns of the Mao era often shared an international modernist aesthetic, particularly with Soviet propaganda, the aesthetics of this campaign emphasizes pre-communist and distinctly Chinese traditions. The art in these posters comes from well-known folk art institutions – peasant paintings from Henan's Wuyang, woodblock prints from the Yangliuqing workshops outside Tianjin and paintings by late Shanghai artist Feng Zikai (Johnson, 2013).

For this reason, commentators have interpreted the Chinese dream poster campaign as 'a redefinition of the state's vision from a Marxist utopia to a Confucian, family-centric nation, defined by a quiet life of respecting the elderly and saving for the future' (Johnson, 2013; also cited in Landsberger, 2014). It is as representations of this vision that Ian Johnson reports of vandalized advertisements in Beijing, where posters from the Chinese dream series, including that of the clay figurine shown above, were tagged by a graffiti artist and slashed. Johnson suggests that this slashing indicates a political motive, perhaps opposition to the growing leftist tendency in official propaganda (where I take 'leftism' to indicate a less liberal and more Maoist position in favour of a strong state; Johnson, 2013).

Stefan R. Landsberger approvingly cites Johnson's comment on a redefined state vision, and continues:

> The shift from ambition to dream in itself is proof of the depoliticisation PRC society has gone through in the past thirty-plus years. While Marxism-Leninism-Mao Zedong Thought remains constitutionally enshrined as the guiding ideologies of the PRC and Deng reappropriated Mao's dictum that practice is the sole criterion of truth as his own, a discursive space has emerged in which (wishful) thinking – or dreaming – no longer can be considered a metaphysical, counterrevolutionary activity.
>
> (Landsberger, 2014: 271)

What I think Landsberger means by 'depoliticization' here is a turn away from revolutionary Maoist ideology. In Mao's China, 'thinking otherwise' was a counterrevolutionary thing to do, based on bourgeois metaphysics as opposed to historical materialism. What has emerged since Mao's death is something more flexible, where some diversity of dreams does not pose as obvious a threat to 'the truth' of the party line as it once did. If this is what Landsberger means, I think he is right. At the same time, I think we can read his comment as an even more pertinent proposition: that the discursive shifts we have noted under the Hu and Xi administrations have ended the possibility of subversive thought, because it has made metaphysics impossible. Put differently, it is no longer possible to imagine any position or organizing principle outside current practices, or any foundation for supporting or opposing the Chinese dream. This is a shift we have already identified with a move from the real to the hyper-real, where there is no distinction between the real and the dream. We can also read this shift in the Chinese dream posters.

The nationalism of the posters is certainly ideological in its mix of dreams and truth claims. Like the Shanghai Expo, the posters are a digest of the Chinese way of life, a panegyric to Chinese values and an idealized transposition of contradictory reality. At the same time, the particularism of China, or the difference between China and other places, is one of equivalence. It recycles a format of nation-branding recognizable from the Shanghai Expo, where each nation repeats the same celebration of its own particularity and heritage, on a pattern that is endlessly the same. What is more, we see here again the exhuming ritual through which the Chinese state engages and denies its own past. There is a desire in these romantic images of rural harmony for an unspoiled past and an origin that would provide a different set of values on which to build the dream of a different, better and harmonious China, and a different, better and harmonious world. As I suggest throughout this book, the co-optation of this past into the present propaganda seems to be enough to slowly exterminate that dream of harmony and of meaningful difference. We recognize, once again, the same recycling pattern of rediscovery and exterminating conversion.

The format is also recognizable from non-state advertising by commercial brands. The 'Chinese values' offered by Xi's slogans are presented as a Chinese and better alternative to Western values of consumerism, individualism and materialism. Simultaneously, they are promoted as consumer goods, advertised by posters that use emotive imagery and catchphrases to make us want to acquire them – just as other commercial advertising does, in the same urban areas, on the same billboards. Scholar Wang Meiqin pertinently notes:

> Turning every Chinese citizen into a consumer, regardless of his or her original social background or class status, has become a widely accepted Chinese dream. Consequently, advertisements have assumed a commanding role, indistinguishably employed by both official entities and private corporations.
>
> (Wang Meiqin, 2015: 180)

Indeed, we may ask, '[w]hat can be more revealing for a society that adopts consumerism as its primary ideology than the ubiquitous presence of political slogans advertised like commercial brands?' (Wang Meiqin, 2015: 178).

A closer look at the medium of advertising the Chinese dream then begins to break down its purported differentiation from the image of a consumerist American dream, blurring once more the attempt at positioning China as the 'other country'. Although the poster campaign's insistence on authenticity does not leave room for much of the self-reflection and irony seen in the Expo, surrounding reflection on these political advertisements bring to the fore the relation between the different functions or orders of images that we have previously discussed – those that dissimulate something and those that dissimulate that there is nothing. A case in point is the artwork of photographer Ni Weihua.

Ni Weihua's photography

Ni, born in 1962, is based in Shanghai and has made party-state slogans and their advertisement in public space the focus of his documentary photography. In series of photographs, of billboards featuring various political 'keywords', Ni has documented the way in which official political slogans have become an indispensable part of the scenery in people's daily life through repetition, spread and infiltration (Wang Nanming and Wang Xueyun, 2008: 26; also described in Wang Meiqin, 2015: 178). He has focused his work on keywords including 'development' (*fazhan* 发展), 'harmony' (*hexie* 和谐) and most recently 'the Chinese dream' (*Zhongguo meng* 中国梦). Ni also refers to these as 'advertising words', emphasizing how they are advertised like commercial products.

Drawing on LeFebvre and other Western Marxists, Ni understands social space as a product of human practice that is full of power struggles (Wang Nanming and Wang Xueyun, 2008: 129; see also Wang Meiqin, 2015: 179). Commercial forces and political ideology collude in this space to form the most powerful form of control over Chinese citizens in contemporary times, manifested through ever-present billboards (Wang Nanming and Wang Xueyun, 2008: 26; see also Wang Meiqin, 2015: 179). For example, many of the photographs in the *Keyword: Harmony* series depict building sites advertising 'harmonious demolition' near the Shanghai Expo, after the forced evictions of previous residents (see Wang Meiqin, 2015: 186 for further commentary). On Wang's interpretation, such slogans have inserted themselves as accepted reality. By capturing them on camera, Ni turns such reality into 'a visual text that allows us to examine the manifestation of political power' (Wang Meiqin, 2015: 186). From such a viewpoint, a tension can be seen to arise in a number of the photographs, between the messages of harmonious dreams purported by the billboards in the background, and individuals who walk into the photographic frame to appear in the foreground. This tension is particularly visible when they highlight disharmony between the consumerist dreams of the wealthy and the real inability of poor workers and rural migrants to access that dream, even as they are literally constructing it.

On one level, we may then understand Ni's work on propaganda posters as revealing a hidden reality: the collusion of consumerism and ideology in China, the way the poor are excluded from the supposedly inclusive Chinese dream, and the chasm between lived reality and virtual dreams. However, Wang also suggests at one point that 'perhaps the artist intends to pose a question here: does it matter anymore whether one confuses the real with the virtual?' (Wang Meiqin, 2015). Intended or not, this is a question that I think Ni's work poses, though not simply because of the visual confusion between the 'real' in the foreground and the 'virtual' that appears on the background billboards.

The collapse of the real and the virtual that I think Ni's photography points us towards is highlighted, in my view, by the sheer volume of photographs generated by his *Keyword* series. Each of his keywords is depicted in thousands of photographs from different sites in Shanghai and other parts of China. This mass highlights the excessive proliferation since the mid-2000s, of harmony and of the Chinese dream, which this book argues robs both of the possibility of meaning. As commentators point out, the definition of the Chinese dream is left deliberately vague, 'embracing everything from a "spirit of rejuvenation" through to the recent revival of low-tech old-fashioned propaganda posters' (Rawnsley, 2015). We have seen how both harmony and the Chinese dream have proliferated into all areas of society, not only through billboard advertising, but through mega events, popular songs, essay competitions, scholarly deployments, train lines, first-aid kits, buildings and a range of commercially available merchandise. In 2013, even before the official discourse had been fully rolled out, the Chinese dream already appeared in provincial versions, like the Henan Dream and the Guangdong Dream, as well as in thematic variants, like the Space Dream, the Aircraft-Carrier Dream and the Sports Dream. Reportedly, a hospital specializing in infertility treatments in Chengdu, Sichuan Province, had already begun promoting 'The China Dream, the Pregnancy Dream' (Murong Xuecun, 2013). The Chinese dream had begun to lose any specificity of meaning as soon as it was formulated. Xi's excessive push of it in advertisements since 2013 has only served to exponentially accelerate this implosion.

Through its sheer scale, Ni's work makes this collapse of meaning appear transparently before us. In a sense, though this may not be Ni's intent, it enacts a strategy of excess that is very similar to what this book employs. It shows up the advertised reproductions of harmony and the Chinese dream as a series of copies of copies without original, a series of self-referential signs with no relation to any reality whatsoever (cf. Baudrillard, 1994 [1981]: 6). As a result, it is not enough to understand the Chinese dream, which Xi so desperately tries to propagate, as ideology. Rather, the distinction between the real China and the Chinese dream has collapsed. This shift has not come about, as is sometimes implied by nationalists and government sources, by the PRC fulfilling real and age-old dreams – staging an Expo, hosting the Olympic Games, surpassing America in terms of GDP, steel production or IR-theorizing. Instead, the collapse of the real China and the Chinese dream has meant the complete eradication, not only of a 'real' authentic China, but of the illusion of a better alternative, of a superior Chinese model, Beijing consensus, or any meaningful 'Chinese characteristics'. Why else would Chinese elites need to push so hard to convince others of their existence and basis in reality?

The Chinese dream in online spoofs

The Chinese dream's dispersal of meaning through excessive proliferation has not only taken form through commercial endeavours and documentary photography, but the Chinese Internet and its spoofing culture has been instrumental in this process, as it was in the case of Hu's harmony. Soon after Xi took over its leadership, the party-state began to advocate a 'cyber "Chinese dream" ', achievable by continuing to build a 'healthy online environment' (*People's Daily Online*, 2013b).[21] This included strengthened clampdowns on undesirable words. Despite the use of homonymous puns in its own propaganda posters, it was announced on 27 November 2014 that the State Administration for Press, Publication, Radio, Film and Television was banning puns and wordplay as part of a wider crackdown on *egao* culture and 'offensive language' (Branigan, 2014).

Despite this crackdown, the Internet has been an important space for articulating the diversity of Chinese dreams, including ones that appear to challenge the party-state. Soon after Xi's launch of the Chinese dream slogan, a trend started on Weibo where people held up pieces of paper with their dreams written for all to see, thereby circumventing pre-programmed keyword blocks. Dreams included messages such as 'My Chinese dream is that Xi Jinping protects my personal safety and reproductive rights', 'My Chinese dream is rights for petitioners' and 'My Chinese dream is to have my home returned'. As such, one commentator notes, 'Chinese citizens have hijacked the phrase and turned it into a symbol of China's civic problems, not its civic ideals' (Kuo, 2013).

From the outset, many netizens expressed scepticism about Xi's Chinese dream. Reflecting the relation to the American dream discussed above, one microblogger wrote:

> 'Chinese Dream' appears on television all the time, but I still don't understand; what the so-called 'Chinese Dream' is really about? Is it about making 1.3 billion Chinese people help one organization or one person to fulfil this dream, or, is it about keeping 1.3 billion Chinese daydreaming? [My] research result indicates that the latter is more convincing: keeping 1.3 billion people in a dreamlike state while sending all your children and relatives to the United States to pursue the 'American Dream!'
>
> (@长话短说, or 'make a long story short', cited in Li, 2012)

Other critical articulations of the Chinese dream echo dreams that we have seen party-state articulations exclude as 'incorrect'. For example, while Chen Sisi's ballad gained popularity by lauding the Chinese dream, satirical singer Li Lei wrote what he called 'the people's take' on Xi's new theme. In his lyrics 'The Chinese dream isn't a dream of forced evictions, but of freedom and elections'. Performing to the camera in his trademark karaoke-like style, Li sang about how 'The Chinese dream is the people's dream, a dream of democracy and constitutional government', and 'China's dream isn't one of dictatorship, or authoritarian government; nor is it a deleted dream'. In comments, Li made his motivations clear: 'The government is really making a big deal of this China dream concept right now, so I thought I'd steal their idea and express our own political views, which are different from the official view' (Li Lei, cited in Qiao Long, 2013). Li, who uses the online nickname 'Red Clothes' because of his trademark attire in music videos, said that large numbers of people left comments when he posted his video online, but that it was taken down twice in the same day. It was subsequently reported that searches for 'red clothes', 'the Chinese dream' or 'the people's dream' on popular video-sharing sites 56.com and Youku yielded no results (Qiao Long, 2013; see also Lim, 2013).

The above examples highlight the discrepancy between the party-state's prescribed dream and the multiplicity of dreams that may contradict it, which many express through the old Chinese saying 'we might share the same bed, but we don't share the same dreams' (*tongchuangyimeng* 同床异梦) (Barmé, 2013: 13).

The attempt to manufacture shared dreaming by censoring alternative dreams has ironically resulted in the shared experience of having one's dreams eradicated by the party-state. For example, independent commentator Zhao Chu shared this experience when his sharply worded online essay compared the Chinese dream unfavourably to the American dream. It argued that the top-down nature of the former deprives ordinary people of the right to dream their own dreams. In later comments, Zhao suggests that the deletion of his essay underscores that it was right: 'This is good evidence to show that the dream that unites the people is such a hypocritical concept. When this dream cannot be discussed, how can it be a real dream?' (Zhao Chu, cited in Lim, 2013). In parallel, when scholar Yu Jianrong, who has championed social causes on social media, received a letter notifying him that his latest book would no longer be published, signed off with the traditional 'please respond', Yu responded publicly on Weibo:

> Who knows the name and contact information for the bureau chief of the General Administration on Press and Publication? I want to treat him (or her) to a cup of coffee and a constitutional study session, where we can also discuss Secretary Xi's Chinese Dream.
>
> (Yu Jianrong cited in Henochowicz, 2013d)

To this comment, one supporter replied: 'The government is not smothering just one book, but smothering our "Chinese Dream"' (cited in Henochowicz, 2013d).

In the context of this type of party-state response, one common strand of satirical commentary has referred to the Chinese dream through the imagery of a prison. This comparison gained momentum after the *China Business Journal* posted a series of Weibo screenshots on 7 July 2013, all depicting articles on educational activities in prisons throughout the country based on the theme 'the Chinese dream, the dream of prison, my dream' (Henochowicz, 2013c). Some commentators suggested similarly creative slogan adaptations, like funeral homes holding a series of 'Chinese dream, the dream of cremation, my dream' events, or the sanitation department holding a 'Chinese dream, rubbish dream' essay contest. The tragicomic nature of the prison variation on Xi's slogan also provoked comparisons to life in China, with one commentator suggesting: 'The Chinese dream, the dream of prison. "One wakes suddenly from one's dream to find oneself confined to a cage"'. Another responds: 'Actually, we are all in prison. This statement, ever so pragmatic, is the most conscientious official pronouncement. The Chinese dream, the dream of prison.' A third commentator suggests, with reference to Chinese online censorship: 'Many Chinese people have similar dreams: to scale the wall, to jailbreak' (all cited in Henochowicz, 2013c)

The prison theme returns in many cartoons that depict the more sinister side to life under the Chinese dream. At online media project *China Digital Times*, cartoonist Crazy Crab has produced a series of satirical cartoons under the title *Hexie Farm* (*xienongchang* 蟹农场) since Hu's time in power. The *China*

Digital Times has been an important forum for bringing *egao* culture and Chinese-language dissident views to an English-speaking audience, and the cartoons of *Hexie Farm* are also published with English-language text. Both the 'crab' name of the cartoonist's pen name, and the '*hexie*' of the series title, refer to the harmony/rivercrab double-meaning that was explored in the previous chapter.

Since Xi's ascension to power, Crazy Crab has published a number of cartoons that reference his Chinese dream. In one of these cartoons, Crazy Crab responds to the detention of activists including lawyer Xu Zhiyong, by depicting Xi as a cage with the text 'dream only'. In the image, Xi tries to cover up his cage-body with the suit of reform, while bell-tipped shoes reveal he is a jester (Crazy Crab, 2013d).

The prison theme returns in a commentary on the state of freedom of expression at the time of the ninety-second anniversary of the founding of the CCP in 2013. This cartoon depicts a human head with the top cut off. A barbed-wire fence surrounds the empty space found where the brain would normally be. The barbs are shaped like the hammer and sickle symbol of the CCP, and the fence is adorned with a sign saying 'dream only' (Crazy Crab, 2013a). The enclosed space of the prison also becomes a reference point for the cartoon in the series that is seen in Figure 5.3. This cartoon depicts frogs in a well, including one that

Figure 5.3 'China dream is the best!' (source: *China Digital Times*, Crazy Crab, 2013c).

wears a crown and resembles President Xi. The well is shaped like Tiananmen, the ground around it is red and yellow like the PRC flag. The frogs turn away from two skulls peering out of a corner of the well, and the Xi-frog declares 'China dream is the best!' The image refers to a fable by philosopher Zhuangzi, where a frog in a well is left speechless when a turtle tells him that the world consists of more than the spot of sky he sees from within his well. The term 'frog in a well' is now used to describe someone narrow-minded and ignorant about the world – characteristics which in the picture lead the frogs to see only the Chinese dream (Crazy Crab, 2013c). On one interpretation, the skulls in the corner remind us of those who died on and around Tiananmen Square in 1989, and those who have been similarly 'harmonized' by a ruthless PRC government before and since. On this view, the frog-leaders are callous and cold, unfazed by the evidence of the deaths they have caused. On a different interpretation, however, the skulls can also be seen as a *memento mori*, a warning or reminder of the death to which the frogs themselves are no doubt fated. After all, the Tiananmen-shaped well with its steep walls appears also as a prison for the frogs, from which they seem to have no way of escaping. The dream is doomed to die before it has even had a chance to encounter the surrounding world.

This theme of self-delusion returns in other cartoons in the series. In one, a ship titled both 'China dream' and 'Titanic' is propelled towards 'economy' icebergs by chimneys painted like the PRC flag, while someone from within it declares: 'Believe me! It's unsinkable!' (Crazy Crab, 2013g). Another depicts Xi sleepwalking over a dreamland of dead pigs, in a nod to an incident in 2013 where thousands of pig carcasses were pulled from the Huangpu river. Arrows point the way with the text 'confidence in pigs', in a reference the 'three confidences' of Xi's Chinese dream: 'we should have firm confidence in our path, in our theories and in our system' (Crazy Crab, 2013b). Yet another cartoon depicts China as a dragon in a hospital bed, with the face and eyes bandaged over. The patient's intravenous drip is marked with a skull and bones to indicate poison, administered by three medics wearing robes that each bears the mark of one of Xi's 'three confidences'. The medics' caps have hammer and sickle emblems, and their noses are growing long like Pinocchio's as they fill in one another's sentences and lie to the patient: 'The great Chinese rejuvenation is coming! All you need is ... another dream! ... and three confidences!' (Crazy Crab, 2013e).

Finally, in a comment on online censorship seen in Figure 5.4, we see Xi walking across a tightrope. He departs from a cliff with a knocked-over sign for 'harmonious society', and heads towards the shore of 'rejuvenation' at the far end of the chasm which he tries to navigate. He uses a double-sided club of 'stability' to prevent him from toppling. His effort is made more precarious by protesting netizens, depicted as angry birds with signs saying 'no censorship' and 'anti-Great Firewall (GFW)' (Crazy Crab, 2013f).

From these and other examples, we can see how netizens are reusing the language of Xi's Chinese dream, but with a satirical twist that draws on a range of less flattering associations. Together, they visualize the multiplicity of humorously

Figure 5.4 'The sit-in' (source: *China Digital Times*, Crazy Crab, 2013f).

critical interpretations of Xi's Chinese dream and the emptiness or absence of any shared 'Chinese dream' behind them.

Netizens clearly want to make the point that they would very much appreciate the freedom to choose their own dreams. Many commentators have lauded this articulation of individual dreams as a form of resistance to the party-state's political vision. However, after our discussion of the individual subject coming apart at the Shanghai Expo and of the complex relation between official discourse and its *egao* metastases, we have reason to be cautious about such claims. In the first instance, individuals are interpellated as subjects of the Chinese dream: my dream is the Chinese dream, and the Chinese dream is my dream. Individuals are repeatedly called upon to participate through writing essays on, illustrating or discussing their Chinese dream in various formats. At the same time, individuals are clearly subjected to the Chinese dream – it is only as dreamers that individuals participate in the Chinese dream, and as we have seen, there is significant pressure to dream correctly. By articulating their own dreams, Chinese netizens are participating in the Chinese dream through the type of cancerous or autoimmune relation that was discussed in the previous chapter.

At the same time, this activity also continues the trend we saw in the previous chapter, where Chinese netizens joined in the 'strategy of excess' by renegotiating the language of harmony in playful and satirical ways. Some even reflect on the relation between the multiplicity of Chinese dreams and disappearance. Cartoonist Zhu Senlin, for example, shows a row of beds with individuals dreaming different dreams, perhaps of musical pursuits, a happy retirement or a good education. One dream, however, has been revoked, leaving only the words 'this dream has been deleted by the dream owner', in an invocation of the message received when a microblog post has been removed (Henochowicz, 2013b).

On the same theme of disappearance, an online exchange that was captured and spread by keen observers in 2013 sees one user ask if another post has just been 'harmonized'. The response from a different user is: 'This doesn't suit the times. Shouldn't it be "done away with by a dream" (*bei meng zuodiaole* 被梦做掉了) or "to be dreamed" (*bei zuomengle* 被做梦了)?' No, says a third user, the new phrase should be 'It was dreamed away! (*bei mengdiao* 被梦掉)' (in Bandurski, 2013b). And so, harmony has been harmonized and replaced by the identically empty and impossible Chinese dream. Through proliferating, morphing and metastasizing, it has long ceased to function as the illusion of an ideal, for both the party-state and its allies, and for those who would once dream of using it as a site of resistance. Both harmony and the Chinese dream have been dreamed away and disappeared.

Conclusion

This book and this chapter have examined the appearance and disappearance of the Chinese dream of a harmonious world. They have suggested that notions of both a 'harmonious world' and a 'Chinese dream' fail to deliver the better way of imagining harmonious difference to which they claim to aspire. The book and chapter have also traced the way in which the excessive mass proliferation of this dream of harmony has charged it with so much meaning that it has collapsed under its own weight and disappeared. This is not because it has failed, but because it has succeeded too well and progressed beyond its limit point. This chapter has suggested that the poster campaigns that advertise the Chinese dream of harmony are fascinating, not simply because they are the sites of meaning or representation, but because they are sites of the disappearance of meaning and representation (cf. Baudrillard, 1987: 29).

This disappearance of meaning, of course, does not mean that the Chinese dream of harmony does not have effects. A recent study of the political attitudes of students who have attended propaganda courses at a Chinese university showed that

> those students with more exposure to the courses, in the sense of being able to recollect more teachings from past courses, will be more likely to believe that the government is strong, but not more likely to believe that the government is good.
>
> (Huang Haifeng, 2015)

As Gary Rawnsley has noted, these results indicate that to those at the receiving end of the party-state's propaganda, 'its very presence and consistency act as a signal to deter dissent' by demonstrating the regime's strength (Rawnsley, 2015). This interpretation is certainly plausible, but I would like to also suggest an alternative reading. Perhaps the party-state's perceived need to demonstrate its strength and its power in this way stems from the absence of power. It knows that there is nothing there behind its Chinese dream. All the talk of 'spreading the Chinese spirit' is merely a signal that there is nothing there to spread, it signals the very lack or absence of a Chinese dream in the first place – so that all the regime can do is try to palm it off on others (cf. Baudrillard, 2006: 5, Nordin, 2014a). If the empire's old clothes once made it possible to imagine a beautiful body underneath, the new garb of overexposure and transparency makes it clear that there is no emperor there in the first place.[22]

The nostalgia we see in the Chinese dream posters, then, is not simply for a time when China was strong, pure and stable under Confucian filial hierarchy or Maoist patriotic fervour. The posters' nostalgia is most importantly for the reality principle, for metaphysics, for the possibility to aspire to something different that may once have existed. It is a nostalgia for something other – and for dreaming as a revolutionary or counter-revolutionary and metaphysical activity. Today, any such collective dream (of harmony, of anything) is gone.

In its wake, the Chinese dream of a harmonious world has not left nothing, but rather a set of empty concepts. As an aspiration, if it was ever there, it has already disappeared – but its concepts remain without principles or ends. If the Chinese dream was once a dream of agency, power, change and a harmonious new world, today it has devoured its own utopia and continues without foundation, diffuse, floating and insubstantial. It has become overexposed. Invested with so much meaning, the Chinese dream of a harmonious world appears anywhere and everywhere and lacks the ability to withdraw. Left transparent and exposed in this way, it is stuck in an empty scene where nothing happens or changes (cf. Baudrillard, 1988 [1987]: 32–3). We are beyond the end of the Chinese dream of a harmonious world.

It is in light of these developments that I propose a re-reading of Landsberger's suggestion. Perhaps alternative dreams are no longer subversive, because there is nothing there to subvert any more. No real harmony, and no illusion or dream of it either. No ground from which we can promote or oppose the Chinese dream or its harmony. Perhaps, as this book has suggested in the case of the Shanghai Expo, the ideology functions as a cover for a simulation: the rhetorical insistence on the Chinese dream in propaganda exists in order to hide that it is the 'real' existing China that is dreamed up in the first place (cf. Baudrillard, 1994 [1981]: 12). Its purpose is to make us think that the rest is real.

In other words, the Chinese dream of a harmonious world has not taken place, is not taking place and will not take place. No amount of GDP growth, strengthening of martial spirit or theorizing with Chinese characteristics will remedy this situation or bring back the possibility of aspiration and seduction of the term. All that remains are versions or layers of simulated dreams, without any meaningful distinction between them. This, then, is the logic of the situation, a situation and logic that also see the PRC government caught in a self-defeating dynamic concerning harmony, from which it cannot easily disengage. Thus we see how the government, and many scholars too, are working hard to eradicate alternative dreams, even as they insist on the Chinese dream's inclusive and harmonious nature. This exclusion desperately tries to make us believe that there is a China there, with the power to harmonize, to dream and to aspire to something that we can either endorse or resist. It tries to convince us that there is something at stake. If people can only be provoked into disagreeing with harmony or the Chinese dream, as articulated by the Chinese party-state, then the semblance of meaning, power and aspiration can be upheld.

In this context of disappearing meaning, as the previous chapter also suggested, antagonistic 'resistance' as we are used to think of it may also have become impossible or meaningless. If there is no distinction between the real and the dream, and nothing there to support or resist and no grounds from which to do so, we no longer have the choice of advancing or of retreating, but only of facing up to this radical illusion (Baudrillard, 1994 [1992]: 122–3).

Notes

1 The materials examined in this chapter mirror the kinds of materials that have been examined in each of the previous chapters, with a focus here on the 'Chinese dream' set phrase. The policy discourse examined in the first section of this chapter is important because it shows how the language of harmony has lived on under Xi Jinping's 'Chinese dream' concept. Data in that section is based on processing official publications, speeches and policy documents, including all Chinese government white papers published from Xi's ascension to leadership to mid-2015 in the Chinese and English languages, as well as the annually published *Reports on the Work of Government* in this period. I have moreover sought out additional speeches made by key figures such as President Xi Jinping, Premier Li Keqiang and Foreign Minister Wang Yi, and I have processed written and video materials from Chinese and international news media.

The academic discourse on the Chinese dream that I examine in the second section is important because it exemplifies how actors more or less closely tied to the state have used and developed the concept and theorized it in more explicitly spatio-temporal terms. I focus on narratives that were developed under Hu Jintao, but that were developed under Xi's 'Chinese dream' rhetoric. The texts in focus are particularly significant because they come from scholars that have been influential both with the Chinese leadership and their academic colleagues in China, and in the international field. As in Chapter 2, I examine a significant volume of academic texts, most of which are in the Chinese language and were available via the Chinese-language academic database CNKI. I have read all the documents that mention the term 'Chinese dream' that are published between 2005 and mid-2015 in any of the most influential Chinese journals in this debate, or authored by any of the 25 scholars identified as the most prominent Chinese IR scholars in a recent study. As in Chapter 2, the 14 journals exhaustively studied include: *Shijie jingji yu zhengzhi*, *Guoji zhengzhi kexue*, *Liaowang*, *Xuezhi luntan*, *Dushu*, *Guoji jingji pinglun*, *Guoji zhengzhi yanjiu*, *Zhongguo fazhan guancha*, *Meiguo yanjiu*, *Jiaoxue yu yanjiu*, *Zhongguo yu shijie guancha*, *Zhanlue yu guanli*, *Xiandai guoji guanxi* and *Guoji zhonglie*. As in Chapter 2, the list of scholars in question is based on scholars' reputation among their peers, assessed through a survey distributed to 305 scholars at China's top universities (Kristensen and Nielsen, 2013: 5). I have also read additional books, articles and conference papers that appear particularly relevant because of a strong focus on the elaboration of the 'Chinese dream'. The literatures I examine are not exhaustive of things written on or referring to the Chinese dream, but they are numerous and influential enough to illustrate some general tendencies in academic imaginaries of China and the world.

The poster campaign examined in the third section is important because it is the most important propaganda effort to propagate and illustrate Xi's 'Chinese dream' idea. Data was collected during visits to Beijing in 2013 and Beijing, Shanghai,

Guangzhou and Chengdu in 2014. A range of posters in the propaganda campaign can be found via www.wenming.cn/jwmsxf_294/zggygg. Ni Weihua's photography is significant because it is internationally widespread and because it deals directly with the kind of official language and propaganda that is the focus of this book.

The form of online expression that I discuss in the fourth section is again important because it is widespread in China, and has come to be understood as an important form of resistance by international scholars and Chinese dissident groups. In my discussion of this playful and critical reference to the Chinese dream, I draw on a quantity of blog posts, images, arts exhibitions and photography that have appeared online since 2012. I focus on examples that have reached a relatively wide audience inside and outside China.

2 One instance of such deployment of the harmony rhetoric was when Xi headed a large central government delegation to the Tibet Autonomous Region between 17 and 22 July 2011, for events to mark the sixtieth anniversary of what the party-state calls the 'peaceful liberation of Tibet'. For examples of Xi promoting harmony during the celebration, see the full text (Xi Jinping, 2011a: 2, 3, 4) or a full length CCTV recording (Xi Jinping, 2011b: 12:27, 24:06, 33:24) of his speech at the anniversary ceremony. Xi's speech was also preceded by others stressing civilizational harmony (*wenming hexie* 文明和谐), and followed by a parade displaying ethnic harmony and unity under the theme 'building harmony', as can be seen in additional CCTV recordings of the ceremony. The broadcast ends by an assertion of the expected harmonious life of ethnic unity under the central government (CCTV, 2011: 19:19, 20:20, 138:50, 147:14).

3 For explicit use of holistic terminology in an official document, see State Council (2014b: V).

4 For example, when Xi visited the Sanya naval base at the edge of the South China Sea in April 2013, he emphasized the need for the navy to focus on the goals of a strong army, to merge individual dreams with the strong army dream and to strengthen the sense of mission (*People's Daily Online*, 2013a). Similarly, during Xi's inspection of the Guangzhou Military Region including its naval reviews, South Sea Fleet Commander Jiang Weilie put forth that 'the over three million square kilometres of territorial waters represents an important strategic resource for the achievement of the great rejuvenation of the Chinese nation and the Chinese Dream' (Bai Ruixue *et al.*, 2013).

5 A number of books and opinion pieces in both Chinese and English had already discussed the idea, and are likely to have given impetus to Xi's use of the term in the first place. For some examples of academic writing that uses the term or discuss the debates about it before November 2012, see Mars and Hornsby (2008), Liu Mingfu (2010), Wang (2010) and Callahan (2013). Some even claimed Xi's use of the term was a response to an article in the *New York Times* (Friedman, 2012).

6 The Central Propaganda Department Theory Bureau issued a 2013 notice to research institutions around China to register research on this topic. A break-down into 15 suggested topics covers almost every purported aspect of the Chinese dream, including its opportunities and challenges, basic content and key characteristics, relation to China's current development, and its origin and contemporary background (National Planning Office of Philosophy and Social Science, 2013; see also Do, 2015: 36).

7 For example Callahan (2014), Sørensen (2015) and Liou and Ding (2015, particularly contributions by Victoria Tin-bor Hui, Chin-fu Hung and Raviprasad Narayanan). This may partly have to do with shifting trends in academic writing over the last decade. It may also be related to shifting functions of set phrases in Chinese politics. Where previously dry phrases like the 'three represents' or the 'scientific outlook on development' were primarily used to describe new approaches in policy and stamp out alternatives, the 'Chinese dream' has been used more as an inspirational slogan to rally the masses to the party cause. As such, it may simply have inspired a greater variety of individual responses than previous slogans. What is

clear is that the academic debates around the Chinese dream have displayed a diverse range of opinions and positions.

8 Failure to understand the true meaning of the Chinese dream, Wang said, would have potentially devastating consequences. In his text, Wang seems to recognize that differences between nations, which translate into foreign policy issues such as disputes over borders in the South China Sea, fall back on different historical memories. Yet, ultimately, questions of divergent understandings are reduced to the problem of *mis*-understanding. The solution offered is better, or correct, understanding (Wang Zheng, 2013).

9 As in government discourse on the Chinese dream, an engagement with those who appear to disagree with the government regularly takes shape in correcting such misunderstandings (see for examples Gao Xin and Sun Laibin, 2015: 174; Zhou Junjun, 2014: 1; Zhang Xiaoming, 2014: 17–21). The party-state also helped with this effort, by issuing guidelines to scholars outlining what they and their students can promote – and more importantly cannot criticize – in what is known as 'Document number 9', at the same time as high-profile cases emerged against faculty failing to stay within acceptable boundaries (ChinaFile, 2013; *Chronicle of Higher Education*, 2013; Mahoney, 2014: 29).

10 Mu is among the minority of scholars who point out that 'the West' also has some tradition of thinking about harmony (Mu Ren, 2014: 30). Most scholars simply state the point he also makes that harmony is a fundamental part of Chinese traditional thought or culture and of the Chinese dream (for example Mu Ren, 2014: 30; Zhou Junjun, 2014: 1; Sun Laibin and Xie Chengyu, 2014: 159–60; Zeng Xiangming, 2014: 5–6; Tao Shaoxing, 2015: 19).

11 However, Liu Mingfu points out in a comment:

> I'm [just] a scholar at [China's] National Defense University, but when I talked about China wanting to be No. 1 in the world, Americans were very unhappy. If China's president talked about being No. 1 in the world, Americans would be unable to bear it ... We can't use the same language. But my Chinese dream and the president's Chinese dream are in essence the same.
>
> (Lim, 2013)

Whether or not Liu is right is not entirely clear from official Chinese documents and speeches, but his claim is certainly not implausible. Some argue that Chinese academics play a more important role to policy making than their counterparts in other parts of the world (Leonard, 2008: 17).

12 Xi Jinping has tended to avoid public talk of surpassing the United States, and when he has mentioned the American dream it has been to emphasize its compatibility with the Chinese dream. Academic writing has, by contrast, paid very much attention to comparing the United States and China. This is not a surprise, as the Chinese slogan clearly plays off the associations and legacy of the American term. For the argument that this Chinese identity is constructed negatively against a bad and barbarian West through the Chinese dream discourse, see Callahan (2015b). Callahan has been a key analyst of the Chinese dream discourse in recent years, and has commented at greater length on a number of the scholars whose work is discussed in this section (Callahan, 2013, 2015a). For a selection of texts that compare the Chinese and the American dream in this way, see Shi Yuzhi (2013), Han Qingxiang (2013), Wang Yiwei (2014) and Lu Chunlong (2015).

13 Mao Zedong and his calamitous Great Leap Forward are important to Hu because they exemplified the dream of catching up to and surpassing America in a number of measurable areas like GDP and steel production (Hu Angang, 2011: 14, 2013a, 2013b: 191–209).

14 Just as Zhao Tingyang and others argued in the Hu Jintao era, Hu Angang and others have suggested that China needs to oppose 'universal values' advocated by 'the West'

in order to underpin its position as a new type of superpower with a 'Chinese perspective', a 'Chinese voice' and its own 'discursive power' (Hu Angang *et al.*, 2011: 201–5). At the same time, Hu Angang and his colleagues clearly claim that the Chinese dream of a World of Great Harmony is also 'the world's dream' and the goal of the PRC leadership (Hu Angang *et al.*, 2011: 188; Hu Angang, 2013a).

15 The publishers quickly published a second edition, the book was translated into English (Liu Mingfu, 2015) and Liu's work has become widely debated in global English-language scholarship.

16 A key lesson he draws from Mao's period in power, and the calamitous Great Leap Forward in particular, is the necessity to destroy old rules in order to break new paths (Liu Mingfu, 2010: 10–11, 13).

17 The first of Wang's points refers to the debates around the English-language translation of the term – whether it should be the Chinese dream, the China dream, China's dreams or even Chinese dreams. In his list of misconceptions, Wang argues that 'President Xi Jinping has elaborated the Chinese dream, stressing its essence is the trinity of the fulfilment of Chinese people, the revival of the Chinese nation and the prosperity of the country' (Wang Yiwei, 2013). To Wang, then, the idea that the Chinese dream may represent the aspirations of the party-state and that these may not represent or be compatible with the individual dreams of all people is simply wrong. Where the Chinese term *Zhongguo meng* had originally been translated as both 'China dream' and 'Chinese dream' in official and unofficial publications, the party-state eventually settled for the latter, partly it seems because it appeared less statist. It bears noting, however, that to my knowledge the party-state never considered translating its slogan as 'Chinese dreams' in the plural. The second point rejects the idea that the Chinese dream will replace the American dream, but only in the sense that Chinese culture is inclusive – and, as argued by Zhao Tingyang, the American and European dreams are 'fading away' anyway. Subsequent points assert that the Chinese dream is realistic, is wedded to socialism and the Party and is pragmatic. Although the Chinese dream 'accommodates all kinds of legitimate, reasonable and fair voices', an excessive emphasis on 'some specific "dreams"' or individuals' 'own desires' for constitutionalism, human rights or democracy would constitute a misconception (Wang Yiwei, 2013). The Chinese dream is not about full Westernization, about returning to China's tributary past or about simple domestic economic construction. Finally, the Chinese dream is incorrectly understood in terms of a 'new nationalism', because 'the Chinese dream is so inclusive that it will be conducive to other countries, especially developing countries, to help them realize their own dreams' (Wang Yiwei, 2013).

18 Wang's colleague Zhang Xiaoming sums up this attitude to diversity when he writes that the Chinese dream possesses great scope and inclusiveness, but is not all-encompassing (Zhang Xiaoming, 2014). As in previous expressions of 'harmonious world', Chinese elites have privileged access to correct understanding of how to build a better world, which means they need to lead or eliminate foreign views that are prone to misunderstanding. Again, this correct understanding of the good is heavily tied to Chineseness, as one article put it: 'the multicoloured dreams of individual happiness possess a common undertone – "ethnic yellow" (*gongtong de dise – "minzu huang"*, 共同的底色 – "民族黄")' (Sun Laibin and Wang Ping, 2014: 10).

19 An English translation from local Beijing directives can be seen in *Beijing Daily* (2013).

20 This makes poster campaigns somewhat different from the propaganda of the Shanghai Expo discussed in Chapter 3 of this book. Although the chapter argued that circumscribed notions of time and space deconstructed through the Expo, it was simultaneously clearly identifiable in time and space, and therefore quite possible to largely avoid for most, even if its effects were not. Because of their infiltration of the everyday spaces of a majority of Chinese people, propaganda posters are not escapable for most of the PRC's population.

21 One example of the Chinese authorities' attempt to enlist influential public intellectuals in such an endeavour can be seen in *The Forum of Social Responsibilities of Internet Celebrities*, which was held in August 2013. The forum gathered so-called 'big V' online celebrities (*da V*, 大V), whose Sina Weibo microblogging accounts have more than ten million followers. The gathered 'big V' agreed to 'Seven baselines' for their online conduct, as well as recommending them to all people. The seven baselines were those of laws and regulations, the socialist system, the national interest, the citizens' legal rights and interests, public order, morals and information accuracy (Jia Yue, 2013).

22 Jeremy Paltiel (2007) has a different take on 'the empire's new clothes' in his book by that name, which also discusses the tensions between particularism and universalism in PRC attempts to build its global status.

Conclusion

Dreaming of future harmonies and multiplicities

> What is necessary is to rectify names.... If names be not correct, language is not in accordance with the truth of things. If language be not in accordance with the truth of things, affairs cannot be carried on to success.
>
> (Confucius in the Analects, Book 13)

> We need to do more to refine and explain our culture, and to expand external communication platforms and channels.
>
> (Xi Jinping in *Xinhua*, 2013c)

> In the beginning before the government used this word, this was a good word. Now when everyone says 'harmony,' there's a little bit of a humorous, joking feeling.
>
> (Beijing student in interview, 2011)[1]

The Chinese dream of a harmonious world has not taken place, is not taking place and will not take place. This has been shown in this book by tracing the notion from Hu Jintao's policy discourse, through Chinese academic theorizations, in the art and architecture of official propaganda, via mocking online spoofs and finally into the proliferation of the Chinese dream under Xi Jinping. This disappearance of harmony may be new, but it reflects back to age-old attempts to pin down meaning, reality and politics into rules and principles. Confucius famously insisted that words or symbols can and should correspond in a correct and truthful way to a real 'thing' that they designate. The threat to harmonious governance, on this understanding, is if rulers call something harmony which in fact is not, thereby causing misunderstanding so that people do not understand how to do what is right. If meaning is unclear, this can and should be remedied by stricter use of words by the rulers or the 'rectification of names'.

Following on from this understanding, Xi Jinping calls for more and improved communication and explanation of such words, and of the Chinese culture to which they are said to be intrinsic. In this way of understanding language, the possibility of mass-reproducing false copies of reality threatens to replace the 'original' or 'true' versions with such copies. On this understanding, mass communication may threaten the authority of the government's original version of harmony, because mass-produced copies appear just as 'real' as their prototype. The threat to harmonious governance, on this understanding, is that bad representations or propaganda might win out over the government's good representation and propaganda. If it does, the risk is that the people turn away from harmony (because they do not understand its goodness), or that they embrace a 'bad' understanding of harmony and thereby erroneously behave in ways that are not 'harmonious' in the way the government would like them to be. If in this way meaning appears unclear, or conducive to the wrong kind of behaviour, this can and should be remedied by more and better communication and illustration – in other words, more and better government propaganda.

However, if the rectification of meaning, understanding and behaviour has been the purpose of propaganda, it has not always worked. From the comment above by a Beijing university student, we see that the definition of 'correct' harmony and the efforts at promoting it have not led to the 'correct' understanding and harmonious behaviour that rectification and propaganda were intended to produce. On the contrary, for people who may once have been attracted to the notion of harmony, like the Beijing student cited here, definition and communication by the state have made that attraction disappear. The positive 'harmony' that could once have been conjured has disappeared into a joke. 'Harmony', on this view, is no longer a word or sign that represents or even dissimulates something, but a word or sign that dissimulates that there is nothing behind it; no harmony, no reality, no true original to fall back on. It is the People's Republic of China (PRC) government that has pushed harmony to that point. If once it was possible to imagine a real or attractive harmony there behind the propaganda, that possibility has disappeared.

This Conclusion will summarize the operations through which harmony has been brought to the collapse described by the Beijing student above. In doing so, it will also answer the three research questions outlined in the Introduction to this book. Together, these three operations show how the Chinese dream of a harmonious world that has been articulated through the contemporary discourse of harmonism is a profoundly self-contradictory concept, which has undermined itself and made itself disappear. The rest of the Conclusion will focus on turning the question of disappearance and fragmentation back on the analysis in this book. It will suggest that the question of the possibility of harmony is in fact less clear-cut than previously indicated. Harmony may have symbolically disappeared as an ideal, it may not be real and it may not be possible to make it fully present or self-same. However, the Chinese dream of a harmonious world continues to proliferate in empty form. Moreover, its impossibility is no more coherent or stable than harmony itself. This book has argued that a cancerous or autoimmune logic is fundamental to the disappearance of the Chinese dream of a harmonious world. It will conclude by suggesting that that logic simultaneously opens the Chinese dream of a harmonious world up to repoliticization of harmony, and thereby to other futures. By doing so, it keeps the dream alive and open to other readings, and to a different harmony to come. Before making this argument more fully, however, we need to sum up the three key points that have been demonstrated by the analysis in this book, which together suggest that the Chinese dream of a harmonious world is impossible and has disappeared. They indicate in turn that (1) the Chinese dream of a harmonious world repeats an allochronizing logic, which makes harmony impossible; (2) there is an aporia at the heart of the Chinese dream of a harmonious world, which makes harmony impossible; and (3) the Chinese dream of a harmonious world has disappeared through mass proliferation, and is now impossible.

The Chinese dream of a harmonious world is impossible

The Chinese dream of a harmonious world repeats an allochronizing logic, which makes harmony impossible

The first question asked in the Introduction to this book was: what are the assumptions behind and political consequences of different ways of articulating the Chinese dream of a harmonious world, particularly in terms of ordering time and space? This book has shown some diversity in the assumptions about time and space that underpin party-state documents, academic writing and the visualizations of harmonious world at the Shanghai Expo. Some articulations rely on a unit-based political cosmology, including civilizations, regions and states. Others are based in holistic assumptions, deploying International Relations (IR)-terms such as 'network space', holistic globalization (specifically *quanqiu yitihua* 全球一体化) and an understanding of 'All-under-heaven' (*Tianxia* 天下) that similarly conceives of a space where everything is already connected to everything else. Both of these ways of imagining space, however, marry their spatializations with notions of progress, modernization, or 'turning the bad into the good', that imply a linear timeline. Such imaginations organize difference in epochs, and binaries such as advanced/behind, modern/traditional, developed/developing and good/bad. One of the key things that the discourse of harmonism does is to deploy these concepts to align multiplicity in a historical queue with Chinese elites at the head. In this story, others are not properly different, they are just behind. 'They' are imagined as though located in a different time than 'we' are. Eventually, 'they' will become like 'us'. In this way, the unit-based and holistic political cosmologies are not mutually exclusive with one replacing the other, but are deployed together in contemporary China in ways that are mutually supportive in underpinning an allochronic world imaginary. Therefore, the diversity of accounts is undermined in that they all fall back on allochronizing assumptions.

An important implication of this is that scholars must stop treating China as the 'other country'. China is not 'behind' as some infant being socialized, as Johnston and others would have it. Nor is it a radical other to 'the West' that naturally escapes the problems of allochronic thought, as in Chinese exceptionalist narratives. What is more, the allochronic imagination of multiplicity that Chinese harmonist discourses share with much 'Western thought' reduces not only the challenge, but the opportunity that time and space could present us with: actual multiplicity in the here and now. At the same time, these same accounts of harmonism assert that such diversity or difference in the here and now is a necessary precondition of harmony, because harmony is about balance between different things. Therefore, by writing in a way that relegates others to a different time, those who promote harmony through this discourse ironically make it impossible, because they deny the multiplicity in the here and now that is said to be a precondition of harmony.

There is an aporia at the heart of the Chinese dream of a harmonious world, which makes harmony impossible

This leads us to the second question asked in the Introduction to this book: are there contradictions in or between different articulations of the harmonious world? How are these made visible? As just summarized, the diversity of more or less official accounts of the Chinese dream of a harmonious world are undermined in that they all fall back on allochronizing assumptions. However, this book has also shown how official language migrates and morphs in different contexts through which the harmonious world is undone – subverted, deconstructed and changed – by its own logic. A reading of China's mega events as both ideology and simulation has revealed how notions of inside/outside, now/then and subject/object come apart. Moreover, netizen and artistic play with the Chinese dream of harmony makes visible certain contradictions, both between different articulations of the harmonious world and within the concept itself.

Throughout the examination of the Chinese dream of a harmonious world, this harmony has also revealed itself to be impossible in the sense that the harmony concept is more profoundly aporetic. Harmony must *by definition* be universal, but its universalization *by definition* makes harmony impossible. The discourse of harmonism claims that unless all parts are harmonious it makes no sense to speak of harmony at all. At the same time, the universalization of harmony – the incorporation of everything into the one harmonious system – would mean there was no outside or other that could balance against that system, and so the multiplicity that is simultaneously harmony's alleged precondition would be impossible. What we have, then, is an aporia at the heart of the dream of a harmonious world, despite attempts to conceal it. This book has aimed to question little by little the attempts at harmonious organization of time and space as belonging to the sovereign that this concealment has implied. It has examined different strategies of reading and using 'harmony' in ways that reveal the excluded other of Hu's Chinese dream of harmony – discord and competition – to be always already there within the political and linguistic system of harmony itself. The harmonious world has never been, is not and could never be made fully present or self-same. The completion or achievement of harmony is impossible.

The Chinese dream of a harmonious world has disappeared through mass proliferation, and is now impossible

The third and final question asked in the Introduction to this book was: what is the overall effect of the proliferation of 'harmony' in contemporary Chinese society? Through the studies in this book we have seen the idea of harmony, in both the 'harmonious world' and 'Chinese dream' slogans, amass so much meaning that the possibility of using it as a meaningful concept has disappeared. Its meaning has been shown to designate total cooperation, total subjugation, total respect for difference, total control, totally moral leadership and so on. Where other scholars have tried to find out its true meaning, this book has shown instead how the illusion of this possibility has disappeared – not into meaninglessness, but into what we may by Baudrillardian analogy think of as transparent 'hyper-meaning', the more meaningful than the meaningful. As an effect of this mass proliferation the term has become overripe and collapsed under the weight of its own meaning to the point where it can no longer function as a dream or an ideal, as indicated by the Beijing student cited above. The dream and the reality of harmonious world have collapsed into one another and the seduction of the concept has been lost. The proliferation of harmony has made it disappear as an imagined metaphysical possibility.

Some scholars have, quite reasonably, called for caution with regard to the oppressive and homogenizing aspects of Chinese harmonization. In the context of its 'hyper-meaning', this threat of the Chinese dream of a harmonious world must be thought of differently. The threat posed by proliferating harmonization is not only the policing of boundaries that this book has described on the level of ideology: cracking down on dissidents, blocking words online, preventing people from tweeting. Indeed, we might want to reflect on why many of us are so obsessed with condemning the limitation of communication: will the (counter-) revolution really be tweeted? Instead, a more spectacular threat to the Chinese dream of a harmonious world comes from the excess of communicating the Chinese dream and harmony themselves, which destroys the illusion of the real in these concepts. In that sense the mass communication of the Chinese dream of a harmonious world is dangerous on a larger metaphysical plane. The party-state is working towards the dream of a controlled hierarchical harmony, but it becomes something completely different. They are the ones who are destroying the Chinese dream, and robbing harmony of its appeal.

What remains after the disappearance of the Chinese dream of a harmonious world

Through these three arguments, this book has demonstrated that the Chinese dream of a harmonious world has not taken place, is not taking place and will not take place. To an extent, Xi Jinping's very rapid launch of his Chinese dream slogan can be understood as a recognition that 'harmonious world' and 'harmonious society' had reached their use-by date (and should therefore be revoked by the dream owner). When I spoke to scholars, students and ordinary people in Beijing in the summer of 2013, a majority echoed the Beijing student and told me that harmonious world was now a joke and that the Chinese dream was the new articulation of China's vision of the future. It seemed as though 'harmonious world' may indeed already have disappeared into the Chinese dream. By summer 2015, a similar fate appeared to have befallen Xi's 'Chinese dream', which no longer seemed to enthuse anyone. In quantitative terms, academic discussion of 'harmonious world' peaked in 2008 and has slowly declined since (Huang Wei, 2015: 74). Even state-owned media soon left both 'harmony' and the 'Chinese dream' to the side – its use of these terms peaked in 2006 and 2013 respectively, before quickly fading to a low level of use (Qian Gang, 2015). However, as we have seen, this does not mean that the Chinese dream of harmony has vanished from the rhetorical scene. Rather, it has continued to have traction in Chinese international and diplomatic relations, where it had already been entrenched.

Before Xi's leadership takeover, the term 'harmonious world' had been written into the Chinese Communist Party (CCP) constitution and numerous official strategy documents. Foreign representatives to the PRC had been taken on Confucius-themed trips by the Chinese party-state, accompanied by academic promoters of harmonious world through whom the envoys 'acquired a deeper understanding of China's traditional cultural philosophy such as "seeking for harmony but not uniformity," "living in harmony with all other nations"' (Ministry of Foreign Affairs of the PRC, 2011a). The PRC establishment had also urged other countries, like Vietnam (*Xinhua*, 2012d), the Maldives (*Xinhua*, 2012a) and India (*Xinhua*, 2012b), to be harmonious. As we have seen, after he became supreme leader, Xi continued to deploy the notion of harmony as part of his Chinese dream, including to international audiences. In international speeches, Xi has stressed his role as a communicator of Chinese history and culture, with the aim of proper understanding, transparency and truth. For example, in 2014 Xi told staff and students at the College of Europe that:

> To observe and *understand China properly*, one needs to bear in mind both China's past and present and draw reference from both China's accomplishments and the Chinese way of thinking.... I hope what I just shared with you could draw for you a more *transparent picture of China*.... In China, we value the idea of preserving 'harmony without uniformity.'
>
> (Xi Jinping, 2014b, my emphasis)

Along similar lines, when Xi spoke to German audiences in 2015, he emphasized that his communication would enable others to see an authentic China in an objective way, and would thereby want to join him or it in striving to fulfil the Chinese dream of a harmonious world:

> China has set the goal for its future development, which is to realize the Chinese Dream of the great rejuvenation of the Chinese nation.... China also expects the outside world to look more into China in an *objective*,

> historical, and multidimensional perspective, so as to *really understand China* in a *comprehensive, authentic* and tridimensional way.... We sincerely hope that all countries in the world will follow the path of peaceful development, joining hands together to build a harmonious world with lasting peace and common prosperity.
>
> (Xi Jinping, 2014c, my emphasis)

These speeches exemplify Xi's attempt to heed his own advice quoted at the outset of this Conclusion: to present a 'rectified' narrative of the Chinese dream and the harmonious world, and to communicate or propagate this more widely and in a clearer way. One commentator lauds the speech to the College of Europe as a sign that Xi is a 'great communicator', comparing him to former US President Ronald Reagan because he is a similarly good actor with a keen sense of rhetorical efficiency and flair. Many commentators have praised Xi's laid-back and plain-speaking image, contrasting it to Hu Jintao's wooden public persona. One analyst refers to Xi's above comment about the need for more and better (international) communication, to approvingly suggest that stepping up such a propaganda effort 'will help extensively promote Chinese culture and ideology ... helping China gain more acceptance and recognition from the international community' (Yang Jiemian, 2015).

And indeed, there is evidence that the dream of a harmonious world had already been well received by a number of foreign dignitaries in the Hu era. In this period, it had already spread into the language use of leaders ranging from Syrian President Bashar Al-Assad (CNTV, 2012) to Kevin Rudd, Australia's former minister of foreign affairs. The latter declared, in a speech given to the Asia Society in New York in 2012: 'there is something in China's concept of a "harmonious world"; which the US, the rest of the region and the rest of the world can work with' (Rudd, 2012). Chinese officials have also been keen to play up such endorsement, most notably perhaps the promotion of harmony by UN Secretary-General Ban Ki-moon (*Xinhua*, 2012c, 2012e).

The notion of a harmonious world, and the traditional strategic culture with which it has been associated, then, has not only been deeply entrenched in PRC policy documents, but has also been given positive play by other influential individuals and organizations. Consequently, as we also saw in Chapter 5, its concept has continued to orbit Chinese politics as an integral part of the Chinese dream, even as that dream has also collapsed and continued its proliferation in empty form. This supports Joseph Cheng's expectation that harmony will remain a major element of China's public diplomacy in the foreseeable future: '[a]s China pursues an increasingly ambitious role in regional leadership and international institution-building, its publicity work on building a "harmonious world" will likely be stepped up' (Cheng, 2012: 183). Indeed, the disappearance of harmony from Chinese politics is unlikely to stop its proliferation, but will only fuel the party-state's insistence on it as part of its empty Chinese dream. However, with the domestic context in mind, Xi might be well advised to proceed with caution in his attempt at providing foreigners with transparent access to the 'objective' or 'authentic' Chinese dream of a harmonious world. In the domestic context, more communication quickly led to the collapse of both harmony and the Chinese dream. Their diplomatic redeployment by non-Chinese actors may be cynical and empty in the first place, but more communication might well destroy any illusion of harmonious sincerity that remains.

Alongside this transplantation of harmony in diplomacy, the morphing of the official term in the cat-and-mouse game with online dissidents also continues. A search for banned terms on Sina Weibo on 2 November 2011 showed the term 'Hexie farm' (*xienongchang* 蟹农场) to be censored, presumably because of its reference to the cartoon series encountered in the previous chapter (Hernandez, 2011). New puns are constantly created, then censored, giving rise to further new terms. The rivercrabs have now morphed into new humorous words that are deployed in *egao* culture online. One such replacement word for harmony/rivercrabs is *shuichan* (水产), meaning 'aquatic product'. Another is the evocative near-homonym *hēxuè* (喝血, also pronounceable as *hēxiě*), which means to 'drink blood'. A third is the homonymous 'fitting shoes' (*he xie* 合鞋), which puns on Xi's attempted use of this term as a metaphor to explain (the lack of) multiplicity in his Chinese dream, and which has led to jibing elaborations of a 'theory of suitable shoes' (*he xie lun* 合鞋论) to replace 'harmony theory' (*hexie lun* 和谐论).[2] Through such terms, harmony/rivercrabs continue to morph, metastasize and proliferate, even as they are 'dreamed away' and the Chinese dream of a harmonious world continues to disappear.

Repoliticizing the Chinese dream of a harmonious world

That harmony as an ideal or a principle is impossible and is not taking place, then, does not mean the term does not persist (cf. Nordin and Öberg, 2015; Öberg, 2013). Moreover, it should be stressed, it does not mean it does not have effects. Decriers of harmonization need not be alarmed by talk of its disappearance. The fact that harmonization is not taking place makes no difference to those who are victimized under the PRC government's harmonious policies and dreams – they suffer just the same, and their nightmares count no more or less because harmony has appeared and disappeared.

What, then, should we make of harmony's simultaneous proliferation and disappearance – should we lament or celebrate it? Baudrillard writes concerning the Gulf War – which he famously declared was not taking place – that it is stupid to be for or against the war if you do not for one moment question its credibility or level of reality (Baudrillard, 1991). Therefore, those who promote the truth of it as a war and historical event are the warmongers, the accomplices (Baudrillard, 1991; Merrin, 1994: 440). On the same logic, it is misplaced to be for or against harmony, if we fail to question its level of reality. We have seen various aspects of the 'hyper-meaning' of harmony and harmonization (total cooperation, total subjugation, total respect for difference, totally moral leadership, total control). None of these things are taking place in contemporary China or its relations to the world. If something is taking place, it is not harmony or harmonization. My task here has not been to promote or oppose this term, but rather to question its credibility and indeed level of reality.

Having gone along with the claims of harmony promoters, we have reason to be cautious about the resulting claims about its credibility, its reality and its politics. Two academic commentators claim with regard to its policy formulation that 'it is implicit that a harmonious world is one where supposed "heresies" are tolerated' (Guo Sujian and Blanchard, 2008: 4). Based on the finding that harmonious world repeats an allochronizing logic, I am less certain that such tolerance is implied in the notion of a harmonious world and the discourse of harmonism. Relegating 'heresies' (or 'others') to a different time from our own means denying them coevalness in the here and now. The implication in the texts examined in this book is that 'they' will eventually come around to seeing the world as 'we' do. The effect of this move is a depoliticization of harmony, because it denies the possibility and necessity of choice in the here and now. The future is already inscribed in this story, so that all we need to do is apply principles of harmony in an appropriate manner in order to get there. There may be a space here for *politics*, in the narrow sense of 'government business' that was introduced at the outset of this book. However, the *political* dimension of this, the 'ontological dimension of undecidability and contingency, agonism and difference underlying political reality' is denied (Viriasova, 2011; cf. Baudrillard, 1990 [1983]: 162, 182). We are presented with what has been referred to in a different context of harmony-speak as a 'post-political vision of politics and governance that tends to eliminate power and antagonism' (Torfing, 2010: 257).

Having said this, this book has suggested that the proliferating metastases of harmony (rivercrabs, aquatic products, suitable shoes) embody an excess of meaning to which we cannot do justice in our interpretations. Instead, it has proposed, this is what pushes these terms back into the political, where multiple competing meanings or doings – of words and purported significance – lead to instances of openness where we need to make 'impossible decisions' with regards to their use and interpretation. And the same is true for the Chinese dream of a harmonious world more generally. Because harmony deconstructs, because a multiplicity of possible meanings is always there, we need to make choices in the here and now about how to interpret them. These are political choices, and they highlight the necessarily political nature of harmony. The choice to interpret the Chinese dream of a harmonious world in what I have argued are depoliticizing ways is ironically, then, a political choice, even if it is not recognized as such.

This indicates two significant points for thinking about harmony and the political. First, because it is necessary to choose how to interpret or communicate harmony, harmony is always already a product of political choice. It is never simply natural, neutral or given. The aporetic and autoimmune logic of harmony described in this book underscores its necessarily political character. Second, it is nonetheless possible to deny that political character, and to avert one's gaze from the cracks, the fuzziness and the irresolvable contradictions that inhabit the Chinese dream of a harmonious world.

As suggested above, such a post-political vision of harmony is theoretically unsustainable, because we cannot escape the need to make choices about how to interpret and 'do' harmony. What is more, insisting on that post-political vision of harmony is politically dangerous. Choosing some ways of understanding and doing harmony inevitably means eliminating or *not choosing* other ways of understanding and doing it. Every inclusion is simultaneously a separation that implies multiple exclusions. In other words, exclusion is the condition of possibility of any semblance of meaning at all: in order to say something I need at that moment to *not* say all the other things that I could be saying. Put differently, in order for a word to make any sense to anyone, it needs to be separated from other words (words that are different or not same). Otherwise, all we would have would be one big word that would mean everything, and therefore would mean nothing. Such is language.

However, that separation, as we have seen, is never stable or secure. Ultimately, we can give no unquestionable definition of or reason for the separation between what something is and what it is not. Although we base our decisions (about what something means in a given context, about what policy to pursue) on reasons and may have strong motivations for choosing what we choose, we will never be able to provide an ultimate ground for any given choice – in Derridean terms, such grounds will always be indefinitely deferred. Therefore, in the shared realm of politics, 'the ultimate decision will have to rely on a skilful combination of rhetorical strategies and the use of force' (Torfing, 2010: 258). As this book has demonstrated, this choice, exclusion and force are intimate parts of harmony that were always already there in the term. What is more, the process of exclusion that is part and parcel of the production of harmony leads to antagonism between those who identify with the included options and those who do not. Denying this antagonism (this political dimension of politics) tends to alienate those who are disqualified from consideration – those who count as 'no one' when everyone wins and no one loses. This, Torfing writes, will tend to displace antagonistic struggles from the realm of the political to the realm of morals, 'where conflicts are based on non-negotiable values and the manifestation of "authentic" identities' (Torfing, 2010: 258). Such non-negotiable values would be the opposite of the cooperative harmony sought (cf. Nordin, 2016). Again, we are led back to an aporia of the Chinese dream of a harmonious world, where harmony may be a 'necessary glue without which neither a society nor a polity are sustainable', but where 'complete social harmony is ultimately suffocating and illiberal' and therefore disharmonious (Rockman, 2010: 207). Again, the Chinese dream of a harmonious world is impossible.

In this way, the depoliticizing denial of discord, competition and disharmonious elements produces more entrenched and non-negotiable discord, competition and disharmony. A repoliticizing recognition of these elements in harmony would indeed 'challenge what have, through discursive practices, been constituted as normal, natural, and accepted ways of carrying on' (Edkins, 1999: 12). By doing so, however, it might also avoid pushing antagonism further into the disharmonious realm of the non-negotiable, the uncooperative and the violent.

Recognizing this political dimension of the Chinese dream of a harmonious world, or repoliticizing it, means reintroducing the necessity of choice, excess of meaning and the radical undecidability of harmony. In other words, it suggests the existence of multiple, contradictory and incomplete stories about what harmony can mean, do and undo. It makes the term embody a coeval multiplicity of meanings, a 'plurality of trajectories' or a 'simultaneity of stories-so-far'.

Dreaming of a harmonious world to come

If harmony, in this way, represents a 'mutual contamination of "nows"' or a 'simultaneity of stories-so-far', where does this leave the rest of those stories, the futures of the Chinese dream of a harmonious world?

Through tracing the simultaneous appearance and disappearance of the Chinese dream of a harmonious world, this book has shown how it works on a logic that I have called 'cancerous' or 'autoimmune'. The discourse of harmonism demands that harmony be excluded, rejected and sent off elsewhere. It must be expelled under the pretext of protecting it, by sending the disharmonious elements inside it off to the outside (cf. Derrida, 2005 [2003]-a: 35–6). This is the expulsion of internal ills that has been promoted by party-state versions of harmonism, and by both Traditional Chinese Medicine and biomedical approaches to cancer. Autoimmunity also calls for putting off the coming of harmony, where the sovereign's truly 'harmonious' behaviour is postponed until later, until more harmonious times. China needs to become strong *first*, be in control of harmony on the inside *first*, use hard power *first* (Nordin, 2016). This move reinforces my claim that there is no self with which harmony can be self-same, no essence to harmony – there is simply no harmony there. This absence of the self-same defines harmony. Again, in a slightly different sense, harmony has not taken place, is not taking place and will not take place.

As we have seen, the cancerous Chinese system is not merely or simply a process by which harmony attacks a part of itself. Its deferral or referral of the other is also a deferral or referral to the other. As such, it marks the undeniable experience of multiplicity and heterogeneity, of the alterity of the other, of the not-same (Derrida, 2005 [2003]-a: 38). At the same time, it is only through denying this undeniable that we can have meaning. Harmony is therefore what it is only by deferring and differing from itself. It can never accomplish the unity that is claimed to be its precondition. To the extent that it tries to accomplish such unity, it has to enforce its principle with violence (disharmony). In this sense, again, it is impossible (Nordin, 2016).

At this point, the perceptive reader may well ask, do the traces and cracks that make harmony come apart not also appear in the argument of this book? Could the same not be said about the argument that the Chinese dream of a harmonious world is impossible? Indeed, a successful failure. And the same is true for 'coeval multiplicities', 'heterotemporalities' or the 'mutual contamination of nows'. This book has questioned whether it is possible to imagine a harmonious world that allows for such multiplicities. The temptation set up by this question is to answer in terms of the dichotomy it implies: it is *either* possible, *or* impossible.

However, the undoing of the harmonious world that this book has examined exposes the need to think otherwise about the dichotomy of possibility/impossibility and to displace it. Following Derrida, both 'harmonious world' and 'coeval multiplicity' are best conceived as *both* possible *and* impossible, never simply one or the other. Any harmonious or coeval relation to otherness is also always a disharmonious and allochronizing relation. That harmony or coeval multiplicities are not *simply possible* is then not an excuse to treat them as *simply impossible*, but calls instead for the opposite of abandoning harmony and coeval multiplicities. The point that harmonious world is not uniquely liberating, but repeats the politically problematic and allochronizing logic of more established writing in what is referred to as 'Western tradition', simply means that it cannot escape the restraints and problems recognizable in other terms. Therefore, retreating to other (old, comfortable) terms is not a solution. Perhaps, instead, we should use the notion of harmony in acknowledgement of a tradition and aspiration to a way of doing things differently. Derrida writes of autoimmunity as holding open the future for a 'democracy to come', in recognition of his debt to the historical and intellectual heritage of a democratic European tradition. I have argued that 'harmony' operates in a similarly autoimmune manner, and its legacy too should be recognized (Nordin, 2016). However, rather than contribute to clarifying and communicating a post-political version of harmony, I have suggested that we can acknowledge this legacy by reading the political back into harmony. Its universal claim that all conceivable elements of a situation need to be in harmony for the situation to be harmonious conjures up the question of exclusions and exceptions. Despite itself, it invites questions about what or who has been excluded, why and on what grounds. I therefore take it as an invitation to question and challenge the *reality*, precisely, of the divisions that deployments of harmony have made visible to us, and to emphasize their political and contingent nature (cf. Pin-Fat, 2010: 119–20). Part of this effort at repoliticization has been to observe the disappearance of the Chinese dream of a harmonious world through excessive proliferation, and to performatively join in with a wider 'strategy of excess' that has contributed to the acceleration of that disappearance. In its wake, we can observe the continuation of its concepts in empty form, but perhaps also the space for the emergence or arrival of something new.

The reason that I have kept insisting on such openness (autoimmunity, undecidability, the other and so on) is because it makes the political, and indeed any futures at all, imaginable. To Derrida, '[w]ithout the absolute singularity of the incalculable and the exceptional, no thing and no one, nothing *other* and thus *nothing*, arrives or happens' (2005 [2003]-b: 148, emphasis in original). And again, '[w]ithout autoimmunity, with absolute immunity, nothing would ever happen or arrive; we would no longer wait, await or expect, no longer expect one another, or expect any event' (2005 [2003]-b: 152, see also 157; Nordin, 2016). This is why Derrida insists on the future 'to come'. This places focus on what comes, rather than that which begins from the self or the one. The Chinese language has the same connotations of the future as that which comes, where the character *lai* 来, meaning precisely 'to come', is part of the term for future, *weilai* 未来. This places it in a chain of meanings of the 'to come' as 'future' (*weilai* 未来 or *jianglai* 将来), 'return' (*huilai* 回来) and 'original' (*yuanlai* 原来). This echoes with a temporality where the future is to come as a return of the other that is also its (non)origin. As we have seen *weilai*, the future, was itself harmonized in conjunction with Ai Weiwei's detention, making it deferred in more than one sense.

Through these ways of rethinking harmony, we see how the undecidability at work in the very concept of harmony leaves open the chance (or threat) of a future, for both the term itself and for singular decisions to be taken. This future is not just *in* the future, something we can hope for, but it imposes itself with absolute urgency in the form that the imperative of harmony takes here and now. Because of its cancerous and (im)possible character, 'harmony' is structurally open to the other – an other that does not await us as the unified ideal of a programmable or predictable future, but that presses upon us (with all the force of its self-difference) in the here and now (cf. Wortham, 2010: 131–2; Derrida, 1994).

The point of retaining the (im)possibility of a harmony to come is partly about retaining the term 'harmony', but it is also about opening up to the possibility of its continued destruction and disappearance. By opening itself up to the other, harmony threatens to further destroy itself and disappear, but also gives it the chance to receive the other – in the here and now, in coeval multiplicity. The point of the 'to come' is a future that cannot be identified in advance, since it would break with all the old names. Without countries, civilizations, progress, we may ask whether it would still make sense to speak of a harmonious world under that name. As a term, then, 'harmony' is not sacred. Some other context, some day, may demand that we use a different word in other sentences. Just as the Chinese party-state (or perhaps any state) works on a cancerous or (auto) immune logic, so too does language attempt to remain immune to anything that may threaten its logical syntax. The definition of a term, by definition, is a border and immune protection from what it is not, but we can read its simultaneous autoimmunity through reading deconstruction and simulation taking place.

Therefore, at the same time as the future is unpredictable, it is at work today, in the Chinese dream of a harmonious world: it is what is coming, what is happening. The responsibility for what remains to be decided or done cannot consist in following rules, rites or proper conduct of harmony, nor in a prescriptive theory for how to think and write about the Chinese dream of a harmonious world. Disputed, multifaceted and a point of contention, it must remain within the realm of the political.

Notes

1 A longer excerpt of this interview exchange can be found in Nordin and Richaud (2014: 57).

2 This pun emerged under Hu Jintao, but received a new lease of life after Xi Jinping tried to explain multiplicity in the Chinese dream through the metaphor of fitting

shoes. Speaking in Moscow on 23 March 2013, Xi defended the CCP's continued dominance of Chinese politics as 'the right of each country in the world independently to choose its own path of development'. He further illustrated this statement by continuing: 'Only the wearer knows if the shoe fits his foot' (*xiezi he bu he jiao chuanzhe cai zhidao* 鞋子合不合脚穿着才知道). Chinese netizens were quick to hijack his metaphor. One commentator quipped: 'You let your family wear comfortable shoes while compelling ours to wear worn-out shoes of the wrong size.' Another rhetorically asked: 'If the shoe doesn't fit what is to be done? Give me a new pair or cut my foot down to size?' Yet another responded:

> Yes, indeed. So, when I'm at a store shopping for shoes, I'll first try them on. If they don't fit, I'll immediately abandon them, no matter what brand they are. If you want to stick to a certain brand, finding the correct size becomes a bit more difficult, does it not?
>
> (All cited in Davies, 2013)

This take on the metaphor was also visualized by cartoonist Rebel Pepper, who depicted his avatar being hypnotized by Xi Jinping with a pendulum saying 'Chinese dream'. Xi holds up a tiny shoe for Rebel Pepper's large webbed feet and says: 'Follow my watch swinging back and forth. Soon you will be able to put it on' (Henochowicz, 2013a). In this way, the Theory of Suitable Shoes (*he xie lun* 合鞋论), which was already in ironic circulation under Hu's homonymous Harmony Theory (*hexie lun* 和谐论), received a new lease of life under Xi's Chinese dream (BBC Chinese, 2013; Davies, 2013; see Nordin and Richaud, 2014: 57 for similar use under Hu).

Bibliography

Abbate, Skya (2006) *Advanced Techniques in Oriental Medicine*, Stuttgart: Georg Thieme Verlag.

AFP (2011) China's Xinjiang 'Isolated' by Email, Phone Blocks, *AFP*, 23 February 2009.

Agnew, John (1998) *Geopolitics: Re-visioning World Politics*, London: Routledge.

Agnew, John and Stuart Corbridge (1995) *Mastering Space: Hegemony, Territory and International Political Economy*, London: Routledge.

Ai Weiwei (2013) *Ai Weiwei – Dumbass*. Last updated 21 May 2013, retrieved 1 August 2015, from www.youtube.com/watch?v=lyQZ-oLshOQ.

Alison (2010) *River Crab 2*. Last updated 8 November 2010, retrieved 11 June 2011, from http://chinadigitaltimes.net/space/File:River_crab2.jpg.

Annas, George J. (1995) Reframing the Debate on Health Care Reform by Replacing Our Metaphors, *New England Journal of Medicine*, 332, 745–8.

Apter, David E. and Tony Saich (1994) *Revolutionary Discourse in Mao's Republic*, Cambridge, MA and London: Harvard University Press.

Arsène, Severine (2010) *La Satire, ou la Ringardisation de la Censure sur le Web Chinois* [Satire, or the Tackiness of Censorship on the Chinese Web], CERI. Retrieved 14 January 2012, from www.ceri-sciences-po.org/cerifr/kiosque.php.

Ashley, Richard K. (1987) The Geopolitics of Geopolitical Space: Toward a Critical Social Theory of International Politics, *Alternatives*, 12(4), 403–34.

Ashley, Richard K. (1988) Untying the Sovereign State: A Double Reading of the Anarchy Problematique, *Millennium*, 17(2), 227–62.

Austin, John L. (1979 [1961]) *How to Do Things with Words: The William James Lectures Delivered at Harvard University in 1955*, 2nd edn, Oxford: Oxford University Press.

Ba Xiang (2010) *Hexielun* [On Harmony], Beijing: Shijie zhishi chubanshe.

Bai Ruixue, Gao Yi and Gan Jun (2013) Nanhai Dalianbing: Zhuanfang Yuanhai Xunlian Biandui Zhihuiyuan Jiang Weilie [Large-Scale Training in the South China Sea: An Exclusive Interview with Jiang Weilie, Commander of the South Sea Fleet Distant Sea Training Formation], *Xinhua*. Last updated 1 April 2013, retrieved 15 June 2015, from http://news.xinhuanet.com/mil/2013-04/01/c_124530104.htm.

Bakhtin, Mikhail M. (1984 [1965]) *Rabelais and His World*, Iswolsky, Helene (Trans.), Bloomington: Indiana University Press.

Bakken, Børge (2000) *The Exemplary Society: Human Improvement, Social Control, and the Dangers of Modernity in China*, Oxford: Oxford University Press.

Bandurski, David (2013a) *A New Year's Greeting Gets Axed in China*. Last updated 3 January 2013, retrieved 17 July 2015, from http://cmp.hku.hk/2013/01/03/30247.

Bandurski, David (2013b) *Will We All Be 'Dreamed Away'?* Last updated 24 April 2013, retrieved 17 July 2015, from http://cmp.hku.hk/2013/04/24/32799.

Bao Ting, Lao Lixing and Aditya Bardia (2010) Cancer Pain Control with Traditional Chinese Medicine. In Cho, William C. S. (Ed.) *Supportive Cancer Care with Chinese Medicine*, Dordrecht: Springer Science and Business Media B.V.

Barabantseva, Elena (2009) Development as Localization: Ethnic Minorities in Official Discourse on China's Western Development Project, *Critical Asian Studies*, 41(2), 225–54.

Barabantseva, Elena (2012) In Pursuit of an Alternative Model? The Modernisation Trap in China's Official Development Discourse, *East Asia*, 29(1), 63–79.

Barboza, David (2010) Shanghai Expo Sets Record with 73 Million Visitors, *New York Times*, 2 November 2010.

Barmé, Geremie R. (2012) History Writ Large: Big-Character Posters, Red Logorrhoea and the Art of Words, *PORTAL: Journal of Multidisciplinary International Studies*, 9(3).

Barmé, Geremie R. (2013) Chinese Dream (Zhongguo Meng). In Barmé, Geremie R. and Jeremy Goldkorn (Eds) *China Story Yearbook 2013: Civilising China*, Canberra: Australian National University, 4–13.

Barnes, Linda L. (2005) *Needles, Herbs, Gods, and Ghosts: China, Healing, and the West to 1848*, London: Harvard University Press.

Barr, Michael D. (2010) Harmony, Conformity or Timidity? Singapore's Overachievement in the Quest for Harmony. In Tao, Julia, Anthony B. L. Cheung, Martin Painter and Chenyang Li (Eds) *Governance for Harmony in Asia and Beyond*, London and New York: Routledge, 73–102.

Barriaux, Marianne (2011) Three Babies Die in New China Milk Scare, *AFP*, 8 April 2011.

Baudrillard, Jean (1981 [1972]) *For a Critique of the Political Economy of the Sign*, Levin, Charles (Trans.), St Louis, MO: Telos Press.

Baudrillard, Jean (1987) *The Evil Demon of Images*, Patton, Paul and Paul Foss (Trans.), Sydney: Power Institute.

Baudrillard, Jean (1988 [1987]) *The Ecstasy of Communication*, Lotringer, Sylvere (Ed.), Schutze, Bernard and Caroline Schutze (Trans.), New York: Semiotext(e).

Baudrillard, Jean (1990 [1983]) *Fatal Strategies: Crystal Revenge*, Fleming, Jim (Ed.), Beitchman, Philip and W. G. J. Niesluchowski (Trans.), New York/London: Semiotext(e)/Pluto.

Baudrillard, Jean (1990 [1987]) *Cool Memories*, Turner, Chris (Trans.), London: Verso.

Baudrillard, Jean (1991) La Guerre du Golfe N'a Pas Eu Lieu [The Gulf War Did Not Take Place], *Libération*, 29 March 1991, 6.

Baudrillard, Jean (1993 [1976]) *Symbolic Exchange and Death*, Grant, Iain Hamilton (Trans.), London: Sage.

Baudrillard, Jean (1993 [1990]) *The Transparency of Evil: Essays on Extreme Phenomena*, Benedict, James (Trans.), New York: Verso.

Baudrillard, Jean (1994 [1981]) *Simulacra and Simulation*, Glaser, Sheila Faria (Trans.), Ann Arbor: University of Michigan Press.

Baudrillard, Jean (1994 [1992]) *Illusion of the End*, Turner, Chris (Trans.), Stanford, CA: Stanford University Press.

Baudrillard, Jean (1996 [1990]) *Cool Memories II*, Durham, NC: Duke University Press.

Baudrillard, Jean (2001) Symbolic Exchange and Death. In Poster, Mark (Ed.) *Jean Baudrillard: Selected Writings*, Cambridge: Polity Press.

Baudrillard, Jean (2001 [1999]) *Impossible Exchange*, Turner, Chris (Trans.), New York: Verso.

Baudrillard, Jean (2002 [1997]) Aids: Virulence or Prophylaxis? In Baudrillard, Jean (Ed.) *Screened Out*, Turner, Chris (Trans.), New York: Verso.
Baudrillard, Jean (2002 [2000]) *Screened Out*, Turner, Chris (Trans.), New York: Verso.
Baudrillard, Jean (2005 [2004]) *The Intelligence of Evil or the Lucidity Pact*, Turner, Chris (Trans.), London: Verso.
Baudrillard, Jean (2006 [2005]) The Pyres of Autumn, *New Left Review*, 37, 5–7.
Baudrillard, Jean and Rex Butler (1997) Baudrillard's List: Jean Baudrillard Interview with Rex Butler. In Zurbrugg, Nicholas (Ed.) *Jean Baudrillard: Art and Artefact*, London and Thousand Oaks, CA: Sage.
BBC Chinese (2013) *Zhongguo Wangmin Reyi Xi Jinping 'Xiezi Hejiao Lun'* [Chinese Netizens Hotly Discuss Xi Jinping's 'Fitting Shoes Theory']. Last updated 23 March 2013, retrieved 2 August 2015, from www.bbc.com/zhongwen/simp/china/2013/03/130323_xi_speech_weibo.shtml.
Beck, Lindsay (2007) From Struggle to Harmony, China Slogans Mark Hu Era, *Reuters*, Beijing, 7 September 2007.
Beijing Daily (2013) *CCP Beijing Municipal Committee Recommendations for Developing 'Chinese Dream' Education and Propaganda Work*. Last updated 5 April 2013, retrieved 17 July 2015, from http://chinadigitaltimes.net/2013/04/translation-chinese-dream-campaign-in-beijing.
Bially Mattern, Janice (2005) Why 'Soft Power' Isn't So Soft: Representational Force and the Sociolinguistic Construction of Attraction in World Politics, *Millennium*, 33(3), 583–612.
Billioud, Sébastien (2011) Confucianism, 'Cultural Tradition', and Official Discourse in China at the Start of the New Century. In Callahan, William A. and Elena Barabantseva (Eds) *China Orders the World? Soft Power, Norms and Foreign Policy*, Washington, DC: Woodrow Wilson Center Press, 215–48.
Birth, Kevin (2008) The Creation of Coevalness and the Danger of Homochronism, *Journal of Royal Anthropological Institute*, 14, 3–20.
Blanchard, Ben (2009) China Tightens Web Screws after Xinjiang Riot, *Reuters*, 6 July 2009.
Blanchard, Jean-Marc F. (2008) Harmonious World and China's Foreign Economic Policy: Features, Implications, and Challenges, *Journal of Chinese Political Science*, 13(2), 165–92.
Blanchard, Jean-Marc F. and Lu Fujia (2012) Thinking Hard about Soft Power: A Review and Critique of the Literature on China and Soft Power, *Asian Perspective*, 36(4), 565–89.
Blaney, David L. and Naeem Inayatullah (2010) *Savage Economics: Wealth, Poverty and the Temporal Walls of Capitalism*, London: Routledge.
Bleiker, Roland (2000) *Popular Dissent, Human Agency and Global Politics*, Cambridge: Cambridge University Press.
Bleiker, Roland (2009) *Aesthetics and World Politics*, Basingstoke: Palgrave Macmillan.
Bloch, Maurice (Ed.) (1975) *Political Language and Oratory in Traditional Society*, London: Academic Press.
Boutonnet, Thomas (2009) *Vers une 'Société Harmonieuse' de Consommation? Discours et Spectacle de l'Harmonie Sociale dans la Construction d'une Chine 'Civilisée' (1978–2008)* [Towards a 'Harmonious Society' of Consumption? Discourse and Spectacle of Social Harmony in the Construction of a 'Civilized' China (1978–2008)], Unpublished doctoral thesis, Université de Lyon – Jean Moulin Lyon 3.

Brady, Anne-Marie (2008) *Marketing Dictatorship: Propaganda and Thought Work in Contemporary China*, London: Rowman & Littlefield.

Brady, Anne-Marie (2011) *China's Thought Management*, Abingdon: Routledge.

Branigan, Tania (2010) Ai Weiwei Supporters Gather for Party at Condemned Studio, *Guardian*, 7 November 2010.

Branigan, Tania (2011) Ai Weiwei Released from Detention, *Guardian*, 22 June 2011.

Branigan, Tania (2014) China Bans Wordplay in Attempt at Pun Control, *Guardian*. Last updated 28 November 2014, retrieved 1 August 2015, from www.theguardian.com/world/2014/nov/28/china-media-watchdog-bans-wordplay-puns.

Breslin, Shaun (2011) The 'China Model' and the Global Crisis: From Friedrich List to a Chinese Mode of Governance?, *International Affairs*, 87(6), 1323–43.

Breslin, Shaun and Simon Shen (2010) Online Chinese Nationalism(s): Comparisons and Findings. In Shen, Simon and Shaun Breslin (Eds) *Online Chinese Nationalism and China's Bilateral Relations*, Lanham, MD: Rowman & Littlefield, 263–82.

Brownell, Susan (2008) *Beijing's Games: What the Olympics Mean to China*, Boulder, CO: Rowman & Littlefield.

Bulley, Dan (2009) *Ethics as Foreign Policy: Britain, the EU and the Other*, Abingdon: Routledge.

Bureau International des Expositions (2011) *Port au Prince 1949*. Retrieved 20 January 2011, from www.bie-paris.org/site/en/component/docman/cat_view/100-expo-documents.html?start=30.

Burke, Anthony (2007) *Beyond Security, Ethics and Violence: War against the Other*, New York: Routledge.

Cai Liang and Song Lilei (2010) *Kongzi Xueyuan: Quanqiu Tixi xia Zhongguo Zhishi Quanli de Waihua* [Confucius Institute: Discussion of China's Knowledge Power in the Global System], *International XXX*, 6, 38–48.

Cai Mingzhao (2013) *Zhongguo Meng Zhengzai Fahui Juda Ganzhaoli* [The Chinese Dream Is Exerting Enormous Appeal]. Last updated 7 December 2013, retrieved 30 June 2015, from http://news.china.com.cn/txt/2013-12/07/content_30828033.htm.

Callahan, William A. (2004) Remembering the Future: Utopia, Empire and Harmony in 21st Century International Theory, *European Journal of International Relations*, 10(4), 569–601.

Callahan, William A. (2007) *Tianxia, Empire and the World: Soft Power and China's Foreign Policy Discourse in the 21st Century*, Document no. 1, British Inter-University China Centre.

Callahan, William A. (2008) Chinese Visions of World Order: Post-Hegemonic or a New Hegemony?, *International Studies Review*, 10(4), 749–61.

Callahan, William A. (2009) The Cartography of National Humiliation and the Emergence of China's Geobody, *Public Culture*, 21(1), 141–73.

Callahan, William A. (2010) *China: The Pessoptimist Nation*, Oxford: Oxford University Press.

Callahan, William A. (2011) Conclusion: World Harmony or Harmonizing the World? In Callahan, William A. and Elena Barabantseva (Eds) *China Orders the World? Soft Power, Norms and Foreign Policy*, Washington, DC: Woodrow Wilson Center Press, 249–68.

Callahan, William A. (2012) Sino-Speak: Chinese Exceptionalism and Politics of History, *The Journal of Asian Studies*, 71(1), 33–55.

Callahan, William A. (2013) *China Dreams: 20 Visions of the Future*, Oxford: Oxford University Press.

Callahan, William A. (2014) The China Dream and the American Dream, *Economic and Political Studies*, 2(1), 143–60.
Callahan, William A. (2015a) History, Tradition and the China Dream: Socialist Modernization in the World of Great Harmony, *Journal of Contemporary China*, 24(96), 983–1001.
Callahan, William A. (2015b) Identity and Security in China: The Negative Soft Power of the China Dream, *Politics*, 35(3–4), 216–29.
Calon (2007) *GFW*, Urban Dictionary. Last updated 7 August 2007, retrieved 4 August 2011, from www.urbandictionary.com/define.php?term=GFW&defid=2543620.
Campbell, David (1996) Political Prosaics, and the Anarchical World. In Shapiro, Michael J. and Hayward R. Alker (Eds) *Challenging Boundaries: Global Flows, Territorial Identities*, Minneapolis: University of Minnesota Press.
Campbell, David (1998) *Writing Security: United States Foreign Policy and the Politics of Identity*, 2nd edn, Manchester: Manchester University Press.
Cao Zhi and Li Xuanliang (2013) *Jiefangjun Daibiao Biaoshi: Jiakuai Tuijin Guofang He Jundui Xiandaihua* [PLA Delegates Talk about Accelerating the Modernization of National Defence and the Armed Forces]. Last updated 6 March 2013, retrieved 15 June 2015, from www.gov.cn/2013lh/content_2347555.htm.
Caulhiaco, Guigonis de and Michael R. McVaugh (1997) *Inventarium Sive Chirurgia Magna*, Vol. 1, Leiden: Brill.
CCP Central Committee (2004) *Zhonggong Zhongyang guanyu Jiaqiang Dang de Zhizheng Nengli Jianshe de Jueding* [Decision on Strengthening the Building of Governing Capacity of the Party], Fourth Plenum of the Sixteenth Party Conference, Beijing, 19 September.
CCTV (2011) *Tibet Celebrates 60th Anniversary of Peaceful Liberation*. Last updated 19 July 2011, retrieved 27 February 2012, from http://english.cntv.cn/special/tibet/60th_anniv/live/index.shtml.
CCTV Documentary (2010) *The Opening Celebration and Site Opening Ceremony of Expo 2010 Shanghai China*, PRC, CCTV.
Central People's Government of the PRC (2008) *China's Policy Paper on Latin America and the Caribbean*, Central People's Government of the PRC, 28 February 2012.
Central Propaganda Department of the CCP [Theory Section] (2013) *Zhongguo Meng: Chanshi 'Zhongguo Meng' Wenzhang Xuanbian* [The China Dream: Selected Articles to Explain 'the China Dream'], Beijing: Zhongyang wenxian.
Chase, Michael S. and James C. Mulvenon (2002) *You've Got Dissent: Chinese Dissident Use of the Internet and Beijing's Counter-Strategies*, Santa Monica, CA: Rand.
Chen, Andrea and Zhuang Pinghui (2015) *Chinese Universities Ordered to Ban Textbooks That Promote Western Values*. Last updated 31 January 2015, retrieved 15 June 2015, from www.scmp.com/news/china/article/1695524/chinese-universities-instructed-ban-textbooks-promote-western-values?page=all.
Chen Duqing (2007) *Parceria Estratégica entre a China e o Brasil* [Strategic Partnership between China and Brazil], speech given at XIX National Forum, Rio de Janeiro, 14 May 2007.
Chen Zhi and Qian Tong (2013) *Xi Jinping: Zhongguomeng Yu Meiguomeng Xiangtong, Yaoqing Aobama Fanghua* [Xi Jinping: Chinese Dream and American Dream Are Interlinked, Invites Obama to Visit China]. Last updated 8 June 2013, retrieved 29 June 2015, from http://world.huanqiu.com/regions/2013-06/4014859.html.
Cheng, Joseph Y. S. (2012) Convincing the World of China's Tradition to Pursue Universal Harmony, *Journal of Chinese Political Science*, 17, 165–85.
Cheung, Kelvin Chi-Kin (2011) Conception of Threat in Chinese Strategic Culture:

Medicine as Analogy, paper presented at 'Representing China: From the Jesuits to Zhang Yimou', University of Manchester, 18–20 May 2011.

Cheung, Kelvin Chi-Kin (2012) Away from Socialism, towards Chinese Characteristics: Confucianism and the Futures of Chinese Nationalism, *China Information*, 26(2), 205–18.

Cheung, Kelvin Chi-Kin (2014) China's Rise and the International Politics of East Asia: The Development of Chinese IR Theory, *China: An International Journal*, 12(2), 31–45.

Chiaramonte, Delia and Lao Lixing (2010) Integrating Chinese and Western Medicine in Cancer Treatment. In Cho, William C. S. (Ed.) *Supportive Cancer Care with Chinese Medicine*, Dordrecht: Springer Science & Business Media B.V.

Chin, Josh (2010) The Most 'Chinese' Chinese Character?, *Wall Street Journal*, 15 October 2010.

China Digital Space (2011a) *Grass-Mud Horse Lexicon*. Retrieved 5 August 2011, from http://chinadigitaltimes.net/space/Grass-Mud_Horse_Lexicon.

China Digital Space (2011b) *Green Dam Girl*. Retrieved 5 August 2011, from http://chinadigitaltimes.net/space/Green_dam_girl.

The China Story (2013) *Xinhua's Top Ten Popular Words of 2013*. Last updated 20 December 2013, retrieved 15 June 2015, from www.thechinastory.org/dossier/xinhuas-top-ten-popular-words-of-2013.

ChinaFile (2013) *Document 9: A Chinafile Translation*. Last updated 8 November 2013, retrieved 30 June 2015, from www.chinafile.com/document-9-chinafile-translation.

Chow, Elaine (2010) *Changchun Is First Chinese City to Become GFWed*. Last updated 8 June 2010, retrieved 4 August 2011, from http://shanghaiist.com/2010/06/08/changchun_is_first_chinese_city_to.php.

Chow, Rey (1991) Violence in the Other Country: China as Crisis, Spectacle, and Woman. In Russo, Ann, Lourdes Torres and Chandra Talpade Mohanty (Eds) *Third World Women and the Politics of Feminism*, Bloomington: Indiana University Press, 81–100.

Chronicle of Higher Education (2013) Professor Says Peking U. May Expel Him in Political Crackdown. Last updated 13 September 2013, retrieved 30 June 2015, from http://chronicle.com/article/Professor-Says-Peking-U-May/141593/?cid=gn&utm_source=gn&utm_medium=en.

Clarke, Juanne (1996) *Health, Illness, and Medicine in Canadian Society*, 2nd edn, Toronto: Oxford University Press.

Clarke, Juanne and Julie Robinson (1999) Testicular Cancer: Medicine and Machismo in the Media (1980–94), *Health*, 3(3), 263–82.

CNTV (2012) Assad Vows to Continue Hard Line. Last updated 12 January 2012, retrieved 27 February 2012, from http://english.cntv.cn/program/newshour/20120112/115377.shtml.

Cohen, Ed (2009) *A Body Worth Defending: Immunity, Biopolitics, and the Apotheosis of the Modern Body*, Durham, NC: Duke University Press.

Committee to Protect Journalists (2011) *China Releases Artist Ai Weiwei, Questions Remain*. Last updated 22 June 2011, retrieved 31 July 2011, from http://cpj.org/2011/06/china-releases-artist-ai-weiwei-questions-remain.php.

Communist Party of China (2007) *Constitution of Communist Party of China*. Last updated 21 October 2007, retrieved 5 March 2011, from www.china.org.cn/english/congress/229722.htm.

Confucius (1979) *The Analects*, Lau Din Cheuk (Trans.), London: Penguin.

Coulter, Gerry (2004) Reversibility: Baudrillard's 'One Great Thought', *International Journal of Baudrillard Studies*, 1(2).

Coulter, Gerry (2005) Passings: Taking Derrida Seriously, *International Journal of Baudrillard Studies*, 2(1).

Crang, Mike and Nigel Thrift (2000) Introduction. In Crang, Mike and Nigel Thrift (Eds) *Thinking Space*, London: Routledge, 1–30.

Crazy Crab (2013a) *Hexie Farm: Barbed Wire*. Last updated 1 July 2013, retrieved 2 August 2015, from http://chinadigitaltimes.net/2013/07/hexie-farm-%E8%9F%B9%E5%86%9C%E5%9C%BA-barbed-wire.

Crazy Crab (2013b) *Hexie Farm: Dreamland*. Last updated 25 March 2013, retrieved 17 July 2015, from http://chinadigitaltimes.net/2013/03/hexie-farm-%E8%9F%B9%E5%86%9C%E5%9C%BA-dreamland.

Crazy Crab (2013c) *Hexie Farm: Frogs in the Well*. Last updated 7 August 2013, retrieved 17 July 2015, from http://chinadigitaltimes.net/2013/08/hexie-farm-%E8%9F%B9%E5%86%9C%E5%9C%BA-frogs-in-the-well.

Crazy Crab (2013d) *Hexie Farm: Mr Cage*. Last updated 17 July 2013, retrieved 2 August 2015, from http://chinadigitaltimes.net/2013/07/hexie-farm-%E8%9F%B9%E5%86%9C%E5%9C%BA-mr-cage.

Crazy Crab (2013e) *Hexie Farm: The Chinese Patient*. Last updated 9 May 2013, retrieved 2 August 2015, from http://chinadigitaltimes.net/2013/05/hexie-farm-%E8%9F%B9%E5%86%9C%E5%9C%BA-the-chinese-patient.

Crazy Crab (2013f) *Hexie Farm: The Sit-in*. Last updated 14 January 2013, retrieved 2 August 2015, from http://chinadigitaltimes.net/2013/01/hexie-farm-%E8%9F%B9%E5%86%9C%E5%9C%BA-the-sit-in.

Crazy Crab (2013g) *Hexie Farm: The Unsinkable*. Last updated 1 July 2013, retrieved 2 August 2015, from http://chinadigitaltimes.net/2013/06/hexie-farm-%E8%9F%B9%E5%86%9C%E5%9C%BA%EF%BC%9Athe-unsinkable.

Cui Jia, Liu Lu and Chen Jia (2012) Self-Immolation Acts Condemned by Deputies, *China Daily*, 8 March 2012, 5.

Cui Yong, Shu Xiao-Ou, Gao Yutang, Wen Wanqing, Ruan Zhi-Xian, Jin Fan and Zheng Wei (2004) Use of Complementary and Alternative Medicine by Chinese Women with Breast Cancer, *Breast Cancer Research and Treatment*, 85(3), 263–70.

Cunningham-Cross, Linsay (2014) Narrating a Discipline: The Search for Innovation in Chinese International Relations. In Horsburgh, Nicola, Astrid H. M. Nordin and Shaun Breslin (Eds) *Chinese Politics and International Relations: Innovation and Invention*, Abingdon: Routledge, 75–96.

Dai Bingguo (2011) China Is Committed to the Path of Peaceful Development, paper presented at Symposium on China's Peaceful Development White Paper, Diaoyutai State Guesthouse, Beijing, 15 September 2011.

Dai Bingguo (2012) A Brighter Future When China and India Work Hand in Hand, paper presented at 15th Meeting of the Special Representatives on the China–India Boundary Question, New Delhi, 16 January 2012.

Dallmayr, Fred (1993) *The Other Heidegger*, Ithaca, NY: Cornell University Press.

Daubigny, Corinne (2003) Pourquoi la Guerre? [Why War?], *Le Coq-Héron*, 173, 151–4.

Davies, Gloria (2007) *Worrying about China: The Language of Chinese Critical Inquiry*, Cambridge, MA: Harvard University Press.

Davies, Gloria (2013) *Fitting Words*. Retrieved 2 August 2015, from www.thechinastory.org/yearbooks/yearbook-2013/chapter-7-fitting-words.

Davis, Kathleen (2008) *Periodization and Sovereignty: How Ideas of Feudalism and*

Secularization Govern the Politics of Time, Philadelphia: University of Pennsylvania Press.

Dayan, Daniel (2008) Beyond Media Events: Disenchantment, Derailment, Disruption. In Price, Monroe E. and Daniel Dayan (Eds) *Owning the Olympics: Narratives of the New China*, Ann Arbor: University of Michigan Press, 391–401.

Delaney, David (2005) *Territory: A Short Introduction*, London: Blackwell.

Deleuze, Gilles and Félix Guattari (1988 [1980]) *A Thousand Plateaus: Capitalism and Schizophrenia*, Minneapolis: University of Minnesota Press.

Demaitre, Luke (1998) Medieval Notions of Cancer: Malignancy and Metaphor, *Bulletin of the History of Medicine*, 72(4), 609–37.

Deng Li (2009) *'Hexie Shijie' Shijiao xia de Zhongguo Haiquan* [China's Sea Power under the Perspective of 'Harmonious World'], *Zhonggong Tongren diwei dangxiao xuebao* [Journal of Tongren Prefectural Committee Party School of CPC], 4(38).

Derrida, Jacques (1976 [1967]) *Of Grammatology*, Spivak, Gayatri Chakravorty (Trans.), London: Johns Hopkins University Press.

Derrida, Jacques (1981 [1972]) *Dissemination*, Johnson, Barbara (Trans.), Chicago, IL: University of Chicago Press.

Derrida, Jacques (1982 [1972]) *Margins of Philosophy*, Bass, Alan (Trans.), Brighton: Harvester.

Derrida, Jacques (1982) Sending: On Representation, *Social Research*, 49(2), 294–326.

Derrida, Jacques (1987 [1972]) *Positions*, Bass, Alan (Trans.), London: Athlone Press.

Derrida, Jacques (1988) *Limited Inc*, Weber, Samuel (Trans.), Evanston, IL: Northwestern University Press.

Derrida, Jacques (1993) *Aporias: Dying – Awaiting (One Another at) the 'Limits of Truth'*, Dutoit, Thomas (Trans.), Stanford, CA: Stanford University Press.

Derrida, Jacques (1994) *Specters of Marx: The State of the Debt, the Work of Mourning, and the New International*, Kamuf, Peggy (Trans.), London: Routledge.

Derrida, Jacques (1995 [1989]-a) The Rhetoric of Drugs. In Weber, Elisabeth (Ed.) *Points…: Interviews, 1974–1994*, Kamuf, Peggy and Michael Israel (Trans.), Stanford, CA: Stanford University Press, 228–54.

Derrida, Jacques (1995 [1989]-b) 'There Is No *One* Narcissism' (Autobiophotographies). In Weber, Elisabeth (Ed.) *Points…: Interviews, 1974–1994*, Kamuf, Peggy and Michael Israel (Trans.), Stanford, CA: Stanford University Press.

Derrida, Jacques (1998 [1996]) *Resistances of Psychoanalysis*, Kamuf, Peggy, Pascale-Anne Brault and Michael Naas (Trans.), Stanford, CA: Stanford University Press.

Derrida, Jacques (1998) Faith and Knowledge: The Two Sources of 'Religion' at the Limits of Reason Alone. In Derrida, Jacques and Gianni Vattimo (Eds) *Religion*, Weber, Samuel (Trans.), Cambridge: Polity, 1–78.

Derrida, Jacques (2002) *Negotiations: Interventions and Interviews 1971–2001*, Rottenberg, Elizabeth (Trans.), Stanford, CA: Stanford University Press.

Derrida, Jacques (2003) Autoimmunity: Real and Symbolic Suicides – A Dialogue with Jacques Derrida. In Borradori, Giovanna (Ed.) *Philosophy in a Time of Terror: Dialogues with Jürgen Habermas and Jacques Derrida*, Chicago, IL: University of Chicago Press.

Derrida, Jacques (2005 [2003]-a) The Reason of the Strongest (Are There Rogue States?). In Derrida, Jacques, Pascale-Anne Brault and Michael Naas (Eds) *Rogues: Two Essays on Reason*, Brault, Pascale-Anne and Michael Naas (Trans.), Stanford, CA: Stanford University Press, 6–114.

Derrida, Jacques (2005 [2003]-b) The 'World' of the Enlightenment to Come (Exception,

Calculation, and Sovereignty). In Derrida, Jacques, Pascale-Anne Brault and Michael Naas (Eds) *Rogues: Two Essays on Reason*, Brault, Pascale-Anne and Michael Naas (Trans.), Stanford, CA: Stanford University Press, 115–59.

Di Dongsheng (2007) Continuity and Changes: A Comparative Study on China's New Grand Strategy, *Historia Actual Online*, 12, 7–18.

Diamond, Larry (2010) Liberation Technology, *Journal of Democracy*, 21(3), 69–83.

Ding Sheng (2008) To Build a 'Harmonious World': China's Soft Power Wielding in the Global South, *Journal of Chinese Political Science*, 13(2), 193–213.

Ding Wei and Giovanni Cubeddu (2010) Quarant'anni D'amicizia 'Parlarsi Sinceramente, Ascoltarsi Reciprocamente' [Forty Years of Friendship 'Speaking Frankly, Listening to Each Other'], *30 Giorni*, 06/07.

Do, Thuy T. (2015) China's Rise and the 'Chinese Dream' in International Relations Theory, *Global Change, Peace and Security*, 27(1), 21–38.

Dorsher, Peter and Peng Zengfu (2010) Chinese Medicinal Herbs Use in Managing Cancer. In Cho, William C. S. (Ed.) *Supportive Cancer Care with Chinese Medicine*, Dordrecht: Springer Science & Business Media B.V.

Dunn, Kevin C. (2003) *Imagining the Congo: The International Relations of Identity*, New York: Palgrave Macmillan.

DZS manyin (2010) *Lv Ba Niang de Xinyang* [Green Dam Girl's Wishes]. YouTube. Last updated 19 July 2010, retrieved 5 August 2011, from www.youtube.com/watch?v=gtE_n2CdPpg&feature=related.

The Economist (2013) Chasing the Chinese Dream. Last updated 4 May 2013, retrieved 15 June 2015, from www.economist.com/news/briefing/21577063-chinas-new-leader-has-been-quick-consolidate-his-power-what-does-he-now-want-his.

Edkins, Jenny (1999) *Poststructuralism and International Relations: Bringing the Political Back in*, London and Boulder, CO: Lynne Rienner Publishers.

Embassy of the PRC in Barbados (2010) *Chinese Watercolor Painting Exhibition in Barbados*. Last updated 19 January 2010, retrieved 10 March 2012, from http://bb.china-embassy.org/eng/xwdt/t652350.htm.

Embassy of the PRC in Chile (2011) *Se Inaugura Salón Confucio en el Instituto Nacional* [Confucius Exhibition Opens at the National Institute]. Last updated 7 April 2011, retrieved 10 March 2012, from http://cl.china-embassy.org/esp/sghd/t813046.htm.

Embassy of the PRC in Commonwealth of Dominica (2011) *Speech by H. E. Wang Zonglai, Ambassador of the People's Republic of China, at the Welcome Reception*. Retrieved 10 March 2012, from http://dm.china-embassy.org/eng/zyxw/t791031.htm.

Embassy of the PRC in FDR of Nepal (2011) *Chinese Ambassador to Nepal Yang Houlan Introduced the White Paper of China's Peaceful Development to Nepal's Chief Editors of Four Main Media*. Last updated 28 September 2011, retrieved 10 March 2012, from http://np.china-embassy.org/eng/News/t863333.htm.

Embassy of the PRC in Germany (2010) *Photoausstellung über Expo 2010 in UN-Außenstelle in Genf* [Photo Exhibition on Expo 2010 in the UN Office in Geneva]. Last updated 27 April 2010, retrieved 10 March 2012, from http://de.china-embassy.org/det/gdxw/t687875.htm.

Embassy of the PRC in Mexico (2011) *Celebran Aniversario del EPL en la Embajada de China en México* [Anniversary of PLA held at the Embassy of China in Mexico]. Last updated 2 August 2011, retrieved 10 March 2012, from www.embajadachina.org.mx/esp/sgjs/t845992.htm.

Embassy of the PRC in PR Bangladesh (2011) *Ambassador Zhang Xianyi Gave a Speech at Bangladesh Defense Services Command and Staff College*. Last updated 10 October

2011, retrieved 10 March 2012, from http://bd.china-embassy.org/eng/xwdt/t865901.htm.
Embassy of the PRC in the UK (2011a) *Chinese Embassy Holds Film Reception in Commemoration of the 66th Anniversary of the Chinese People's Victory against Japanese Aggression and the 80th Anniversary of the 'September 18th Incident'*. Last updated 27 August 2011, retrieved 28 February 2012, from www.chinese-embassy.org.uk/eng/EmbassyNews/2011/t852901.htm.
Embassy of the PRC in the UK (2011b) *'Fashion Shenzhen' Won Great Popularity in Britain: Ambassador Liu Xiaoming Couples Attend the 'Fashion Shenzhen' Event at London Fashion Week*. Last updated 23 September 2011, retrieved 27 February 2012, from www.chinese-embassy.org.uk/eng/EmbassyNews/2011/t868724.htm.
Embassy of the PRC in the USA (2010) Chinese Embassy Spokesman Wang Baodong: Don't Politicize the Nobel Peace Prize, *USA Today*, 10 December 2010.
Embassy of the PRC in the USA (2011) *Symposium on 'China's Peaceful Development' Is Held in Beijing*. Last updated 16 September 2011, retrieved 10 March 2012, from www.china-embassy.org/eng/zt/zhongguodehepingfazhan/t862099.htm.
Erickson, Robert A. (1997) *The Language of the Heart 1600–1750*, Philadelphia: University of Pennsylvania Press.
Esarey, Ashley and Xiao Qiang (2008) Political Expression in the Chinese Blogosphere: Below the Radar, *Asian Survey*, 48(5), 752–72.
Expo 2010 (2006a) *1949 Port au Prince – Haiti*. Last updated 26 August 2006, retrieved 20 January 2011, from http://en.expo2010.cn/a/20080614/000094.htm.
Expo 2010 (2006b) *New Research Reveals China Took Part in First World Expo*. Last updated 25 August 2006, retrieved 20 January 2011, from http://en.expo2010.cn/expo/expo_english/oe/awe/cwe/userobject1ai35918.html.
Expo 2010 (2008) *Brief Introduction of World Expo Shanghai*. Last updated 26 January 2008, retrieved 15 September 2010, from http://en.expo2010.cn/a/20081116/000004.htm.
Expo Shanghai Online (2010a) *China Pavilion*. Retrieved 18 September 2010, from http://pavilion.expo.cn/z0001/ssize/explainchinavenue/index.html.
Expo Shanghai Online (2010b) *Expo 2010 Shanghai China Official Homepage*. Retrieved 26 February 2012, from http://en.expo2010.cn.
Expo Shanghai Online (2010c) *My Expo Dream Home*. Retrieved 18 September 2010, from http://en.expo.cn/jnh/dreamwall/index.html.
Expo Shanghai Online (2010d) *Site Tour*. Retrieved 11 December 2010, from http://en.expo.cn/indexn.html.
Expo Shanghai Online (2010e) *Tibet in the Heaven*. Retrieved 11 December 2010, from http://pavilion.expo.cn/p6006/ssize/cn/index.html.
Expo Shanghai Online (2010f) *Vanke Pavilion*. Retrieved 19 September 2010, from http://pavilion.expo.cn/e1016/ssize/index.html.
Expo Shanghai Online (2010g) *Xinjiang Pavilion*. Retrieved 19 September 2010, from http://pavilion.expo.cn/p8006/ssize/index.html.
Fabian, Johannes (1983) *Time and the Other: How Anthropology Makes Its Object*, New York: Columbia University Press.
Fang Xiaojiao (2008) *Hexie Shijie Linian yu Zhongguo Ruanshili Jianshe* [The Harmonious World Concept and China's Building of Soft Power], *Jiaoxue yu yanjiu* [Education and Research], 4, 67–72.
Festa, Paul E. (2006) Mahjong Politics in Contemporary China: Civility, Chineseness, and Mass Culture, *Positions*, 14(1), 7–35.
Foreign Ministry of the PRC (2011) *President Hu Jintao Attends the Welcome Ceremony*

Hosted by U.S. President Obama at the White House 2011/01/20. Last updated 20 January 2011, retrieved 10 March 2012, from www.china-embassy.org/eng/gdxw/t788873.htm.

Foucault, Michel (1990) *The History of Sexuality: An Introduction*, Vol. I, Hurley, Robert (Trans.), New York: Vintage Books.

Friedman, Thomas L. (2012) China Needs Its Own Dream, *New York Times*. Last updated 2 October 2012, retrieved 15 June 2015, www.nytimes.com/2012/10/03/opinion/friedman-china-needs-its-own-dream.html?_r=0.

Fu, Sandra (2011) Two New Lists of Sina Weibo's Banned Search Terms, *China Digital Times*. Last updated 7 November 2011, retrieved 8 November 2011, from http://chinadigitaltimes.net/2011/11/two-new-lists-of-sina-weibos-banned-search-terms.

Fuchs, Chris (2014) Old Stomping Grounds, *Taipei Times*. Last updated 4 May 2014, retrieved 1 August 2015, from www.taipeitimes.com/News/feat/archives/2014/05/04/2003589511.

Gang Lin (2005) *China's 'Good Neighbor' Diplomacy: A Wolf in Sheep's Clothing?*, Document no. 126, Asia Program Special Report, Woodrow Wilson International Center for Scholars.

Gao Xin and Sun Laibin (2015) Lun Zhongguomeng de Dazhong Rentong: Jiyu Jiazji Rentong de Weidu [On the Public Recognition of the Chinese Dream: The Dimension of Value Basis Identification], *Dangdai shijie yu shehui zhuyi* [Contemporary World and Socialism], 2, 171–6.

Gaofudev (2011) *Insect Necklace – River Crab – Potamon Denticulatum*. Retrieved 8 August 2011, from www.ebay.co.uk/itm/Insect-Necklace-River-Crab-Potamon-denticulatum-/190320365027.

Gardels, Nathan (2014) Xi Launches Cultural Counter-Revolution to Restore Confucianism as China's Ideology, *Huffington Post*. Last updated 18 December 2014, retrieved 28 September 2015, from www.huffingtonpost.com/nathan-gardels/xi-jinping-confucianism_b_5897680.html.

Gell, Alfred (1992) *The Anthropology of Time: Cultural Constructions of Temporal Maps and Images*, Oxford: Berg.

Gilley, Bruce (2004) *China's Democratic Future: How It Will Happen and Where It Will Lead*, New York: Columbia University Press.

Gilman, Sander L. (1988) Medical Colonialism and Disease: Lam Qua and the Creation of a Westernized Medical Iconography in 19th-Century China. In Gilman, Sander L. (Ed.) *Disease and Representation: Images of Illness from Madness to Aids*, London: Cornell University Press, 140–54.

Glaser, Bonnie S. and Evan S. Medeiros (2007) The Changing Ecology of Foreign Policy-Making in China: The Ascension and Demise of the Theory of 'Peaceful Rise', *The China Quarterly*, 190, 291–310.

Goldkorn, Jeremy (2010) *Ai Weiwei's River Crab Banquet*, Danwei.org. Last updated 7 November 2010, retrieved 4 March 2011, from www.danwei.org/art/ai_weiweis_river_crab_banquet.php.

Gow, Mike (2015) Universities Find It Difficult to Grasp China's Dream, *Times Higher Education*. Last updated 12 February 2015, retrieved 15 June 2015, from www.timeshighereducation.co.uk/comment/opinion/universities-find-it-difficult-to-grasp-chinas-dream/2018398.article.

Grace, Victoria (2003) Medical Visualisation: Ontological Politics and Paradoxes. In Grace, Victoria, Heather Worth and Laurence Simmons (Eds) *Baudrillard West of the Dateline*, Palmerston North, New Zealand: Dunmore Press, 189–206.

Grammaticas, Damian (2013) China's New President Xi Jinping: A Man with a Dream, BBC News. Last updated 14 March 2013, retrieved 30 June 2015, from www.bbc.co.uk/news/world-asia-china-21790384.
Guicciardini, Francesco (1984) *The History of Italy by Francesco Guicciardini*, Princeton, NJ: Princeton University Press.
Guo Jianning (2006) The Scientific Outlook on Development and the Building of a Harmonious Society, *Journal of Peking University (Philosophy & Social Sciences)*, 3.
Guo Sujian and Jean-Marc F. Blanchard (Eds) (2008) *'Harmonious World' and China's New Foreign Policy*, Lanham, MD: Lexington Books.
Haddad, Samir (2004) Derrida and Democracy at Risk, *Contretemps*, 4, 29–44.
Hale, David George (1971) *The Body Politic: A Political Metaphor in Renaissance English Literature*, The Hague: Mouton.
Hall, David L. and Roger T. Ames (1998) *Thinking from the Han: Self, Truth, and Transcendence in Chinese and Western Culture*, Albany, NY: SUNY Press.
Han Qingxiang (2013) *Zhongguomeng Beijing, Shizhi Yu Neihan* [The Backdrop, Essence and Content of the Chinese Dream]. Last updated 17 June 2013, retrieved 18 June 2015, from http://theory.people.com.cn/n/2013/0617/c112851-21868421-2.html.
Hang Lihua (2010) *Hexie Shijie Shijiao xia de Zhongguo Waijiao* [Chinese Foreign Policy from the Viewpoint of Harmonious World], *Gaige yu chuangxin* [Reform and Innovation], 20–1.
Hanyu da zidian (Ed.) (1995) *Hanyu Da Zidian* [Comprehensive Chinese Character Dictionary], corrected ed., Wuhan: Hubei cishu chubanshe.
Harvey, Penelope (1996) *Hybrids of Modernity: Anthropology, the Nation State and the Universal Exhibition*, London: Routledge.
Have, Henk Ten (1987) Medicine and the Cartesian Image of Man, *Theoretical Medicine*, 8(2), 235–46.
He Zhou (2008) SMS in China: A Major Carrier of the Nonofficial Discourse Universe, *The Information Society*, 24(3), 182–90.
Hecaitou (2009a) *80 Hou zhi Manhua Nixi: Lv Ba Tiaojiao* [Cartoon Counter-attack of the Post-80s: Green Dam Discipline]. Last updated 14 June 2009, retrieved 5 August 2011, from www.hecaitou.net/?p=5770.
Hecaitou (2009b) *Wangyou Banbu yi pi Xin Hanzi* [Netizens Publish a Set of New Characters]. Last updated 31 August 2009, retrieved 5 August 2011, from www.hecaitou.com/blogs/hecaitou/archives/134100.aspx.
Hegarty, Paul (2004) *Jean Baudrillard: Live Theory*, London: Continuum.
Heifenbrug, Attila (2008) *Hexie Shijie* [Rivercrab World]. Last updated 29 November 2008, retrieved 11 June 2011, from http://picasaweb.google.com/A.Heifenbrug/JtDCaK#5274053782376715458.
Heinrich, Larissa (2008) The Pathological Body. In Heinrich, Larissa (Ed.) *The Afterlife of Images: Translating the Pathological Body between China and the West*, Durham, NC: Duke University Press, 39–71.
Henochowicz, Anne (2013a) Drawing the News: Kung Fu, Ninjas, Dreams, *China Digital Times*. Last updated 29 March 2013, retrieved 2 August 2015, from http://chinadigitaltimes.net/2013/03/drawing-the-news-kung-fu-ninjas-dreams.
Henochowicz, Anne (2013b) Drawing the News: Silly Old Bear, *China Digital Times*. Last updated 19 June 2013, retrieved 2 August 2015, from http://chinadigitaltimes.net/2013/06/drawing-the-news-silly-old-bear.
Henochowicz, Anne (2013c) Netizen Voices: Chinese Dream, the Dream of Prison, *China Digital Times*. Last updated 16 July 2013, retrieved 17 July 2015, from

http://chinadigitaltimes.net/2013/07/netizen-voices-chinese-dream-the-dream-of-prison.

Henochowicz, Anne (2013d) Netizen Voices: Don't Smother Our 'Chinese Dream', *China Digital Times*. Last updated 1 May 2013, retrieved 2 August 2015, from http://chinadigitaltimes.net/2013/05/netizen-voices-dont-smother-our-chinese-dream.

Herold, David K. (2011) Noise, Spectacle, Politics: Carnival in Chinese Cyberspace. In Herold, David K. and Peter Marolt (Eds) *Online Society in China: Creating, Celebrating, and Instrumentalising the Online Carnival*, Abingdon: Routledge, 1–20.

Herold, David K. and Peter Marolt (2011) *Online Society in China: Creating, Celebrating, and Instrumentalising the Online Carnival*, Abingdon: Routledge.

Herzlich, Claudine and Janine Pierret (1987) *Illness and Self in Society*, London: Johns Hopkins University Press.

Hexie Farm (2011) *Xienongchang* [Hexie Farm]. Last updated 8 November 2011, retrieved 8 November 2011, from http://hexiefarm.wordpress.com.

Hilal, Khalid (2001) Theoretical Perspectives from China on International Relations, *Public Organization Review*, 1(3), 375–7.

Ho, Benjamin (2014) Understanding Chinese Exceptionalism: China's Rise, Its Goodness, and Greatness, *Alternatives: Global, Local, Political*, 39(3), 164–76.

Hoad, Terry F. (1993) Harmony. In Hoad, Terry F. (Ed.) *The Concise Oxford Dictionary of English Etymology*, Oxford: Oxford University Press.

Hobbes, Thomas (1996) *Leviathan*, Tuck, Richard (Ed.), Cambridge: Cambridge University Press.

Horsburgh, Nicola, Astrid H. M. Nordin and Shaun Breslin (2014) Introduction. In Horsburgh, Nicola, Astrid H. M. Nordin and Shaun Breslin (Eds) *Chinese Politics and International Relations: Innovation and Invention*, Abingdon: Routledge, 1–21.

Hrehnr (2009a) *Lv Ba Niang Lv zhi Ge* [Green Dam Girl Green Song]. YouTube. Last updated 5 July 2009, retrieved 5 August 2011, from www.youtube.com/watch?v=5zeuhpiz-lQ&feature=player_embedded.

Hrehnr (2009b) *Lv Ba Niang zhi Wu* [Green Dam Girl Dance]. YouTube. Last updated 7 July 2009, retrieved 5 August 2011, from www.youtube.com/watch?v=vxnc6ng-rnI&NR=1.

Hu Angang (2011) *China in 2020: A New Kind of Superpower*, Washington, DC: Brookings Institution Press.

Hu Angang (2013a) *Shijie Datong de 'Zhongguomeng'* ['The Chinese Dream' of the World of Great Harmony]. Last updated 11 December 2013, retrieved 30 June 2015, from http://theory.people.com.cn/n/2013/1211/c359405-23812773.html.

Hu Angang (2013b) *Zhongguo Daolu Yu Zhongguo Mengxiang* [Chinese Path and Chinese Dream], Hangzhou: Zhejiang renmin chubanshe.

Hu Angang (2014) Qingnian Chengcai Yu 'Zhongguomeng' [Youth Growth and 'China Dream'], *Xueshujiaoliu*, 239(2), 5–13.

Hu Angang and Yan Yilong (2010) *Zhongguo: Zou Xiang 2015* [China: Moving toward 2015], Hangzhou: Zhejiang People's Publishing House.

Hu Angang, Yan Yilong and Wei Xing (2011) *2030 Zhongguo: Maixiang Gongtong Fuyu* [2030 China: Towards Common Prosperity], Beijing: Renmin University Press.

Hu Dingxian (2010) Remarks by H. E. Ambassador Hu Dingxian at the Reception of the 61st Anniversary of the Founding of the PRC, speech given at Reception of the 61st Anniversary of the Founding of the PRC, Nassau, 28 September 2010.

Hu Dingxian (2012) Remarks by H. E. Ambassador Hu Dingxian at the Official Performance by the China National Acrobatic Troupe, speech given at the Official Performance by the China National Acrobatic Troupe, Lesotho Convention Center, Lesotho, 6 February 2012.

Hu Jintao (2005a) *Build towards a Harmonious World of Lasting Peace and Common Prosperity*. Retrieved 15 February 2011, from www.china-un.org/eng/zt/shnh60/t212915.htm.

Hu Jintao (2005b) *Hu Jintao guanyu Goujian Shehuizhuyi Hexie Shehui Jianghua Quanwen* [Full Text of Hu Jintao's Speech on Building Socialist Harmonious Society]. Zhongguowang [Chinanet]. Last updated 26 June 2005, retrieved 14 January 2012, from www.china.com.cn/chinese/news/899546.htm.

Hu Jintao (2005c) Making an Effort to Build a Sustainable, Peaceful, and United Prosperous Harmonious World, speech at the United Nations 60 Year Celebration, *Renmin ribao*, 16 September 2005, 1.

Hu Jintao (2007) *Report at 17th Party Congress*. Last updated 15 October 2007, retrieved 16 February 2011, from http://news.xinhuanet.com/english/2007-10/24/content_6938749.htm.

Hu Jintao (2009) Jointly Create a Better Future for World Peace and Development, New Year Address Delivered by Hu Jintao, President of the People's Republic of China, Beijing, 31 December 2009.

Hu Jintao (2010) Address by Hu Jintao at the Opening Session of the Second Round of the China–US Strategic and Economic Dialogues, speech given at Second Round of the China–US Strategic and Economic Dialogues, Beijing, 24 May 2010.

Hu Jintao (2011a) Broad Vision, Shared Prosperity, speech given at BRICS Leaders Meeting, Sanya, Hainan, 14 April 2011.

Hu Jintao (2011b) Speech at a Meeting Commemorating the 90th Anniversary of the Founding of the CCP, speech given at Grand Gathering Marking the 90th Founding Anniversary of the CPC, Great Hall of the People, Beijing, 1 July 2011.

Hu Shan (2011) Remarks by Chinese Ambassador H. E. Mr. Hu Shan at the Reception Celebrating the 62nd Anniversary of the Founding of the PRC, speech given at Reception Celebrating the 62nd Anniversary of the Founding of the PRC, Bahamas, 5 October 2011.

Hua Shiping (2013) *Bainian 'Zhongguomeng' Yu 'Datong' Chuantong* [100 Years of 'Chinese Dream' and 'Great Harmony' Tradition]. Last updated 27 June 2013, retrieved 29 June 2015, from http://theory.people.com.cn/n/2013/0627/c112851-21998307.html.

Huang Chiung-Chiu and Shih Chih-yu (2014) *Harmonious Intervention: China's Quest for Relational Security*, Farnham: Ashgate.

Huang Haifeng (2015) Propaganda as Signaling, *Comparative Politics*, 47(4), 419–44.

Huang Wei (2015) From Reservation to Ambiguity: Academic Debates and China's Diplomatic Strategy under Hu's Leadership, *East Asia*, 32, 67–81.

Huang Xiaoming (2001) The Zen Master's Story and an Anatomy of International Relations Theory. In Chan, Stephen, Peter Mandaville and Roland Bleiker (Eds) *The Zen of International Relations: IR Theory from East to West*, Basingstoke: Palgrave, 222–43.

Hughes, Chris (2011) The Recycling of Time and the End of History, *International Journal of Baudrillard Studies*, 8(1).

Huliang zhoukan (2002) *Women de Dianzi Zhengfu* [Our E-Government], *Huliang zhoukan* [Internet Weekly], 42, 35.

Human Rights Watch (2010) *'I Saw It with My Own Eyes': Abuses by Security Forces in Tibet, 2008–2010*. Last updated 21 July 2010, retrieved 15 January 2016, from www.

hrw.org/report/2010/07/21/i-saw-it-my-own-eyes/abuses-chinese-security-forces-tibet-2008-2010.

Hung, Kenneth Tin-Kin (2011) *Nao Can Youji/The Travelogue of Dr. Brain Damages*. Retrieved 4 August 2011, from www.tinkin.com/arts/the-travelogue-of-dr-brain-damages.

Hutchings, Kimberly (2008) *Time and World Politics: Thinking the Present*, Manchester: Manchester University Press.

I. C. R. (2007) Jean Baudrillard, 1929–2007, *Science Fiction Studies*, 34(3), 525–7.

Inayatullah, Naeem and David L. Blaney (2004) *International Relations and the Problem of Difference*, New York: Routledge.

Inkster, Nigel (2010) China in Cyberspace, *Survival*, 52(4), 55–66.

Jacques, Martin (2009) *When China Rules the World: The Rise of the Middle Kingdom and the End of the Western World*, London: Allen Lane.

Jia Yue (2013) *Wangluo Mingren Gongshi Gongshou 'Qitiao Dixian'* [Online Celebrities Agree to Defend 'Seven Baselines']. Last updated 11 August 2013, retrieved 18 June 2015, from http://society.people.com.cn/n/2013/0811/c1008-22522366.html.

Jian Zhang (2007) *Building a Harmonious World? Chinese Perceptions of Regional Order and Implications for Australia*, Document no. 35, Australian Strategic Policy Institute.

Jiang Aitao (2009) *Revision of 44 Chinese Characters in Hot Debates*, CRI English. Last updated 31 August 2009, retrieved 5 August 2011, from http://english.cri.cn/6909/2009/08/31/189s512590.htm.

Jiang Zemin (1997) *Enhance Mutual Understanding and Build Stronger Ties of Friendship and Cooperation*. Retrieved 25 February 2011, from http://us.china-embassy.org/eng/zmgx/zysj/jzxfm/t36252.htm.

Jin Chunming, Huang Yuchong and Chang Huimin (Eds) (1989) *'Wenge' Shiqi Guaishi Guaiyu* [Weird Things and Weird Words from the Time of the 'Cultural Revolution'], Beijing: Qiushi chubanshe.

Johnson, Ian (2013) *Old Dreams for a New China*. Last updated 15 October 2013, retrieved 16 July 2015, from www.nybooks.com/blogs/nyrblog/2013/oct/15/china-dream-posters/?printpage=true.

Johnston, Alastair I. (1995) *Cultural Realism: Strategic Culture and Grand Strategy in Chinese History*, Princeton, NJ: Princeton University Press.

Johnston, Alastair I. (2008) *Social States: China in International Institutions, 1980–2000*, Princeton, NJ: Princeton University Press.

Johnston, Alastair I. and Robert S. Ross (Eds) (1999) *Engaging China: The Management of an Emerging Power*, London: Routledge.

jozjozjoz (2009) *The Green Dam Youth Escort: Not an Environmentalist 'Dating' Service for Young People*. Last updated 19 June 2009, retrieved 5 August 2011, from www.8asians.com/2009/06/19/the-green-dam-youth-escort-not-an-environmentalist-dating-service-for-young-people.

Kaltman, Blaine (2007) *Under the Heel of the Dragon: Islam, Racism, Crime and the Uighur in China*, Athens: Ohio University Press.

Kang, David (2007) *China Rising: Peace, Power and Order in East Asia*, New York: Columbia University Press.

Kaptchuk, Ted J. (2000) *Chinese Medicine: The Web That Has No Weaver*, London: Ebury Press.

Karlgren, Bernhard (1974 [1923]) *Analytic Dictionary of Chinese and Sino-Japanese*, New York: Dover Publications.

Kerr, David (2011) Paradoxes of Tradition and Modernity at the New Frontier: China, Islam, and the Problem of 'Different Heavens'. In Callahan, William A. and Elena Barabantseva (Eds) *China Orders the World? Soft Power, Norms and Foreign Policy*, Washington, DC: Woodrow Wilson Center Press, 143–79.

Koman, Richard (2009) *Green Dam Built on Copyright, Open Source Violations*. Last updated 15 June 2009, retrieved 5 August 2011, from www.zdnet.com/blog/government/green-dam-built-on-copyright-open-source-violations/4961.

Krasner, Steven (2001) Rethinking the Sovereign State Model, *Review of International Studies*, 27(5), 17–42.

Kristensen, Peter Marcus and Ras Tind Nielsen (2013) Constructing a Chinese International Relations Theory: A Sociological Approach to Intellectual Innovation, *International Political Sociology*, 7(1), 19–40.

Ku Chieh-Kang (1938 [1935]) A Study of Literary Persecution during the Ming, Goodrich, L. Carrington (Trans.), *Harvard Journal of Asiatic Studies*, 3(3/4), 254–311.

Kuhn, Anthony (2010) In Changing China, Being 'Suicided' or 'Harmonized', *NPR*. Last updated 19 March 2010, retrieved 1 March 2010, from www.npr.org/templates/story/story.php?storyId=124913011.

Kuhn, Robert L. (2013) *Only a Nationalist Can Reform China*. Last updated 6 March 2013, retrieved 14 July 2015, from www.digitalnpq.org/articles/global/642/06-03-2013/robert_lawrence_kuhn.

Kuo, Lily (2013) *Chinese Citizens Are Hijacking Xi Jinping's Latest Propaganda Tool*. Last updated 18 May 2013, retrieved 30 June 2015, from http://qz.com/83181/chinese-citizens-are-hijacking-xi-jinpings-latest-propaganda-tool.

Kurlantzick, Joshua (2004) Dictatorship.Com: The Web Won't Topple Tyranny, *The New Republic*, 25 March 2004.

Laclau, Ernesto and Lilian Zac (1994) Minding the Gap: The Subject of Politics. In Laclau, Ernesto (Ed.) *The Making of Political Identities*, London: Verso, 11–39.

Lacoue-Labarthe, Philippe (1990) *Heidegger, Art and Politics: The Fiction of the Political*, Oxford: Blackwell.

Lafitte, Gabriel (1999) Tibetan Futures: Imagining Collective Destinies, *Futures*, 31(2), 155–69.

LaFountain, Marc J. (2008) Obscene Ethics: A Baudrillardian View of Spurlock's Super Size Me, *International Journal of Baudrillard Studies*, 5(2).

Lagerkvist, Johan (2005) The Techno-Cadre's Dream: Administrative Reform by Electronic Governance in China Today?, *China Information*, 19(2), 189–216.

Lagerkvist, Johan (2008) Internet Ideotainment in the PRC: National Responses to Cultural Globalization, *Journal of Contemporary China*, 17(54), 121–40.

Lagerkvist, Johan (2010) *After the Internet, before Democracy: Competing Norms in Chinese Media and Society*, New York: Peter Lang.

Lahans, Tai (2008) The Treatment of Colorectal Cancer Using Chemotherapy and Chinese Herbal Medicine, *Chinese Medical Times*, 3(4).

Landsberger, Stefan R. (2014) Dreaming the Chinese Dream: How the People's Republic of China Moved from Revolutionary Goals to Global Ambitions, *International Journal for History, Culture and Modernity*, 2(3), 245–74.

Landsberger, Stefan R. and Marien van der Heijden (2008) *Chinese Propaganda Posters*, Amsterdam: AD Druk, Zeist.

Lane, Richard J. (2000) *Jean Baudrillard*, London: Routledge.

Lee, Sean (2011) *Shrimp Soldiers and Crab Generals*. Last updated 1 May 2011, retrieved 31 July 2011, from www.seanleedesign.com/2011/05/shrimp-soldiers-and-crab-generals.html.

Lefort, Claude (1988) *Democracy and Political Theory*, Macey, David (Trans.), Cambridge: Polity.

Leonard, Mark (2008) *What Does China Think?* New York: Public Affairs.

Lewis, Leo (2010) Shanghai Expo Organisers Ripped off Theme Tune from 1997 Japanese Hit, Say Critics, *The Times*. Last updated 28 March 2010, retrieved 27 April 2010, from www.timesonline.co.uk/tol/news/world/asia/article7109948.ece.

Li Baojun and Li Zhiyong (2008) *'Hexie Shijieguan' yu 'Baquan Wendinglun': Yi Xiang Bijiao Fenxi* ['Harmonious World Outlook' and 'Hegemonic Stability Theory': A Comparative Analysis], *Jiaoxue yu yanjiu* [Education and Research], 6, 79–85.

Li Chenyang (2010) Harmony as a Guiding Principle for Governance. In Tao, Julia, Anthony B. L. Cheung, Martin Painter and Chenyang Li (Eds) *Governance for Harmony in Asia and Beyond*, London and New York, Routledge, 37–57.

Li, Ellen (2012) Chasing the 'Chinese Dream', *The Atlantic*. Last updated 13 December 2012, retrieved 17 July 2015, from www.theatlantic.com/international/archive/2012/12/chasing-the-chinese-dream/266236.

Li Hongmei (2011) Parody and Resistance on the Chinese Internet. In Herold, David Kurt and Peter Marolt (Eds) *Online Society in China: Creating, Celebrating, and Instrumentalising the Online Carnival*, Abingdon: Routledge, 71–88.

Li Huaxin (2013) Chinese Dream, People's Dream and the World's Dream, speech by Consul General Li Huaxin at China Studies Centre, University of Sydney, 30 September 2013.

Li Keqiang (2014) *Report of the Work of the Government (2014)*, delivered at the Third Session of the Twelfth National People's Congress, Beijing, 5 March 2014.

Li Keqiang (2015) *Report of the Work of the Government (2015)*, delivered at the Third Session of the Twelfth National People's Congress, Beijing, 5 March 2015.

Lim, Louisa (2013) Chasing the Chinese Dream – If You Can Define It, *NPR*. Last updated 29 April 2013, retrieved 17 July 2015, from www.npr.org/2013/04/29/179838801/chasing-the-chinese-dream-if-you-can-define-it?sc=tw&cc=share.

Lindqvist, Cecilia (1991) *China: Empire of Living Symbols*, Tate, Joan (Trans.), Reading, MA: Addison-Wesley Publishing Company.

Link, Perry, Richard P. Madsen and Paul G. Pickowicz (2001) Introduction. In Link, Perry, Richard P. Madsen and Paul G. Pickowicz (Eds) *Popular China: Unofficial Culture in a Globalizing Society*, Lanham, MD: Rowman & Littlefield, 1–8.

Liou, Chih-Shian and Arthur S. Ding (Eds) (2015) *China Dreams: China's New Leadership and Future Impacts*, Singapore: World Scientific.

Liu Dongjian (2006) Hexie Shehui Yanjiu Shuping [Review of Research on Harmonious Society], *Jiaoxue yu yanjiu* [Education and Research], 2, 42–7.

Liu Guijin (2010) Speech by Ambassador Liu Guijin, Special Representative for African Affairs of Chinese Government, at Seminar on China–Ethiopia and China–Africa Relations in a Mutually Beneficial and Win–Win Manner, FDR Ethiopia, 23 November 2010.

Liu Guoli (2008) Economic Development, Political Stability, and Social Harmony: Can All Good Things Go Together? In Guo Sujian and Guo Baogang (Eds) *China in Search of Harmonious Society*, Lanham, MD: Lexington Books, 129–61.

Liu Hanming (2011) Remarks by H. E. Mr. Liu Hanming, speech given at Reception in Celebration of the 62nd Anniversary of the Founding of the PRC, St John's, Antigua, 29 September 2011.

Liu Huanxing (2011) Speech by H. E. Mr. Liu Huanxing, Chinese Ambassador to Botswana, at Botswana Defence Command and Staff College, 21 February 2011.

Liu Jianfei (2006) Heping Jueqi Shi Zhongguo de Zhanlve Xuanze [Peaceful Rise Is China's Strategic Choice], *Shijie jingji yu zhengzhi* [World Economics and Politics], 1, 36–40.

Liu Mingfu (2010) *Zhongguo Meng: Hou Meiguo Shidai de Daguo Siwei Zhanlue Dingwei* [The China Dream: The Great Power Thinking and Strategic Positioning of China in the Post-American Age], Beijing: Zhongguo youyi chuban gongsi.

Liu Mingfu (2014) Zhongguomeng – Yingxiongmeng [Chinese Dream – Hero Dream], *Juece yu xinxi* [Policy Making and Information], 353(2).

Liu Mingfu (2015) *The China Dream: Great Power Thinking and Strategic Posture in the Post-American Era*, New York: CN Times Books.

Liu Xiaoming (2011a) The 12th Five-Year Plan: China's Scientific and Peaceful Development, speech given at Royal Institute of International Affairs, Chatham House, London, 18 March 2011.

Liu Xiaoming (2011b) China's Perspective on Cybersecurity, speech given at Second Worldwide Cybersecurity Summit, 2 June 2011.

Liu Xiaoming (2011c) Towards a New Partnership: China and the West, speech given at Towards a New Partnership: China and the West, the Chinese University of Hong Kong, 23 November 2011.

Liu Xiaoming (2015) Speech by H. E. Ambassador Liu Xiaoming, speech given at Book Launch of Xi Jinping, The Governance of China, Chinese Embassy, London, 15 April 2015.

Liu Xinsheng (2010) China's Domestic and Foreign Policies, speech given at UDSM, UR of Tanzania, 16 April 2010.

Liu Xinyu (2005) Gongying Zhongguo Waijiao Zhaogao Shijie [China's Win–Win Diplomacy Proclaimed to the World], *Liaowang*, 51, 40–2.

Liu Zhanwen and Liu Liang (2009) Formation of the Chinese Medicine Theoretical System and Its Philosophical Basis. In Liu Zhanwen (Ed.) *Essentials of Chinese Medicine: Foundations of Chinese Medicine*, Vol. 1, London: Springer, 3–32.

Liu Zhiguang (1992) *Dongfang Heping Zhuyi: Yuanqi, Liubian ji Zouxiang* [Oriental Pacificism: Its Origins, Development and Future], Changsha, Hunan: Hunan chubanshe.

Lo, Vivienne and Christopher Cullen (2005) *Medieval Chinese Medicine: The Dunhuang Medical Manuscripts*, London: Routledge Curzon.

Lotahk (2011) *Green Dam Girl Cosplay Wig Dark Gary Mixed Purple*. Retrieved 8 August 2011, from http://cgi.ebay.com/Green-Dam-Girl-Cosplay-WIG-Dark-Gary-Mixed-Purple-/180546668749.

Lu Chunlong (2015) Urban Chinese Support for the Chinese Dream: Empirical Findings from Seventeen Cities, *Journal of Chinese Political Science*, 20, 143–61.

Lu, Henry C. (1986) *Chinese System of Food Cures: Prevention & Remedies*, New York: Sterling Pub. Co.

Lupton, Deborah (2003) *Medicine as Culture: Illness, Disease and the Body in Western Societies*, 2nd edn, London: Sage.

Lvshi chunqiu (1996) *Lvshi Chunqiu* [Spring and Autumn Annals], Shanghai: Shanghai guji chubanshe.

Lynch, Daniel C. (1999) *After the Propaganda State: Media, Politics, and 'Thought Work' in Reformed China*, Stanford, CA: Stanford University Press.

McMillan, Karen and Heather Worth (2003) In Dreams: Baudrillard, Derrida and September 11. In Grace, Victoria, Heather Worth and Laurence Simmons (Eds) *Baudrillard West of the Dateline*, Palmerston North, New Zealand: Dunmore Press, 116–37.

Mahoney, Joseph G. (2014) Interpreting the Chinese Dream: An Exercise of Political Hermeneutics, *Journal of Chinese Political Science*, 19, 15–34.

Manzenreiter, Wolfram (2010) The Beijing Games in the Western Imagination of China: The Weak Power of Soft Power, *Journal of Sport and Social Issues*, 34(1), 29–48.

Marcovitch, Harvey (2005) *Black's Medical Dictionary*, 41st edn, London: Black Publishers.

Marianini, Desiree and Janek Zdzarski (2011) *Dancing with Shackles on*, Danwei.org, broadcast 1 March 2011.

Mars, Neville and Adrian Hornsby (2008) *The Chinese Dream: A Society under Construction*, Rotterdam: 010 Publishers.

Martinsen, Joel (2006) *Explicating Harmony: Logo from the Economic Observer for Its Feature Section on the 2006 NPC and CPPCC Sessions*, Danwei.org. Last updated 7 March 2006, retrieved 11 June 2011, from www.danwei.org/trends_and_buzz/explicating_harmony.php.

Martinsen, Joel (2007) *You've Been Harmonized!* Danwei.org. Retrieved 2 February 2011, from www.danwei.org/featured_video/youve_been_harmonized.php.

Massey, Doreen B. (2005) *For Space*, London: Sage.

Massumi, Brian (2005) The Future Birth of the Affective Fact, *Proceedings of the 'Genealogies of Biopolitics' Conference.*

Mendis, Patrick (2013) *What Does the 'Chinese Dream' Really Mean?* Last updated 14 March 2013, retrieved 30 June 2015, from www.scmp.com/comment/insight-opinion/article/1189936/what-does-chinese-dream-really-mean.

Meng Bingchun (2009) Regulating *E Gao*: Futile Efforts of Recentralization? In Zhang Xiaoling and Zheng Yongnian (Eds) *China's Information and Communications Technology Revolution: Social Changes and State Responses*, London and New York: Routledge, 52–67.

Meng Bingchun (2011) From Steamed Bun to Grass Mud Horse: E Gao as Alternative Political Discourse on the Chinese Internet, *Global Media and Communication*, 7(1), 33–51.

Merrin, William (1994) Uncritical Criticism? Norris, Baudrillard and the Gulf War, *Economy and Society*, 23(4), 433–58.

Miller, Joseph E. (2013) China's Dream Army, *SITC Bulletin Analysis*, June 2013.

Ming Wan (2013) *Xi Jinping's 'China Dream': Same Bed, Different Dreams?* Last updated 2 August 2013, retrieved 24 November 2013, from www.theasanforum.org/xi-jinpings-china-dream-same-bed-different-dreams.

Ministry of Foreign Affairs of the PRC (2011a) *A Journey of Culture, Cooperation and Communication: Vice Foreign Minister Fu Ying Invites Diplomatic Envoys of European Countries to Visit Shandong*. Last updated 12 April 2011, retrieved 23 May 2012, from www.fmprc.gov.cn/eng/zxxx/t815074.htm.

Ministry of Foreign Affairs of the PRC (2011b) *Xi Jinping and Le Hong Anh Jointly Meet with the Youth Representatives of China and Vietnam*. Last updated 22 November 2011, retrieved 12 March 2012, from www.fmprc.gov.cn/eng/zxxx/t890389.htm.

Ministry of Foreign Affairs of the PRC and the Ministries of Foreign Affairs of the Caribbean Countries Having Diplomatic Relations with China (2010) *Joint Communiqué on the Fourth Round of Consultations between the Ministry of Foreign Affairs of the PRC and the Ministries of Foreign Affairs of the Caribbean Countries Having Diplomatic Relations with China*. Last updated 12 May 2010, retrieved 10 March 2012, from http://bs.china-embassy.org/eng/sbgxyw/t724359.htm.

Mitchell, Timothy (1988) *Colonizing Egypt*, Cambridge: Cambridge University Press.

Mu Ren (2014) Qiantan 'Zhongguomeng' Yu 'Hexie Shehui' 'Hexie Shijie' de Goujian [Discussing the Construction of the 'Chinese Dream', and 'Harmonious Society' and 'Harmonious World'], *Lilun yanjiu* [Theoretical Research], 326(6), 28–33.

Murong Xuecun (2013) The New Face of Chinese Propaganda, *New York Times*. Last updated 20 December 2013, retrieved 17 July 2015, from http://mobile.nytimes.com/2013/12/21/opinion/sunday/murong-the-new-face-of-chinese-propaganda.html?_r=0.

Musolff, Andreas (2003) Ideological Functions of Metaphor: The Conceptual Metaphors of *Health* and *Illness* in Public Discourse. In Dirven, René, Roslyn M. Frank and Martin Pütz (Eds) *Cognitive Models in Language and Thought: Ideology, Metaphors and Meaning*, Berlin: Mouton de Gruyter, 327–52.

Mythical Realm (2011) *Oriental/Chinese Dragon*. Retrieved 4 August 2011, from www.mythicalrealm.com/creatures/chinese_dragon.html.

Naas, Michael (2006) 'One Nation ... Indivisible': Jacques Derrida on the Autoimmunity of Democracy and the Sovereignty of God, *Research in Phenomenology*, 36(1), 15–44.

Nancy, Jean-Luc (1991 [1983]) *The Inoperative Community*, Minneapolis: University of Minnesota Press.

National People's Congress of the PRC (2004) *Constitution of the People's Republic of China*. Last updated 14 March 2004, retrieved 2 March 2012, from www.npc.gov.cn/englishnpc/Constitution/node_2825.htm.

National Planning Office of Philosophy and Social Science (2013) from www.npopss-cn.gov/n/2013/1024/c221360-23311531.html.

Neville, Robert Cummings (2010) Harmony in Government. In Tao, Julia, Anthony B. L. Cheung, Martin Painter and Chenyang Li (Eds) *Governance for Harmony in Asia and Beyond*, London and New York: Routledge, 58–70.

Ni Shixiong and Qian Xuming (2008) Xin Diyuan Zhengzhi yu Hexie Shijie [New Regional Politics and Harmonious World], *Qinghua daxue xuebao (Zhexue shehui kexue ban)* [Qinghua University Journal (Philosophy Social Sciences Edition)], 23(5), 123–31.

Ni Shixiong and Xu Jia (1997) Ouzhou Guoji Guanxi Lilun Yanjiu: Lishi Huigu yu Sikao [Chinese International Relations Theory Research: Historical Overview and Reflections], *Ouzhou* [Europe], 6.

Noesselt, Nele (2015a) China's Foreign Strategy after the 18th Party Congress: Business as Usual?, *Journal of Chinese Political Science*, 20, 17–33.

Noesselt, Nele (2015b) Revisiting the Debate on Constructing a Theory of International Relations with Chinese Characteristics, *The China Quarterly*, 222, 430–48.

Nordin, Astrid H. M. (2012a) How Soft Is 'Soft Power'? Unstable Dichotomies at Expo 2010, *Asian Perspective*, 36(4), 591–613.

Nordin, Astrid H. M. (2012b) Space for Coeval Multiplicity: A Response to Doreen Massey's Critique of Derridean Deconstruction. In Smith, Shilinka and Shauna Hill (Eds) *Space and Place* (e-book), ID Press.

Nordin, Astrid H. M. (2014a) Bordering on the Unacceptable in China and Europe: 'Cao Ni Ma' and 'Nique Ta Mère'. In Liu, Joyce C. H. and Nick Vaughan-Williams (Eds) *European–East Asian Borders in Translation*, Abingdon: Routledge, 166–81.

Nordin, Astrid H. M. (2014b) Radical Exoticism: Baudrillard and Other's Wars, *International Journal of Baudrillard Studies*, 11(2).

Nordin, Astrid H. M. (2014c) Un-Innovative Censorship, Innovative Resistance: The Internet, Forbidden Words and the Humorous Homonyms of Egao. In Horsburgh, Nicola, Astrid H. M. Nordin and Shaun Breslin (Eds) *Chinese Politics and International Relations: Innovation and Invention*, Abingdon: Routledge, 175–98.

Nordin, Astrid H. M. (2016) Futures beyond 'the West'? Autoimmunity in China's Harmonious World, *Review of International Studies*, 42(1), 156–77.

Nordin, Astrid H. M. (forthcoming a) Hegemony in Chinese? *Ba* in Chinese International Relations. In Koenig, Lion and Bidisha Chaudhuri (Eds) *The Politics of the 'Other' in India and China: Western Concepts in Non-Western Contexts*, Abingdon: Routledge, 204–13.

Nordin, Astrid H. M. (forthcoming b) Ironic 'Resistance' in Chinese Citizen Media Online. In Baker, Mona and Bolette Blaagaard (Eds) *Citizen Media and Public Spaces: Diverse Expressions of Citizenship and Dissent*, Abingdon: Routledge.

Nordin, Astrid H. M. and Dan Öberg (2015) Targeting the Ontology of War: From Clausewitz to Baudrillard, *Millennium: Journal of International Studies*, 43(2), 392–410.

Nordin, Astrid H. M. and Lisa Richaud (2014) Subverting Official Language and Discourse in China? Type River Crab for Harmony, *China Information*, 28(1), 47–67.

Nyíri, Pál (2006) The Yellow Man's Burden: Chinese Immigrants on a Civilizing Mission, *The China Journal*, 56, 83–106.

Öberg, Dan (2013) The Disappearance of the Face: Servility and Social Media, *International Journal of Baudrillard Studies*, 10(2).

Öberg, Dan (2014) Forget Clausewitz, *International Journal of Baudrillard Studies*, 11(3).

Oksenberg, Michel and Elizabeth Economy (Eds) (1999) *China Joins the World: Progress and Prospect*, New York: Council of Foreign Relations.

Osuri, Goldie (2006) Imploding Singularities: For a Critique of Autoimmunity as Political Future, *Social Semiotics*, 16(3), 499–519.

Oxford Dictionaries (2011a) *Cancer 1*. Retrieved 26 July 2011, from http://oxforddictionaries.com/definition/Cancer?rskey=kliUUI&result=1.

Oxford Dictionaries (2011b) *Cancer 2*. Retrieved 26 July 2011, from http://oxforddictionaries.com/definition/cancer?rskey=kliUUI&result=2.

Oxford Dictionaries (2011c) *Harmony*. Oxford Dictionaries. Retrieved 31 May 2012, from http://oxforddictionaries.com/definition/harmony#m_en_gb0365750.

Paltiel, Jeremy T. (2007) *The Empire's New Clothes: Cultural Particularism and Universal Value in China's Quest for Global Status*, New York: Palgrave Macmillan.

Pan Mingji (1992) *Cancer Treatment with Fuzheng Peiben Principle*, Fuzhou: Fujian Science and Technology Press.

Patience, Martin (2013) What Does Xi Jinping's China Dream Mean?, BBC News. Last updated 6 June 2013, retrieved 29 June 2015, from www.bbc.co.uk/news/world-asia-china-22726375.

People's Daily (2006) Wu Jianmin: 'Harmonious World' Helps Rebut 'China Threat', 20 March 2006.

People's Daily Online (2013a) *Laoji Qiangjun Mubiao Xianshen Qiangjun Shijian* [Remember the Goal of a Strong Army, Be Devoted to Strong Army Practice]. Last updated 12 April 2013, retrieved 15 June 2015, from http://politics.people.com.cn/n/2013/0412/c1024-21107503.html.

People's Daily Online (2013b) *Wangluo Mingren Jushou Yangshi, Taolun Weibo Da V de Shehui Zeren* [Internet Celebrities Gather, Discuss the Social Responsibility of Microblogging 'Big Vs']. Last updated 12 August 2013, retrieved 18 June 2015, from http://media.people.com.cn/n/2013/0812/c40606-22528296.html.

People's Daily Online (2014) *Renmin You Xinyang, Guojia Caiyou Liliang: Yi Lun Hongyang Shehuizhuyi Hexin Jiazhiguan* [The People Has Belief, the Country Has

Strength: On Carrying Forward Socialism Core Value System]. Last updated 12 February 2014, retrieved 17 July 2015, from http://paper.people.com.cn/rmrb/html/2014-02/12/nw.D110000renmrb_20140212_2-01.htm.

Perry, Elizabeth (2007) Studying Chinese Politics: Farewell to Revolution?, *The China Journal*, 57, 1–22.

Pierre, Jon (2010) Consensual but Not Confucian: Resolving the Paradox of Consensual Politics in Scandinavia. In Tao, Julia, Anthony B. L. Cheung, Martin Painter and Chenyang Li (Eds) *Governance for Harmony in Asia and Beyond*, London and New York: Routledge, 228–42.

Pin-Fat, Véronique (2010) *Universality, Ethics, and International Relations*, Abingdon: Routledge.

Porter, Roy (1997) *The Greatest Benefit to Mankind: A Medical History of Humanity from Antiquity to the Present*, London: HarperCollins.

Pouchelle, Marie-Christine (1990) *The Body and Surgery in the Middle Ages*, Cambridge: Polity.

Price, Monroe E. and Daniel Dayan (Eds) (2008) *Owning the Olympics: Narratives of the New China*, Ann Arbor: University of Michigan Press.

PSAAC (2015a) *He, Guoyun Chang* [Harmony, Prosperous National Destiny]. Retrieved 25 July 2015, from www.wenming.cn/jwmsxf_294/zggygg/pml/ctmdxl/201309/t20130929_1500681.shtml.

PSAAC (2015b) *He, Zui Mei de Shipian* [Harmony, the Most Beautiful Poem]. Retrieved 25 July 2015, from www.wenming.cn/jwmsxf_294/zggygg/pml/ctmdxl/201309/t20130929_1500435.shtml.

PSAAC (2015c) *Heman Zhonghua* [China Full of Harmony]. Retrieved 25 July 2015, from www.wenming.cn/jwmsxf_294/zggygg/pml/ctmdxl/201309/t20130929_1500613.shtml.

PSAAC (2015d) *Zhongguo Meng, He Wei Gui* [The Chinese Dream, Treasuring Harmony]. Retrieved 25 July 2015, from www.wenming.cn/jwmsxf_294/zggygg/pml/zgmxl/201309/t20130930_1501247.shtml.

PSAAC (2015e) *Zhongguo Meng, Wode Meng* [The Chinese Dream, My Dream]. Retrieved 25 July 2015, from www.wenming.cn/jwmsxf_294/zggygg/pml/zgmxl/201309/t20130930_1501267.shtml.

PSAAC (2015f) *Zhongguo Xin: He* [Heart of China: Harmony]. Retrieved 25 July 2015, from www.wenming.cn/jwmsxf_294/zggygg/pml/ctmdxl/201309/t20130929_1500624.shtml.

Purdue, Peter C. (2015) The Tenacious Tributary System, *Journal of Contemporary China*, 24(96), 1002–14.

Qian Gang (2015) *Preserving Stability*. Retrieved 28 September 2015, from http://cmp.hku.hk/2012/09/14/27074.

Qiao Long (2013) *Censors Delete 'China Dream' Song*. Last updated 8 April 2013, retrieved 2 August 2015, from www.rfa.org/english/news/china/delete-04082013155845.html.

Qin Yaqing (2006) Hexie Shijie: Zhongguo Waijiao Xin Linian [Harmonious World: Chinese Diplomacy's New Concept], *Qianxian* [Frontline], 12, 30–2.

Qin Yaqing (2007) Why Is There No Chinese International Relations Theory?, *International Relations of the Asia-Pacific*, 7(3), 313–40.

Qin Yaqing (2011) A Chinese School of International Relations Theory: Possibility and Inevitability. In Callahan, William A. and Elena Barabantseva (Eds) *China Orders the World? Soft Power, Norms and Foreign Policy*, Washington, DC: Woodrow Wilson Center Press, 37–53.

Qin Zhiyong (2008) Cultural Construction of a Harmonious Society. In Guo Sujian and Guo Baogang (Eds) *China in Search of Harmonious Society*, Lanham, MD: Lexington Books, 61–74.

Qiu, Jack Linchuan (2006) The Changing Web of Chinese Nationalism, *Global Media and Communication*, 2(1), 125–8.

Qiu Xiaoqi (2011a) *Discurso de S. E. Sr. Embaixador Qiu Xiaoqi na Fundação Dom Cabral* [Speech by H. E. Ambassador Qiu Xiaoqi at Fundação Dom Cabral], speech given at Fundação Dom Cabral, Brazil, 15 August 2011.

Qiu Xiaoqi (2011b) *Palavras do Embaixador Qiu Xiaoqi* [Remarks by Ambassador Qiu Xiaoqi], speech given at Reception Commemorating the 62nd Anniversary of the Proclamation of the PRC, Embassy of the PRC to Brazil, Brasilia, 4 October 2011.

Qiushi (2013) The Chinese Dream Infuses Socialism with Chinese Characteristics with New Energy, *Qiushi*, May.

Rajan, Tilottama (2002) *Deconstruction and the Remainders of Phenomenology*, Stanford, CA: Stanford University Press.

Rawnsley, Gary (2015) *Why China's Propagandists Love the Internet*. Last updated 21 July 2015, retrieved 25 July 2015, from https://foreignpolicy.com/2015/07/21/why-chinas-propagandists-love-the-internet.

Reisfield, Gary M. and George R. Wilson (2004) Use of Metaphor in the Discourse on Cancer, *Journal of Clinical Oncology*, 22(19), 4024–7.

Reynolds, Trish (1987) *Your Cancer, Your Life*, Richmond, Vic.: Greenhouse Publications.

Rockman, Bert A. (2010) Open Politics and Disharmony. In Tao, Julia, Anthony B. L. Cheung, Martin Painter and Chenyang Li (Eds) *Governance for Harmony in Asia and Beyond*, London and New York: Routledge, 189–209.

Roetz, Heiner (2010) Xunzi's Vision of Society: Harmony by Justice. In Tao, Julia, Anthony B. L. Cheung, Martin Painter and Chenyang Li (Eds) *Governance for Harmony in Asia and Beyond*, London and New York: Routledge, 313–28.

Ruan Zongze (2005) Goujian Hexie Shijie de Zhongguo Waijiao [China's Foreign Policy of Building a Harmonious World], *Liaowang*, 46, 13–15.

Rudd, Kevin (2012) The Prospects for Peace in the Pacific: The Future of the Expanded East Asia Summit, speech given at Asia Society, New York, 13 January 2012.

Ruggie, John G. (1993) Territoriality and Beyond: Problematizing Modernity in International Relations, *International Organization*, 47(1), 139–74.

Rydell, Robert W. (1984) *All the World's a Fair: Visions of Empire at American International Expositions 1876–1916*, Chicago, IL: University of Chicago Press.

Santa Anna, Otto (2003) Three Mandates for Anti-Minority Policy Expressed in U.S. Public Discourse Metaphors. In Dirven, René, Roslyn M. Frank and Martin Pütz (Eds) *Cognitive Models in Language and Thought: Ideology, Metaphors and Meaning*, Berlin: Mouton de Gruyter, 199–228.

Saussure, Ferdinand de (1960) *Course in General Linguistics*, Sechehaye, Albert, Albert Riedlinger and Charles Bally (Eds), London: Owen.

Schipper, H., C. R. Goh and T. I. Wang (1995) Shifting the Cancer Paradigm: Must We Kill to Cure?, *Journal of Clinical Oncology*, 13(4), 801–7.

Schneider, Florian (2014) Reconceptualising World Order: Chinese Political Thought and Its Challenge to International Relations Theory, *Review of International Studies*, 40(4), 683–703.

Schoenhals, Michael (1992) *Doing Things with Words in Chinese Politics: Five Studies*, Berkeley, CA: Institute of Asian Studies, University of California.

Shanghai shibohui shiwu xietiaoju (2009) *Bai Nian Shibo Meng* [100 Years of Expo Dream], Shanghai: Dongfang chuban zhongxin.
Shapiro, Michael J. (1997) *Violent Cartographies: Mapping Cultures of War*, London: University of Minnesota Press.
Shen, Simon and Shaun Breslin (2010) When China Plugged in: Structural Origins of Online Chinese Nationalism. In Shen, Simon and Shaun Breslin (Eds) *Online Chinese Nationalism and China's Bilateral Relations*, Lanham, MD: Rowman & Littlefield, 3–12.
Shi Yinhong (2008a) Chengjiu yu Tiaozhan: Zhongguo Heping Fazhan, Hexie Shijie Linian yu Duiwai Zhengce Xingshi [Achievements and Challenges: China's Peaceful Development, Harmonious World and Foreign Policy Terrain], *Dangdai shijie yu shehui zhuyi* [The Contemporary World and Socialism], 2, 81–5.
Shi Yinhong (2008b) China's Peaceful Development, Harmonious World and International Responsibility: Achievements and Challenges, *International Review*, Spring, 19–28.
Shi Yuzhi (2013) Zhongguomeng Qubie Yu Meiguomeng de Qi Da Tezheng [Seven Major Characteristics Differentiating the Chinese Dream and the American Dream], *Qiushi*, 20 May.
Shi Zhongwen (2008) Traditional Culture Embodied in Confucianism and China's Search for Harmonious Society and Peaceful Development. In Guo Sujian and Guo Baogang (Eds) *China in Search of a Harmonious Society*, Lanham, MD: Lexington Books, 35–60.
Shih Chih-yu (2010) The Self That Has No Other: Asia as a Democratic Perspective on Postcolonial Modernity, paper presented at 'Theory vs. Policy? Connecting Scholars and Practitioners', New Orleans Hilton Riverside Hotel, The Loews New Orleans Hotel, New Orleans, LA, 17 February 2010.
Shinn, James (Ed.) (1996) *Weaving the Net: Conditional Engagement with China*, New York: Council of Foreign Relations Press.
Smith, Richard G. (Ed.) (2010) *The Baudrillard Dictionary*, Edinburgh: Edinburgh University Press.
Son, Key-young (2012) Harmony, the Supremacy of Human Agency and East Asia's Mega-Discourses for Governance, *Chinese Journal of International Politics*, 5(4), 395–423.
Sontag, Susan (1991) *Illness as Metaphor; and, Aids and Its Metaphors*, London: Penguin.
Sørensen, Camilla T. N. (2015) The Significance of Xi Jinping's 'Chinese Dream' for Chinese Foreign Policy: From 'Tao Guang Yang Hui' to 'Fen Fa You Wei', *Journal of Chinese International Relations*, 3(1), 53–73.
Southern Metropolis Weekly (2009) *2009 Niandu Shi Da Xinci* [Top 10 Neologisms of 2009]. Retrieved 24 December 2009, from www.nbweekly.com/Print/Article/9353_0.shtml.
Sow Keat Tok and Zheng Yongnian (2007) *'Harmonious Society' and 'Harmonious World': China's Policy Discourse under Hu Jintao*, Document no. 26, Nottingham: University of Nottingham China Policy Institute.
Stacey, Jackie (1997) *Teratologies: A Cultural Study of Cancer*, London: Routledge.
State Council (2004) *China's National Defense in 2004*, Beijing: Information office of the State Council.
State Council (2005a) *China's Endeavors for Arms Control, Disarmament and Non-Proliferation*, Beijing: Information Office of the State Council.

State Council (2005b) *China's Peaceful Development Road*, Beijing: Information Office of the State Council.
State Council (2006) *China's National Defense in 2006*, Beijing: Information Office of the State Council.
State Council (2007) *China's Political Party System*, Beijing: Information Office of the State Council.
State Council (2009a) *China's Ethnic Policy and Common Prosperity and Development of All Ethnic Groups*, Beijing: Information Office of the State Council.
State Council (2009b) *China's National Defense in 2008*, Beijing: Information Office of the State Council.
State Council (2009c) *Report on the Economic and Social Development of Tibet*, Beijing: Information Office of the State Council.
State Council (2010) *China's Human Resources*, Beijing: Information Office of the State Council.
State Council (2011a) *China's Foreign Aid*, Beijing: Information Office of the State Council.
State Council (2011b) *China's National Defense in 2010*, Beijing: Information Office of the State Council.
State Council (2011c) *China's Peaceful Development*, Beijing: Information Office of the State Council.
State Council (2013a) *China–Africa Economic and Trade Cooperation*, Beijing: Information office of the State Council.
State Council (2013b) *The Diversified Employment of China's Armed Forces*, Beijing: Information Office of the State Council, April 2013.
State Council (2014a) *The History and Development of the Xinjiang Production and Construction Corps*, Beijing: Information Office of the State Council, 5 October 2014.
State Council (2014b) *The Practice of the 'One Country, Two Systems' Policy in the Hong Kong Special Administrative Region*, Beijing: Information Office of the State Council, June 2014.
Stchi (2009) *Lv Ba Niang zhi Ge* [The Green Dam Girl Song]. Last updated 1 July 2009, retrieved 5 August 2011, from www.youtube.com/watch?v=hsw23W019SA&feature=player_embedded.
Stern, Maria and Marysia Zalewski (2009) Feminist Fatigue(s): Reflections on Feminism and Familiar Fables of Militarisation, *Review of International Studies*, 35(3), 611–30.
Stibbe, Arren (1997) Fighting, Warfare and the Discourse of Cancer, *South African Journal of Linguistics*, 15(2), 65–70.
Stocking, George W. (1987) *Victorian Anthropology*, New York: Free Press.
Strandsbjerg, Jeppe (2010) *Territory, Globalization and International Relations: The Cartographic Reality of Space*, Basingstoke: Palgrave Macmillan.
Suettinger, Robert L. (2005) The Rise and Descent of 'Peaceful Rise', *China Leadership Monitor*, 12, 1–10.
Summers, Josh (2009) *The Truth about Xinjiang's Internet Situation*. Last updated 6 December 2009, retrieved 31 July 2011, from www.farwestchina.com/2009/12/truth-about-xinjiangs-internet.html.
Sun Laibin and Wang Ping (2014) Zhongguomeng de Secai [The Colours of the Chinese Dream], *Lingdao kexue luntan* [Leadership Science Forum], 9–10.
Sun Laibin and Xie Chengyu (2014) Zhongguomeng de Wenhua Yiyun [The Cultural Implications of the Chinese Dream], *Dangdai shijie yu shehui zhuyi* [Contemporary World and Socialism], 6, 159–64.

Tang Lijun and Syamantak Bhattacharya (2011) Power and Resistance: A Case Study of Satire on the Internet, *Sociological Research Online*, 16(2).

Tang Lijun and Yang Peidong (2011) Symbolic Power and the Internet: The Power of a 'Horse', *Media Culture Society*, 33(5), 675–91.

Tao, Julia, Anthony B. L. Cheung, Martin Painter and Chenyang Li (2010a) *Governance for Harmony in Asia and Beyond*, Abingdon: Routledge.

Tao, Julia, Anthony B. L. Cheung, Martin Painter and Chenyang Li (2010b) Why Governance for Harmony? In Tao, Julia, Anthony B. L. Cheung, Martin Painter and Chenyang Li (Eds) *Governance for Harmony in Asia and Beyond*, London and New York: Routledge, 3–11.

Tao Shaoxing (2015) Jiegou 'Zhongguo Weixie Lun': Zhongguomeng Zhi Yu Hexie Shijie Zhuiqiu [Deconstructing 'China Threat Theory': The Pursuit of Harmonious World in the Chinese Dream], *Nanchang hankong daxue xuebao: shehui kexue ban* [Journal of Nanchang Hangkong University: Social Sciences], 17(1), 14–21.

Teschke, Benno (2003) *The Myth of 1648: Class, Geopolitics and the Making of International Relations*, London: Verso.

Teufel Dreyer, June (2015) The 'Tianxia Trope': Will China Change the International System?, *Journal of Contemporary China*, 24(96), 1015–31.

Thomson, Alexander John Peter (2005) What's to Become of 'Democracy to Come'?, *Postmodern Culture*, 15(3).

Thornton, Patricia M. (2002) Framing Dissent in Contemporary China: Irony, Ambiguity and Metonymy, *China Quarterly*, 171, 661–81.

Tian Wenlin (2013) *'Zhongguo Meng' Ye Shi 'Shijie Meng'* [The 'China Dream' Is Also the 'World Dream'], Zhongshi wangping. Last updated 26 September 2013, retrieved 8 March 2014, from http://opinion.cntv.cn/2013/09/26/ARTI1380197528891824.shtml.

Tianjin shi geming weiyuanhui zhengzhibu (1969 [5 March 1949]) *Zai Zhongguo Gongchandang di qi jie Zhongyang Weiyuanhui di er ci Quanti Huiyi shang de Baogao* [Report to the Second Plenum of the Seventeenth CCP Central Committee]. In Tianjin shi geming weiyuanhui zhengzhibu (Ed.) *Wuchanjieji Wenhua Dageming Zhongyao Wenxian Xuanbian* [Selected Important Documents from the Great Proletarian Cultural Revolution], Tianjin: Tianjin renmin chubanshe.

Torfing, Jacob (2010) Harmony through Network Governance? In Tao, Julia, Anthony B. L. Cheung, Martin Painter and Chenyang Li (Eds) *Governance for Harmony in Asia and Beyond*, London and New York: Routledge, 241–63.

Turner, Bryan S. (2003) Social Fluids: Metaphors and Meanings of Society, *Body & Society*, 9(1), 1–10.

Tutuwan (2009) *Harmony or Die*. Last updated 23 June 2009, retrieved 5 August 2011, from http://vimeo.com/5294725.

Unschuld, Paul (2010) *Medicine in China: A History of Ideas*, 25th anniversary edn, Berkeley: University of California Press.

US Asia Law NYU (2011) *Jerome A. Cohen Responds to Ai Weiwei's Release*. Last updated 22 June 2011, retrieved 31 July 2011, from www.usasialaw.org/?p=5581.

V Saxena (2010) *The Gumbygate Scandal: China's Haibao Versus America's Gumby*. Last updated 11 May 2010, retrieved 27 March 2011, from www.weirdasianews.com/2010/05/11/gumbygate-scandal-chinas-haibao-americas-gumby.

Vanishing Tattoo (2011) *Crab Tattoo Designs*. Retrieved 31 July 2011, from www.vanishingtattoo.com/tattoos_designs_symbols_crab.htm.

Vaughan-Williams, Nick (2007) The Shooting of Jean Charles de Menezes: New Border Politics?, *Alternatives*, 32(2), 177–95.

Viriasova, Inna (2011) Politics and the Political: Correlation and the Question of the Unpolitical, *Peninsula: A Journal of Relational Politics*, 1(1).

Walker, R. B. J. (1993) *Inside/Outside: International Relations as Political Theory*, Cambridge: Cambridge University Press.

Wallis, Cara (2015) Gender and China's Online Censorship Protest Culture, *Feminist Media Studies*, 15(2), 223–38.

Walters, William (2006) Rethinking Borders beyond the State, *Contemporary European Politics*, 4(2/3), 141–59.

Wang, Helen H. (2010) *The Chinese Dream: The Rise of the World's Largest Middle Class and What It Means to You*, Brande, Denmark: Bestseller Press.

Wang Meiqin (2015) Advertising the Chinese Dream: Urban Billboards and Ni Weihua's Documentary Photography, *China Information*, 29(2), 176–201.

Wang Nanming and Wang Xueyun (Eds) (2008) *Guanjianci: Ni Weihua de 'Fazhan' Yu 'Hexie'* [Keywords: 'Development' and 'Harmony' of Ni Weihua], *Exhibition Catalogue*, Beijing: The Wall Museum.

Wang Xuexian (2008) A Harmonious World Begins at People's Heart, paper presented at Second ASEM Interfaith Dialogue, Cyprus, 4 September 2008.

Wang Yingmei and Wang Pujing (2013) *Zhongguo Meng: Dangyuan Ganbu Duben* [The China Dream: A Reader for Party Members and Cadres], Beijing: Yanjiu chubanshe.

Wang Yingwu (2011) *La Chine Suit Fermement la Voie de Développement Pacifique* [China Firmly Follows the Road of Peaceful Development]. Last updated 30 September 2011, retrieved 10 March 2012, from http://cd.china-embassy.org/fra/xw/t863972.htm.

Wang Yiwei (2006) Tanxun Zhongguo de Xin Shenfen: Guanyu Minzuzhuyi de Shenhua [Inquiry into China's New Identity: On the Myth of Nationalism], *Shijie jingji yu zhengzhi* [World Economics and Politics], 2, 14–22.

Wang Yiwei (2013) *Debunking Ten Misconceptions of the Ideal of the Chinese Dream*. Last updated 11 April 2013, retrieved 15 June 2015, from www.globaltimes.cn/content/774320.shtml#.UYLhVCsjoqs.

Wang Yiwei (2014) 'Zhongguomeng' Ye Shi Shehui Zhuyimeng ['Chinese Dream' – Socialist Dream], *Xinjiang shifan daxue xuebao (zhexue shehui kexue ban)* [Journal of Xinjiang Normal University (Philosophy and Social Sciences)], 35(2), 54–8.

Wang Yiwei and Han Xueqing (2013) Guoji Guanxi Lilun de Zhongguomeng [The China Dream of International Relations Theory], *Shijie jingji yanjiu* [World Economy Research], 21–39.

Wang Yizhou (2005) *Zhongguo Guoji Guanxi Lilun: Dui Chengjiu yu Queshi de ji dian Ganshou* [Chinese International Relations Theory: Achievements and Shortcomings], irchina.org. Retrieved 29 November 2011, from www.irchina.org/xueke/inchina/gaikuang/view.asp?id=10.

Wang Yizhou (2008) Zhongguo Waijiao shi Tese [The Ten Characteristics of Chinese Diplomacy], *Shijie jingji yu zhengzhi* [World Economics and Politics], 5, 6–19.

Wang Yizhou (2010) Kongbu Zhuyi Mian Mian Guan [Different Faces of Terrorism]. In Wang Yizhou (Ed.) *Kongbu Zhuyi Suoyuan* [Origins of Terrorism: Perception of Chinese], Beijing: Social Sciences Academic Press.

Wang Yuan-Kang (2011) *Harmony and War: Confucian Culture and Chinese Power Politics*, New York: Columbia University Press.

Wang Zheng (2013) *Not Rising, but Rejuvenating: The 'Chinese Dream'*. Last updated 5 February 2013, retrieved 26 May 2015, from http://thediplomat.com/2013/02/chinese-dream-draft.

Wang Zheng (2014) *Never Forget National Humiliation: Historical Memory in Chinese Politics and Foreign Relations*, New York: Columbia University Press.

Wang Zonglai (2011) *China's Approach to Challenges*. Last updated 1 July 2011, retrieved 10 March 2012, from http://dm.china-embassy.org/eng/zyxw/t836034.htm.

Wei Qiang (2012) Remarks at the Farewell Luncheon Hosted by the Minister of Foreign Affairs and Foreign Trade of Barbados, Senator the Hon. Maxine Mclean, speech given at Farewell Luncheon Hosted by the Minister of Foreign Affairs and Foreign Trade of Barbados, Hilton Barbados, Needham's Point, St Michael, 30 January 2012.

Wen Jiabao (2005) *Report on the Work of the Government (2005)*, delivered at the Third Session of the Tenth National People's Congress, 5 March 2005.

Wen Jiabao (2006) *Report of the Work of the Government (2006)*, delivered at the Fourth Session of the Tenth National People's Congress, Beijing, 5 March 2012.

Wen Jiabao (2007) *Report of the Work of the Government (2007)*, delivered at the Fifth Session of the Tenth National People's Congress, Beijing, 5 March 2007.

Wen Jiabao (2008) *Report of the Work of the Government (2008)*, delivered at the First Session of the Eleventh National People's Congress, Beijing, 5 March 2008.

Wen Jiabao (2009) *Report of the Work of the Government (2009)*, delivered at the Second Session of the Eleventh National People's Congress, Beijing, 5 March 2009.

Wen Jiabao (2010a) Expo Spirit Forever, speech given at Expo 2010 Shanghai China Summit Forum, Shanghai, 31 October 2010.

Wen Jiabao (2010b) *Report of the Work of the Government (2010)*, delivered at the Third Session of the Eleventh National People's Congress, Beijing, 5 March 2010.

Wen Jiabao (2011) *Report of the Work of the Government (2011)*, delivered at the Fourth Session of the Eleventh National People's Congress, Beijing, 5 March 2011.

Wen Jiabao (2012) *Report of the Work of the Government (2012)*, delivered at the Fifth Session of the Eleventh National People's Congress, Beijing, 5 March 2012.

Wen Jiabao (2013) *Report of the Work of the Government (2013)*, delivered at the First Session of the Twelfth National People's Congress, Beijing, 17 March 2013.

Wieger, Léon (1965 [1915]) *Chinese Characters: Their Origin, Etymology, History, Classification and Signification – A Thorough Study from Chinese Documents*, Davrout, L. (Trans.), 2nd edn, New York: Dover Publications.

Wiener, Seth (2011) Grass-Mud Horses to Victory: The Phonological Constraints of Subversive Puns. In Jing-Schmidt, Zhuo (Ed.) *Proceedings of the 23rd North American Conference on Chinese Linguistics.*

Williams, Charles Alfred Speed (1976) Five Poisons. In Williams, Charles Alfred Speed (Ed.) *Outlines of Chinese Symbolism and Art Motives*, 3rd edn, New York: Dover, 187.

Williams Camus, Julia T. (2009) Metaphors of Cancer in Scientific Popularization Articles in the British Press, *Discourse Studies*, 11(4), 465–95.

Wills, Deborah (2009) *At War with Metaphor: Media, Propaganda, and Racism in the War on Terror*, Lanham, MD: Lexington Books.

Winichakul, Thongchai (1994) *Siam Mapped: A History of the Geo-Body of a Nation*, Honolulu: University of Hawai'i Press.

Wong, Edward (2009) Riots in Western China amid Ethnic Tension, *New York Times*, Beijing, 6 July 2009.

Wong, Raimond and Stephen M. Sagar (2010) Supportive Cancer Care Using Chinese Medicine. In Cho, William C. S. (Ed.) *Supportive Cancer Care with Chinese Medicine*, Dordrecht: Springer Science & Business Media B.V.

Wortham, Simon Morgan (2010) *The Derrida Dictionary*, London: Continuum International Publishing Group.

Wu Bangguo (2010) *Report on the Work of the Standing Committee of the National People's Congress*, delivered at the Third Session of the Eleventh National People's Congress, Beijing, 9 March 2010.

Wu Yi (2006) China's Development Road, speech given at the First China–US Strategic Economic Dialogue, Beijing, 14 December 2006.

Xi Jinping (2011a) Speech by Xi Jinping at Tibet's Peaceful Liberation Anniversary Conference, speech given at Tibet's Peaceful Liberation Anniversary Conference, Lhasa, 19 July 2011.

Xi Jinping (2011b) Vice President Xi Jinping Speeches on Ceremony for 60th Anniversary of Tibet's Liberation, CCTV. Last updated 19 July 2011, retrieved 27 February 2012, from http://english.cntv.cn/program/newsupdate/20110719/111943.shtml.

Xi Jinping (2014a) *Tigao Ruan Shili Shixian Zhongguomeng* [Elevate Soft Power, Realize the Chinese Dream]. Last updated 1 January 2014, retrieved 30 June 2015, from http://paper.people.com.cn/rmrbhwb/html/2014-01/01/content_1369744.htm.

Xi Jinping (2014b) *Speech by H. E. Xi Jinping President of the People's Republic of China at the College of Europe*. Last updated 1 April 2014, retrieved 28 September 2015, from www.chinamission.be/eng/jd/t1143591.htm.

Xi Jinping (2014c) *Xi Jinping Delivers Important Speech in Germany, Stressing China Will Unswervingly Adhere to the Path of Peaceful Development*. Last updated 29 March 2014, retrieved 28 September 2015, from www.fmprc.gov.cn/mfa_eng/topics_665678/xjpzxcxdsjhaqhfbfwhlfgdgblshlhgjkezzzbomzb_666590/t1143914.shtml.

Xiao Feng (2005) Constructivism and Chinese Foreign Policy, paper presented at Annual Meeting of the International Studies Association (ISA), Hilton Hawaiian Village, Honolulu, Hawaii, 5 March 2005.

Xiao Qiang (2007) Under the Internet Police's Radar, *China Digital Times*. Last updated 28 April 2007, retrieved 2 March 2011, from http://chinadigitaltimes.net/2007/08/under-the-internet-polices-radar.

Xiao Qiang (2009) *Satire: New Chinese Characters Created by Netizens*. Last updated 31 August 2009, retrieved 5 August 2011, from http://chinadigitaltimes.net/2009/08/satire-new-chinese-characters-created-by-netizens.

Xiao Qiang (2010) CDT Launches the Grass-Mud Horse Lexicon, *China Digital Times*. Last updated 7 December 2010, retrieved 2 March 2011, from http://chinadigitaltimes.net/2010/12/introducing-the-grass-mud-horse-lexicon.

Xiao Qiang (2011a) The Battle for the Chinese Internet, *Journal of Democracy*, 22(2), 47–61.

Xiao Qiang (2011b) Leaked Propaganda Directives and Banned 'Future', *China Digital Times*. Last updated 24 June 2011, retrieved 31 July 2011, from http://chinadigitaltimes.net/2011/06/future-banned-on-sina-weibo-search.

Xie Lei (2014) 'Meili Zhongguo': Hexie Shehui Yu Hexie Shijie Linian de Xin Fazhan ['Beautiful China': The New Development of the Concepts of Harmonious Society and Harmonious World], *Wuhan keji daxue xuebao (shehui kexue ban)* [Journal of Wuhan University of Science and Technology (Social Science Edition)], 16(5), 482–7.

Xin Xu (2006) Modernizing China in the Olympic Spotlight: China's National Identity and the 2008 Beijing Olympiad, *Sociological Review*, 54, 90–107.

Xinhua (2005) Hu Makes 4-Point Proposal for Building Harmonious World, *Xinhua*, 15 September 2005.

Xinhua (2007a) CPC Constitution Amendment Advocates Building of 'Harmonious World'. Last updated 25 October 2007, retrieved 15 February 2011, from www.gov.cn/english/2007-10/25/content_786565.htm.

Xinhua (2007b) Harmonious World: China's Ancient Philosophy for New Int'l Order (5). Last updated 2 October 2007, retrieved 24 February 2011, from http://english.people.com.cn/90001/90776/6275748.html.

Xinhua (2008) Chinese Official: Mutual Appreciation, Peaceful Coexistence Key to World Harmony. Last updated 20 February 2008, retrieved 10 March 2012, from http://news.xinhuanet.com/english/2008-02/20/content_7635460.htm.

Xinhua (2009a) Chinese Political Advisors: Dalai Lama Not Harmony Promoter but Trouble Maker. Last updated 11 March 2009, retrieved 1 March 2011, from http://news.xinhuanet.com/english/2009-03/11/content_10994554.htm.

Xinhua (2009b) Chinese President Calls for Building Harmonious World. Last updated 24 September 2009, retrieved 10 March 2012, from http://news.xinhuanet.com/english/2009-09/24/content_12104060.htm.

Xinhua (2009c) Chinese President Calls on Media to Contribute to Harmonious World. Last updated 9 October 2009, retrieved 10 March 2012, from http://news.xinhuanet.com/english/2009-10/09/content_12198196.htm.

Xinhua (2009d) Thousands of Harmony Makers Sent to Urumqi Communities While Authorities Vow Harsh Punishment against Syringe Attackers. Last updated 6 September 2009, retrieved 1 March 2011, from http://news.xinhuanet.com/english/2009-09/07/content_12006500.htm.

Xinhua (2010a) Passive Voice Employed by Ordinary Chinese to Call for Freedom. Last updated 16 February 2010, retrieved 3 March 2011, from http://news.xinhuanet.com/english2010/indepth/2010-02/16/c_13176690.htm.

Xinhua (2010b) Premier Wen Declares Shanghai World Expo Closed. Last updated 1 November 2010, retrieved 1 November 2010, from http://en.expo2010.cn/a/20101101/000001.htm.

Xinhua (2010c) Shanghai World Expo Wins Worldwide Applause. Last updated 31 October 2010, retrieved 31 October 2010, from http://news.xinhuanet.com/english2010/china/2010-10/31/c_13584040.htm.

Xinhua (2010d) Wen Urges Strategic Perspective, Open Mind in China–EU Cultural Ties. Last updated 7 October 2010, retrieved 3 March 2012, from http://au.china-embassy.org/eng/xw/t759091.htm.

Xinhua (2011) China's President Reaffirms Support to UN. Last updated 1 November 2011, retrieved 10 March 2012, from www.china-embassy.org/eng/gdxw/t765812.htm.

Xinhua (2012a) China Hopes for Stable, Healthy Ties with the Maldives. Last updated 13 February 2012, retrieved 27 February 2012, from http://english.cntv.cn/20120213/117913.shtml.

Xinhua (2012b) China, India Pledge Closer Ties for Common Development. Last updated 12 February 2012, retrieved 27 February 2012, from http://news.xinhuanet.com/english/china/2012-02/09/c_131399214.htm.

Xinhua (2012c) Interview: UN Chief Lauds China's 'Crucially Important Role' in World Peace, Development. Last updated 6 January 2012, retrieved 27 February 2012, from http://english.cntv.cn/20120106/108814.shtml.

Xinhua (2012d) Senior Official Expects Stronger China–Vietnam Ties. Last updated 14 February 2012, retrieved 27 February 2012, from http://english.cntv.cn/20120214/115874.shtml.

Xinhua (2012e) UN Chief Welcomes Chinese New Year by Exhibiting Calligraphy at UN. Last updated 11 January 2012, retrieved 27 February 2012, from http://english.cntv.cn/20120111/115466.shtml.

Xinhua (2012f) *Xi Jinping Zai Guangzhou Zhanqukaochashi Qiangdiaojianchi Fuguo He*

Qiangjun Xiangtongyi Nuli Jianshe Gonggu Guofang He Qiangdajundui [During an Inspection of the Guangzhou Military Region, Xin Jinping Stressed the Unity of Being a Prosperous Nation and a Strong Military and the Need to Strive to Build a Consolidated National Defence and Strong Army]. Last updated 12 December 2012, retrieved 15 June 2015, from http://news.xinhuanet.com/politics/2012-12/12/c_114003822.htm.

Xinhua (2013a) Inventory of 2013's Ten Big Buzzwords [*Pandian 2013 Nian Shi Da Liuxingyu*]. Last updated 20 December 2013, retrieved 15 June 2015, from http://news.xinhuanet.com/politics/2013-12/20/c_125886796.htm.

Xinhua (2013b) President Vows to Press Ahead with 'Chinese Dream'. Last updated 17 March 2013, retrieved 18 June 2015, from http://news.xinhuanet.com/english/china/2013-03/17/c_132239786.htm.

Xinhua (2013c) Xi Jinping: Building a Culturally Advanced Socialist Nation, and Striving to Improve the Nation's Cultural Soft Power, *Xinhuanet.com*, 31 December 2013.

Xinhua (2013d) Youth Urged to Contribute to Realization of 'Chinese Dream'. Last updated 4 May 2013, retrieved 15 June 2015, from http://news.xinhuanet.com/english/china/2013-05/04/c_132359537.htm.

Xinhua (2013e) *Zai Beijing Junqu Diaoyanshi Qiangdiao Qieshi Yong Dang Zai Xin Xingshixia de Qiangjun Mubiao Tongyi Sixiang Ningjuli Liliang Yinling Fazhan* [Xu Qiliang Inspects Beijing Military Region, Emphasizes Unifying Thinking, Gathering Strength, Directing Development According to the Party's Goal of Military Strengthening under the New Situation]. Last updated 12 April 2013, retrieved 15 June 2015, from http://cpc.people.com.cn/n/2013/0412/c64094-21117911.html.

Xu Bo (2009) *Shibo Liyi* [Expo Etiquette], Shanghai: Dongfang chuban zhongxin.

Xu Wei (2010) Zhutiguan Quan Jilu [Full Record of Theme Pavilions], *Shanghai Shibo* [Shanghai Expo], Special Issue 1.

Xu Yuting (2009) *Green Dam Girl & Bunny Full Sets*. Last updated 30 September 2009, retrieved 8 August 2011, from www.dd-anne.com/?p=24.

Xuanlv (2010) *Jianchi san ge Daibiao, Chuangjian Hexie Shehui* [Insist on Three Watches, Establish River Crab Society]. Last updated 28 September 2010, retrieved 3 March 2011.

Yan Xuetong (2006) Hexie Shehui yu Hexie Shijie de Zhengce Guanxi [The Policy Relation of Harmonious Society and Harmonious World], *Guoji zhengzhi yanjiu* [Research in International Politics], 1, 14–15.

Yan Xuetong (2011) *Ancient Chinese Thought, Modern Chinese Power*, Bell, Daniel and Sun Zhe (Eds), Princeton, NJ: Princeton University Press.

Yang Guobin (2009) *The Power of the Internet in China: Citizen Activism Online*, New York: Columbia University Press.

Yang Houlan (2012) Address by H. E. Ambassador Yang Houlan, speech given at Army Command and Staff College, Nepal, 29 February 2012.

Yang Jiechi (2010) *World Expo: A New Stage for Diplomacy – Foreign Minister Yang Jiechi on World Expo Diplomacy*. Last updated 1 November 2010, retrieved 10 March 2012, from http://ie.china-embassy.org/eng/NewsPress/t769239.htm.

Yang Jiechi (2011) Advance China's Diplomacy amid Peaceful Development, speech given at Symposium on China's Peaceful Development White Paper, Diaoyutai State Guesthouse, Beijing, 15 September 2011.

Yang Jiemian (2015) *China's Innovative Diplomatic Strategy in the New Era*. Last updated 27 May 2015, retrieved 28 September 2015, from www.ciis.org.cn/english/2015-05/27/content_7937633.htm.

Yee, Sienho (2008) Towards a Harmonious World: The Roles of the International Law of

Co-Progressiveness and Leader States, *Chinese Journal of International Law*, 7(1), 99–105.

Yellow Bridge (2010) *Yellow Bridge Mandarin–English Talking Dictionary*. Retrieved 22 September 2010, from www.yellowbridge.com/chinese/chinese-dictionary.php.

Yetts, W. Perceval (1923) Pestilence and Leechcraft in Ancient China, *Proceedings of the Royal Society of Medicine*, 17, 1–7.

Yin Hengmin (2007) *El Excmo. Sr. Embajador Yin Hengmin Asiste a la Inauguración de la Exposición 'El Mismo Mundo' en la Biblioteca de México* [H. E. Yin Hengmin Ambassador Attends the Opening of the Exhibition 'The Same World' at the Library of Mexico]. Last updated 25 July 2007, from www.embajadachina.org.mx/esp/sgjs/t344795.htm.

Yoon, Suthichai (2013) *The China Dream: What Does It Really Mean?* Last updated 1 August 2013, retrieved 30 June 2015, from www.nationmultimedia.com/opinion/The-China-Dream-What-does-it-really-mean-30211609.html.

Yu Bin (2008) China's Harmonious World: Beyond Cultural Interpretations. In Guo Sujian and Guo Baogang (Eds) *China in Search of Harmonious Society*, Lanham, MD: Lexington Books, 75–97.

Yu, Kam Por (2010) The Confucian Conception of Harmony. In Tao, Julia, Anthony B. L. Cheung, Martin Painter and Chenyang Li (Eds) *Governance for Harmony in Asia and Beyond*, London and New York: Routledge, 15–36.

Yu Xiaofeng and Wang Jiangli (2006) Fei Chuantong Anquan Weihu de 'Bianjie', 'Yujing' Yu 'Fanshi' [The 'Border', 'Context' and 'Form' Defended by Non-Traditional Security], *Shijie jingji yu zhengzhi* [World Economics and Politics], 11, 55–63.

Yu Zhengliang (2005) Construction of Chinese Theory and Chinese School of International Relations, *Journal of Shanghai Jiaotong University*, 13(4), 5–8.

Yue Daiyun (2013) *The Chinese Dream Can Enrich World Civilization*. Retrieved 30 June 2015, from http://english.cntv.cn/special/newleadership/chinesedream01.html.

Zehfuss, Maja (2007) *Wounds of Memory: The Politics of War in Germany*, Cambridge: Cambridge University Press.

Zeng Xiangming (2014) 'Zhongguomeng' de Ruanshili Jiedu [Interpreting the Soft Power of the 'Chinese Dream'], *Fujian lilun xuexi* [Fujian Theory Studies], 8, 4–6.

Zhang Facai (2008) *Everyone Wins*. Danwei.org. Last updated 28 December 2008, retrieved 8 March 2011 from Joel Martinsen, 'Joke Advertising' entry, www.danwei.org/blogs/joke_advertising.php.

Zhang Guoqing and M. M. Kadieh (2010) *Deux Berceaux de Civilisations* [Two Cradles of Civilizations], Embassy of the PRC in Republic of Djibouti. Last updated 22 November 2010, retrieved 10 March 2012, from http://dj.china-embassy.org/fra/xwdt/t771024.htm.

Zhang Qianfan (2010) Propriety, Law and Harmony: A Functional Argument for the Rule of Virtue. In Tao, Julia, Anthony B. L. Cheung, Martin Painter and Chenyang Li (Eds) *Governance for Harmony in Asia and Beyond*, London and New York: Routledge, 282–314.

Zhang Weidong (2010) Chinese Embassy in the FSM Celebrates the 61st Anniversary of the Founding of the PRC, speech given at Chinese Embassy in the FSM Celebrates the 61st Anniversary of the Founding of the PRC, China Star Restaurant, Pohnpei, Micronesia, 28 September 2010.

Zhang Weidong (2011) Speech by H. E. Ambassador Zhang Weidong, given at Spring Festival Reception, Cliff Rainbow Hotel, Pohnpei, 1 January 2011.

Zhang Weiwei (2014) *Zhongguo Chaoyue: Yige 'Wenmingxing Guojia' de Guangrong Yu Mengxiang* [China Surpasses: The Glory and Dream of a 'Civilization-State'], Shanghai: Shanghai renmin chubanshe.

Zhang Xiaoming (2014) Xuyao Zhongguomeng Yu Zhongguomeng Xuyao [The Need for the Chinese Dream and the Chinese Dream's Needs], *Dalian ganbu xuekan* [Dalian Cadre Journal], 12, 17–21.

Zhang Yunling (2008) Guanyu Goujian Hexie Shijie de Sikao [Reflections on Building a Harmonious World], *Dangdai Yangtai* [Contemporary Asia-Pacific], 2, 4–8.

Zhao Suisheng (2015) Rethinking the Chinese World Order: The Imperial Cycle and the Rise of China, *Journal of Contemporary China*, 24(96), 961–82.

Zhao Tingyang (2003) *Mei You Shijieguan de Shijie* [No Worldview for the World], Beijing: Zhongguo renmin daxue chubanshe.

Zhao Tingyang (2005) *Tianxia Tixi: Shijie Zhidu Zhexue Taolun* [Tianxia System: Philosophical Discussion of World System], Nanjing Shi, Jiangsu jiao yu chu ban she.

Zhao Tingyang (2006a) *Guanyu Hexie Shijie de Sikao* [Reflections on Harmonious World], *Shijie jingji yu zhengzhi* [World Economics and Politics], (9), 1.

Zhao Tingyang (2006b) Meiguo Meng, Ouzhou Meng He Zhongguo Meng [The American Dream, the European Dream and the Chinese Dream], *Kua wenhua duihua* [Transcultural Dialogue], 18, 143–61.

Zhao Tingyang (2006c) Rethinking Empire from a Chinese Concept 'All-under-Heaven' (Tianxia), *Social Identities*, 12(1), 29–41.

Zhao Tingyang (2009) *Huai Shijie Yanjiu: Zuo wei di yi Zhexue de Zhengzhi Zhexue* [Investigations of the Bad World: Political Philosophy as First Philosophy], Beijing: Zhongguo renmin daxue chubanshe.

Zhao Tingyang (2014) The 'China Dream' in Question, *Economic and Political Studies*, 2(1), 127–42.

Zhou Jianming and Jiao Shixin (2008) Cong Dongxi Maodun dao Xifang yu Duoyuan Wenming de Maodun [From East–West Contradiction to the Contradiction between the West and Multiple Civilizations], *Shijie jingji yu zhengzhi* [World Economics and Politics], 6, 21–30.

Zhou Junjun (2014) Zhongguomeng Shijie Jiazhide Benzhi Shuxing [The Essential Attributes of the Chinese Dream World Values], *Zhonggong Nanning shiwei dangxiao xuebao* [CCP Nanning Party Committee school Journal], 3, 1–4.

Zhou Yuxiao (2011) Remarks at the Farewell Reception by H. E. Zhou Yuxiao, speech given at Farewell Reception by H. E. Zhou Yuxiao, Republic of Liberia, 16 March 2011.

Zhu Rongji (2003) *Report on the Work of Government (2003)*, delivered at the First Session of the Tenth National People's Congress, Beijing, 5 March 2003.

Zhuru cilei (2007) *Bei Hexie le*. Last updated 23 August 2007, retrieved 1 March 2011, from www.tudou.com/programs/view/5MBD0_D_lho.

Zou Keyuan (2011) Building a 'Harmonious World': A Mission Impossible?, paper presented at East Asian Peace Program First Annual Conference on Democracy and Peace in East Asia, Uppsala University, Sweden, 16–18 September 2011.

Index